THE MIND
OF THE PAEDOPHILE

Other titles in the
Forensic Psychotherapy Monograph Series

THE MIND
OF THE PAEDOPHILE
Psychoanalytic Perspectives

Edited by

Charles W. Socarides

Associate Editor

Loretta R. Loeb

Forensic Psychotherapy Monograph Series

Series Editor   Honorary Consultant
Brett Kahr   *Estela Welldon*

KARNAC
LONDON   NEW YORK

First published in 2004 by
H. Karnac (Books) Ltd.
6 Pembroke Buildings, London NW10 6RE

British Library Cataloguing in Publication Data

A C.I.P. for this book is available from the British Library

 ISBN: 1-85575-970-5

10 9 8 7 6 5 4 3 2 1

Printed in Great Britain

www.karnacbooks.com

to the Memory of Margaret S. Mahler, M.D.
Psychoanalyst
Researcher
Teacher
Friend
For her discovery of the separation–individuation phases
of human development, the application of which
to the understanding of paedophilia
is only one of its human benefits.

CONTENTS

ACKNOWLEDGEMENTS

We wish to express our thanks to the publisher, Karnac, London, and especially the editor of the Forensic Series, Brett Kahr, for their courage in making it possible to present this material on this hitherto unexplainable sexual perversion that has been so devastating to innocent victims throughout the world.

We believe that further psychoanalytic comprehension of this disorder and its origins and psychodynamics may help the victims and may further our understanding and treatment of those so afflicted and possibly prevent further abuse.

We also owe gratitude to the secretarial services of Tamar Schwartz for her extraordinary efficiency in working on this complex task so important for the world.

SERIES FOREWORD

Brett Kahr

Centre for Child Mental Health, London
and
The Winnicott Clinic of Psychotherapy, London

Throughout most of human history, our ancestors have done rather poorly when dealing with acts of violence. To cite but one of many shocking examples, let us perhaps recall a case from 1801, of an English boy aged only 13, who was executed by hanging on the gallows at Tyburn. What was his crime? It seems that he had been condemned to die for having stolen a spoon (Westwick, 1940).

In most cases, our predecessors have either *ignored* murderousness and aggression, as in the case of Graeco–Roman infanticide, which occurred so regularly in the ancient world that it acquired an almost normative status (deMause, 1974; Kahr, 1994); or they have *punished* murderousness and destruction with retaliatory sadism, a form of unconscious identification with the aggressor. Any history of criminology will readily reveal the cruel punishments inflicted upon prisoners throughout the ages, ranging from beatings and stockades, to more severe forms of torture, culminating in eviscerations, beheadings, or lynchings.

Only during the last one hundred years have we begun to develop the capacity to respond more intelligently and more humanely to acts of dangerousness and destruction. Since the advent of psychoanalysis and psychoanalytic psychotherapy, we now have access to a much deeper understanding both of the aetiology of aggressive acts and of their treatment; and nowadays we need no longer ignore criminals or abuse them—instead, we can provide compassion and containment, as well as conduct research that can help to prevent future acts of violence.

The modern discipline of forensic psychotherapy, which can be defined, quite simply, as the use of psychoanalytically orientated "talking therapy" to treat violent, offender patients, stems directly from the work of Sigmund Freud. Almost one hundred years ago, at a meeting of the Vienna Psycho-Analytical Society, held on 6 February 1907, Sigmund Freud anticipated the clarion call of contemporary forensic psychotherapists when he bemoaned the often horrible treatment of mentally ill offenders, in a discussion on the psychology of vagrancy. According to Otto Rank, Freud's secretary at the time, the founder of psychoanalysis expressed his sorrow at the "nonsensical treatment of these people in prisons" (quoted in Nunberg & Federn, 1962, p. 108).

Many of the early psychoanalysts preoccupied themselves with forensic topics. Hanns Sachs, himself a trained lawyer, and Marie Bonaparte, the French princess who wrote about the cruelty of war, each spoke fiercely against capital punishment. Sachs, one of the first members of Freud's secret committee, regarded the death penalty for offenders as an example of group sadism (Moellenhoff, 1966). Bonaparte, who had studied various murderers throughout her career, had actually lobbied politicians in America to free the convicted killer Caryl Chessman, during his sentence on Death Row at the California State Prison in San Quentin, albeit unsuccessfully (Bertin, 1982).

Melanie Klein concluded her first book, the landmark text *Die Psychoanalyse des Kindes* [*The Psycho-Analysis of Children*], with resounding passion about the problem of violence in our culture. Mrs Klein noted that acts of criminality invariably stem from disturbances in childhood, and that if young people could receive access to psychoanalytic treatment at any early age, then much cruelty could be prevented in later years. Klein expressed the hope that: "If every child who shows disturbances that are at all severe were to be analysed in good time, a great number of these people who later end up in prisons or lunatic asylums, or who go completely to pieces, would be saved from such a fate and be able to develop a normal life" (1932, p. 374).

Shortly after the publication of Klein's transformative book, Atwell Westwick, a Judge of the Superior Court of Santa Barbara, California, published a little-known though highly inspiring article, "Criminology and Psychoanalysis" (1940), in the *Psychoanalytic Quarterly*. Westwick may well be the first judge to commit himself in print to the value of psychoanalysis in the study of criminality, arguing that punishment of the forensic patient remains, in fact, a sheer waste of time. With foresight, Judge Westwick queried, "Can we not, in our well nigh hopeless and overwhelming struggle with the problems of delinquency and crime, profit by medical experience with the problems of health and disease? Will we not, eventually, terminate the senseless policy of sitting idly by until misbehavior occurs, often with irreparable damage, then dumping the delinquent into the juvenile court or reformatory and dumping the criminal into prison?" (p. 281). Westwick noted that we should, instead, train judges, probation officers, social workers, as well as teachers and parents, in the precepts of psychoanalysis, in order to arrive at a more sensitive, non-punitive understanding of the nature of criminality. He opined: "When we shall have succeeded in committing society to such a program, when we see it launched definitely upon the venture, as in time it surely will be—then shall we have erected an appropriate memorial to Sigmund Freud" (p. 281).

In more recent years, the field of forensic psychotherapy has become increasingly well constellated. Building upon the pioneering contributions of such psychoanalysts and psychotherapists as Edward Glover, Grace Pailthorpe, Melitta Schmideberg, and more recently Murray Cox, Mervin Glasser, Ismond Rosen, Estela Welldon, and others too numerous to mention, forensic psychotherapy has now become an increasingly formalized discipline that can be dated to the inauguration of the International Association for Forensic Psychotherapy and to the first annual conference, held at St. Bartholomew's Hospital in London in 1991. The profession now boasts a more robust foundation, with training courses developing in the United Kingdom and beyond. Since the inauguration of the Diploma in Forensic Psychotherapy (and subsequently the Diploma in Forensic Psychotherapeutic Studies), under the auspices of the British Postgraduate Medical Federation of the University of London in association with the Portman Clinic, students can now seek further instruction in the psychodynamic treatment of patients who act out in a dangerous and illegal manner.

The volumes in this series of books will aim to provide both practical advice and theoretical stimulation for introductory students and for senior practitioners alike. In the Karnac Books Forensic Psychotherapy Monograph Series, we will endeavour to produce a regular stream of high-quality titles, written by leading members of the profession, who will share their expertise in a concise and practice-orientated fashion. We trust that such a collection of books will help to consolidate the knowledge and experience that we have already acquired and will also provide new directions for the upcoming decades of the new century. In this way, we shall hope to plant the seeds for a more rigorous, sturdy, and wide-reaching profession of forensic psychotherapy.

As the new millennium begins to unfold, we now have an opportunity for psychotherapeutically orientated forensic mental health professionals to work in close conjunction with child psychologists and with infant mental health specialists so that the problems of violence can be tackled both preventatively and retrospectively. With the growth of the field of forensic psychotherapy, we at last have reason to be hopeful that serious criminality can be forestalled and perhaps, one day, even eradicated.

References

Bertin, C. (1982). *La Dernière Bonaparte*. Paris: Librairie Académique Perrin.
deMause, L. (1974). The evolution of childhood. In: Lloyd deMause (Ed.), *The History of Childhood* (pp. 1–73). New York: Psychohistory Press.
Kahr, B. (1994). The historical foundations of ritual abuse: an excavation of ancient infanticide. In: Valerie Sinason (Ed.), *Treating Survivors of Satanist Abuse* (pp. 45–56). London: Routledge.
Klein, M. (1932). *The Psycho-Analysis of Children*, trans. Alix Strachey. London: Hogarth Press and The Institute of Psycho-Analysis. [First published as *Die Psychoanalyse des Kindes*. Vienna: Internationaler Psychoanalytischer Verlag.]
Moellenhoff, F. (1966). Hanns Sachs, 1881–1947: the creative unconscious. In: F. Alexander, S. Eisenstein, & M. Grotjahn (Eds.), *Psychoanalytic Pioneers* (pp. 180–199). New York: Basic Books.
Nunberg, H., & Federn, E. (Eds.) (1962). *Minutes of the Vienna Psychoanalytic Society. Volume I: 1906–1908*, trans. Margarethe Nunberg. New York: International Universities Press.
Westwick, A. (1940). Criminology and Psychoanalysis. *Psychoanalytic Quarterly*, 9: 269–282.

EDITORS & CONTRIBUTORS

WILFRED ABSE is Professor Emeritus of Psychiatry at the University of Virginia and Faculty, Washington Psychoanalytic Institute, Washington, DC.

WILLIAM F. GREER is an Assistant Professor, Community Faculty, and faculty member of Psychoanalytic Studies of the Medical College of Hampton Road, Norfolk, Virginia. A clinical member of the Virginia Psychoanalytic Society, he also maintains a private practice in Hampton, Virginia.

DANIEL P. JUDA is a psychoanalyst and Associate Professor, Department of Psychology and Thematic Studies Department, John Jay College of Criminal Justice, City University of New York.

BRETT KAHR is Senior Clinical Research Fellow in Psychotherapy and Mental Health at the Centre for Child Mental Health in London and Senior Lecturer in Psychotherapy in the School of Psychotherapy and Counselling at Regent's College. Since 2001 he has been the inaugural Winnicott Clinic Senior Research Fellow in Psychotherapy. He is the author or editor of several books, including *D.W. Winnicott: A Biographical Portrait*, which won the Gradiva Prize for Biography in 1997; *Forensic Psychotherapy and Psychopathology: Winnicottian Perspectives; Exhibitionism*; and *The Legacy of Winnicott: Essays in Infant and Child Mental Health*. A psychotherapist and marital psychotherapist in private practice, he serves as the Series Editor of the Forensic Psychotherapy Monograph Series for Karnac.

Loretta R. Loeb is Clinical Professor of Psychiatry at the Oregon Health Sciences University; Certified in Adult, Child, and Adolescent Psychoanalysis by the American Psychoanalytic Association; and a psychoanalyst in practice in Portland, Oregon. She has received a Recognition Award for Outstanding and Valuable Service to the Children of Oregon, presented by the Oregonian Council of Child and Adolescent Psychiatry, 1995; the Hero to Youth Award from the Oregon Youth Authority for her Gang Tattoo Removal Project, 1997; the Sigmund Freud Award from the National Association for Research and Therapy of Homosexuality, 1999; and the Problem Solving Award for the Gant Study Group from the Portland Police Bureau, 2000.

Charles W. Socarides is Former Clinical Professor of Psychiatry, Albert Einstein College of Medicine (1979–1996) and Chairman, Discussion Group, The Sexual Perversions: Theory and Therapy, American Psychoanalytic Association, 1980–2004. He is a member of the American Psychoanalytic Association and the International Psychoanalytic Association. He is in private practice in New York City. In 1995 he was awarded the Distinguished Professor Award from the Association of Psychoanalytic Psychotherapists in the National Health Service.

Vamik D. Volkan is Professor Emeritus of Psychiatry, University of Virginia, Charlottesville, Virginia; Erik Erikson Scholar, The Austen Riggs Center, Stockbridge, Massachusetts; and Training and Supervising Analyst, the Washington Psychoanalytic Institute, Washington, DC.

Months before the eruption at the start of the Millennium in the Roman Catholic Church over the extent of paedophile practices within the clergy, I was approached by Brett Kahr, the Editor of the Forensic Psychotherapy Monograph Series, about the question of whether psychoanalysis could shed some light on the origin, meaning, and contents of paedophile perversions and paedophile behaviour in general, and whether I could help in doing so.

He had just completed the third volume (Kahr, 2001) of his series, devoted to Winnicottian perspectives on the origins of delinquency, violence, perversion, and the like—a consequence of early maternal deprivation and adolescent breakdown—as well as to the therapeutic techniques employable in the treatment of such children and adolescents.

Pleased with his question and invitation, I readily agreed to further research psychoanalytic findings of my colleagues and myself. Although the consequences of sexual abuse of children have been explored analytically, what immediately confronted me was the knowledge that psychoanalytic studies of paedophile perverts were extremely rare. Over the last forty-five years, only three psychoanalytic case histories have been reported in the English literature in major psychoanalytic journals. One was my own paper, "Meaning and Content of a Pedophiliac Perversion" (1959), another was by Vamık Volkan and William Greer in 1995 entitled "Dogman" (chapter two herein), and the third was by Daniel Juda in 1986 (chapter four herein). Clearly this subject was a stepchild of psychoanalysis, acknowledged but ignored and neglected. Scattered reports of paedophile behaviour have appeared in the literature over the past seventy years, but significant in-depth clinical material derived from psychoanalytic investigations in the consultation-room were essentially missing. Perhaps this was not simply due to the fact that paedophile perverts do not usually—due to their fear of the law—present themselves for analysis, or, alternatively, that psychoanalysts do not accept them for treatment as their activities would ordinarily seem to be outside psychoanalytic enquiry—that is, criminality. Furthermore, the absence of sufficient clinical psychoanalytic reports had made it questionable in the minds of many as to whether paedophilia could be classified as sexual perversion. The answer to this issue is dramatically evident in the material presented. An additional factor may be the analyst's aversion to treat or report on such patients because of the revulsion and anger with which their perversion is viewed by the general public and society.

I enthusiastically accepted Kahr's invitation, and with Loretta Loeb—a child analyst well-known for her studies of gender-identity disorders—as my associate editor, I believed that psychoanalysis could make a definite contribution to the understanding of paedophilia, or at least provide a beginning by shedding light as to the origins of this disorder, by placing it in a classificatory system (which I had been contemplating for some time), as well as by describing its dynamics and its possible therapy in a well-organized manner. For it remains of primary importance to rescue the paedophilias from the hotchpotch of psychological, psychiatric, and legal issues that have made them a quagmire of bits of clinical information, some accurate on one aspect of the problem, but often confusing and ill-conceived as to diagnosis, origins, course in treatment, and prognosis. For example, a major psychiatric expert on the treatment of paedophiles sent to him for institutionalized therapy recently commented in the public press that he considers paedophiles as simply not quite "grown up"—that is, as "immature" individuals.

This book constitutes the first major textbook on the paedophilias, and we trust that it will be a spur to others to analyse paedophile perverts as well as to care tenderly for the wounds of the child victims who are described within its pages.

THE MIND
OF THE PAEDOPHILE

Tribute

Free from illusions, . . . relentless and radical . . . Freud
showed that the impulsive energy of the libido, . . . was an
indestructible part of the human organism, a force that could
not be annulled so long as life and breath remained, and that
the best way of dealing with it was to lift it into the conscious
were its activities to be free from danger. . . . No one can
bridle impulses without perceiving them clearly; no one can
master demons unless he summons them forth from their
lurking-places and looks them boldly in the face. Medicine's
business is, not to maintain silence concerning the secret
places of the heart, but to discover them and tell all the truth
about them.

Stefan Zweig, Mental Healers (1933, pp. 261–262)

Introduction

Charles W. Socarides & Loretta R. Loeb

The authors of the chapters in this book explore the internal world of the paedophile—a little-known region of the mind of adults and juvenile individuals who experience the imperative need for sexual congress with children and act upon it. The psychoanalytic method reveals the unconscious motivations out of which these urges emerge. In this investigative method, psychoanalysts attempt to answer three major questions: (1) where do these urges come from? [cause searching]; (2) what purpose do they serve? [means to ends]; and (3) what can be done about them? [healing function].

Of all the sexual perversions, paedophilia remains among the most unpleasant and repulsive to many, deserving only the harshest condemnation. And yet it cries out for explanation, explanation that would be of benefit to victims and victimizers. However, explanations have been sought, with few exceptions, only in the study of conscious motivations of those afflicted and in the application of behavioural-modification techniques to this condition. Statistical inquiries and compilations of frequency of acts, the study of the recidivism rate, the effect of incarceration, surgical

procedures on the brain, electroshock therapy, the attempt to eliminate the sexual drive through endocrine preparations, various
types of psychotherapy, including group therapy, and so forth,
have yielded little information explanatory of this condition. This
book takes a different direction, in that it utilizes information
derived from the subject himself—a subject willing to reveal the
secrets of his unconscious, provided that he is protected by all the
laws of medicine, psychiatry, and psychoanalysis, in the hope that
somehow he may be alleviated of his condition. The knowledge we
gain is through dream interpretation, examination of the earliest
years of life, fantasies, and memories, as well as the study of his
transferences and his free associations.

Mining of the mind of the paedophile has already produced
considerable yield. It has become apparent that there is no single
paedophilia but, rather, the paedophilias: a group of conditions with
similar sexual aims—sexual relations with prepubertal children—
but with different causative processes, different levels of fixation,
resulting in varying degrees of severity and different prognoses for
recovery. For example, C. W. Socarides puts his case histories into
a classification system on the basis of diagnosis. Does the paedophilia derive from a borderline, a psychotic, or a neurotic personality organization? He separates obligatory paedophilia from
variational and situational types as well as those arising from
oedipal and/or pre-oedipal conflicts and from those that are basi-
cally part and parcel of a schizophrenic process. He describes the
motivational, unconscious forces in each and clarifies what to expect in a well-conducted psychoanalysis of such patients. Classification then becomes of considerable value in that it is a beacon of
orientation for all concerned, not only for the clinician, or for the
judiciary, but for anyone who is in the position of authority to
adjudicate and decide management of a particular type of offender.

Similarly it also informs us that one individual simply engaging
in masturbation watching "kiddie porn", who does not sexually
abuse a child, should not be treated by the authorities as a dangerous sexual offender.

The consequences of child sexual abuse have been widely written about by outstanding psychoanalytic authors for years. Some of
these contributions are noted by my associate editor, Loretta R.
Loeb, in the final chapter, "The Consequences of Child Sexual

Abuse: A Brief Survey". She cites several valuable papers to stand for the entire field of reporting in this short book devoted almost entirely to the paedophile himself. In so doing, we are in no way minimizing the traumatic effects on the child; otherwise, this book would be several volumes in length.

The frequency of paedophilia of the obligatory type is unknown except in exceptional situations similar to that which has surfaced among the Catholic clergy. For many adults have come forth with charges against priests who have sexually abused them as *children*.

Sexual abuse material, however, is plentiful, if not overwhelming, on the Internet, as reported in the *Spectator*, London:

> [Scotland Yard] reports . . . "Operation Barcelona . . . identified 109 groups dealing with child abuse material. Some groups have over 3,000 members. There is a list of 5,000 names, all abusers, on the Internet either because of dealings with images or hands-on paedophiles. There is no official estimate of how many British men view indecent images of children on the web. One police source . . . estimates the figure of 200,000. The percent who have gone on to become hands-on abusers is unknown, but research in the U.S.A. suggests that thirty percent of viewers of this type of material have turned out to be active child abusers" [!]. [J. Gibb, Reporter, *Spectator*, 19 April, 2003, pp. 18–19]

While the prediction that thirty percent of viewers are obligatory paedophile perverts is highly questionable, Freud's two comments on the subject of incidence come to mind. The first may be found in *Three Essays on the Theory of Sexuality* (1905d): "when children are the exclusive sexual object, they usually come to play that part when someone is cowardly or has become impotent and adopts them as substitutes." The second, even more profound, was his 1911 observation: "[These activities] . . . are a living relic of the ancient expression of an adulation and primacy of instinctual discharge processes, in which the belief of the value of the sexual process per se was secondary to instinctual discharge." Such activities remain the "weak spot in our psychical organization" (Freud, 1911b, p. 223). In 1945, Fenichel observed: "Children are weak and in the main approachable when other objects are excluded through anxiety. . . . It is true that sometimes . . . superficial reasons may suffice for persons to be attracted to children" (p. 333).

Chapter one, by Charles W. Socarides, utilizes Mahler's separation–individuation theory of development to shed light on the origins of the disorder. His classification of the various forms of paedophilia can be seen as a giant step forward in the diagnosis of this condition, separating it from the less severe conditions. The correct diagnosis of the type of paedophilia one is dealing with can only be made through a rigorous study of the patient's developmental as well as sexual history. In the two different forms of paedophilia he treated psychoanalytically, each has its own individual psychodynamics.

Chapter two, by Vamık D. Volkan and William Greer, presents the early sexual experiences of a person who later became a paedophile, the difficulty that the therapist had in dealing with his paedophile patient, and the kind of therapeutic relationship that had to be maintained so that the patient could begin to gain some control over his perversion, not interrupt therapy, and simultaneously protect children. The patient's unconscious conflicts are clearly illustrated with examples of acting-out behaviour. The therapist's careful handling of the transference gradually allowed this patient to appear over time more like a neurotic, so that he was then able to gain insight into the nature of the obligatoriness of his behaviour. The psychoanalysis of the patient's psychosomatic symptoms enabled him to separate and free himself from his hostile intrapsychic objects so that he could relate more appropriately to the current people in his environment.

Chapter three, by Brett Kahr, describes the paedophile patient as a juvenile socially disturbed individual. He notes that the vast majority of psychoanalysts have neglected the study of perverse sexual activity in children and adolescents, but that multiple clinics are now developing in the United Kingdom to treat this population. Kahr cites the work of other workers who have an appreciation for the importance of early intervention and points out that approximately a third of all sexual crimes against children have been perpetrated by other youngsters. Kahr and his colleagues have been encouraged by the fact that since they began their psychotherapy programme a number of years ago for young abusers, not one single boy, as of the time of the writing of his paper, had re-offended during the course of their analytic treatment. By working with young children and adults, Kahr concludes that, "we have a rich opportunity to observe the development of paedophilia *in vivo*, before the personality structure has become rigidified". After reviewing how he collected and investigated his data, Kahr then presents the entire course of his treatment of a 16-year-old male sexual offender.

In chapter four, Daniel P. Juda shares with us his experience in dealing with paedophiles in his practice as both psychoanalyst and Associate Professor, Department of Psychology, John J. College of Criminal Justice, City College of the University of New York. He briefly reviews the two predominant psychoanalytic theories regarding the aetiology of homosexual paedophilia—the Freudian-based approach and the Kohutian-based approach. Juda concludes that both theories recognize the importance of the early pre-oedipal (birth to 3 years of age) developmental phase producing this disorder. However, there are important differences in these two early developmental theories, and they influence how the clinical case material can be analysed and interpreted. A case history of a homosexual paedophile is presented to illustrate the usefulness of the self-psychology approach to the understanding of certain cases. Juda places special emphasis on the notion of the *selfobject*—specifically, the use by the offender of the child victim as a mirroring and idealizing object in order to make up for inadequate and destructive internalized archaic selfobjects in his early maternal environment. He is engaging in an act of "self-healing". Juda comments that "homosexual paedophilia is a disorder that signals a serious deficit in the offender's self-formation". "Just as an infant has not developed the capacity to experience reality from the mother's point of view," it prevents him from being able to empathize with his victim/selfobject.

In chapter five, Wilfred Abse presents clinical incidents of child abuse. He also reviews the non-analytic literature dealing with the *ritualized* sexual abuse of children and the lawsuits pertaining to the intensive investigation of Satanic cults. Abse suggests that the World War II war trials and the narratives of many survivors have shown that the sadistic horrors that the Nazis committed towards children can well be perceived as sadistic paedophile acts. Many people are unaware of the material in this chapter.

Chapter six, the final and concluding chapter, by Loretta R. Loeb, shows that the impact of paedophilia on its victims may be enormous, tragic, and horrifying. It causes an interference with the normal psychosexual development of these children and leads to complex and devastating psychological problems in adulthood. These problems include not only sexual problems but disturbed family and social relationships that last for years. By encouraging professionals to work with and help victims as well as victimizers, we may well improve the world in which we raise our children.

Lastly, we must take note of the recent Massachusetts Report of the Massachusetts General's Office and its contents. On 24 July 2003, *The New York Times* reported that 789 children have been abused sexually by priests in the Boston, Massachusetts, area since 1940. In the Bishops' own words, "the [Bishops] felt that once caught a molester would not abuse again" and therefore there was "failure to take any meaningful steps to limit a priest's contact with children in the future". Of course, this assumption is sadly contrary to all psychoanalytic knowledge of an obligatory perversion.

CHAPTER ONE

A psychoanalytic classification of the paedophilias: two clinical illustrations

Charles W. Socarides

THEORETICAL SECTION

In 1967, I first suggested that the genesis of well-structured[1] perversions may well be the result of disturbances that occur earlier than had been generally assumed, namely in the pre-oedipal phase. The challenge confronting us was to understand clinical forms of the same perversion, from the mildest to the well-structured perversion, to that occurring in an individual with a florid psychosis. Paedophilia, for example, could be classified in the following way: oedipal paedophilia, pre-oedipal paedophilia, and schizo-paedophilia. My classification demonstrated that the

Portions of this chapter are an expansion and revision of chapter 12, "Pedophilia: The Case of Jenkins", in my book, *Preoedipal Origin and Psychoanalytic Therapy of Sexual Perversions* (Madison, CT: International Universities Press, 1988), and some portions are adapted or replicated from my diverse writings over a thirty-five-year period. The case material of people who came for help presented here is from the late 1960s. The views expressed are my own and are not those of any organization.

same phenomenology may have different structures in different individuals.

The situational and variational forms of paedophilia are considered non-clinical forms of sexual perversion. The former is characterized by (1) environmental inaccessibility to adult partners of the opposite sex; (2) consciously motivated behaviour; (3) paedophile acts that are not fear-induced but arise out of conscious deliberation and choice; (4) the ability to function with an adult partner of the opposite sex; and (5) a flexible sexual pattern that allows individuals to return to adult opposite-sex partners when they are available.

The motivations underlying the variational form of paedophiliac behaviour are as varied as the motivations driving men and women to pursue dependency, seek security, wreak vengeance, or experience specialized sensations. They may be entirely a product of individual enterprise, contrary to the general social order. The behaviour is consciously motivated, and paedophile acts are not fear-induced but arise out of conscious deliberation and choice. The person is able to function with an adult partner of the opposite sex. The sexual pattern is flexible, and these individuals do return to adult opposite-sex partners when they so prefer. Variational paedophilia may occur in individuals who seek to gratify the desire for an alternation of sexual excitement, often for reasons of impotence or near impotence. In latent forms of paedophilia the patient may live without being aware of this condition in its milder forms, being able for many years to tolerate its various negative influences on his general health. Latent forms of this perversion may erupt into oedipal, pre-oedipal, or schizo-paedophilia. Fleeting sexual impulses towards children occurring in the course of handling or observing the child are frequent, however, and are often reported during psychoanalytic therapy. Such fantasies or even enactments do not necessarily signify that the patient is suffering from a paedophiliac perversion. Considerable numbers of individuals may be engaging in paedophiliac *behaviour*. Often fleeting periodic paedophiliac fantasies are reported by patients with intense fears of the opposite sex, together with suppressed (rarely expressed) paedophiliac tendencies. In this group is the sudden appearance of a paedophile perversion in the elderly or late-middle-aged whose sexual patterns have been altered by multiple psychological or organic brain changes accompanying ageing, trauma, or neoplasm. Often individuals in the course of making a transition from certain psychotic states (often paranoid) to neurotic symptomatology (or in the opposite direction), pass through a transitional-symptom phase of paedophilia or other perverse formation—for example, exhibitionism and voyeurism. This phenomenon was first described by Glover (1933). Rare acts of paedophiliac behaviour, reacted to with anxiety, may appear in the manifest content of dreams of these who temporarily retreat from adult sexuality to a less threatening infantile sexual-object choice. Some adults have engaged in brief and isolated sexual contact with prepubertal children in the context of a seductive, curious child and in the state of drug intoxication. This may represent a loosening of impulse control and regression secondary to frustration. As a rule, these acts are not stereotyped nor are they the sole avenue for the individual's sexual gratification and are transitory. High incidence of sexual abuse of children reported to the authorities beginning in the 1980s leads one to conjecture that there may be a "facultative" or "epidemic" form of non-clinical paedophilia similar to that which has been reported as regards the increase in sexual promiscuity. Such epidemic or facultative forms of behaviour have been known to occur at times of social disequilibrium and where these is no "authoritative prohibition by society" (Freud, 1905d, p. 222) against sexual license. As noted by Fenichel (1945), "children are weak and remain approachable when other objects are excluded through anxiety. . . . It is true that sometimes . . . superficial reasons may suffice for persons to be attracted by children" (p. 333). As Freud (1911b) noted, there is a much longer dominance of the pleasure principle over the reality principle in the evolution of human erotism. They are living relics of the ancient expression, adulation, and primacy of instinctual discharge processes in which the belief in the value of the sexual object *per se* was secondary to instinctual discharge. Such activities constitute the "weak spot in our psychical organization". "An essential part of the psychical disposition to neurosis indeed lies in the delay of educating the sexual instincts to pay regard to reality, and . . . in the condition which makes this delay possible" (Freud, 1911b, p. 223).

In contrast, the true paedophiliac is one who out of inner necessity must engage in sexual relations with a prepubertal child (before the development of secondary sex characteristics) in order

to achieve sexual gratification and to obtain relief from unconscious conflicts. The diagnosis of paedophilia can therefore only be
made after a rigorous study of the patient's sexual history and the
developmental phases that he has traversed.

A brief review of the psychoanalytic literature

Well-structured paedophiliac perversions are not uncommon but
have received scant psychoanalytic attention, for they do not
present themselves for treatment. Those who undergo treatment
greatly fear the possibility that disclosure of their identities and
others who enter it are prone to premature interruption. Fenichel
(1945), in his *Psychoanalytic Theory of Neurosis,* devotes only two
short paragraphs to this perversion. He concluded that this "love"
for children was based on a narcissistic object choice. Karpman
(1950) reported a case of paedophilia in which the patient's conflict
seemed to centre around a fear of pubic hair in women. It constituted a traumatic experience in the patient's childhood which he
avoided by substituting harmless girls of prepubertal age. He
noted the importance of incorporative elements, being swallowed
by the pubic hair, but the developmental aspects of the ego as
defence mechanisms were not clarified. He reported a twenty-year
cure with the enucleation of the traumatic episode. Cassity (1927)
reviewed the literature up to that time, including the contributions
of Krafft-Ebing, Havelock Ellis, Magnan, Bleuler, Stekel, and
Hadley, and presented four cases treated by himself. He underscored the following aetiological factors: (1) the early loss of the
breast (weaning trauma), provoking strong retaliative tendencies,
which were alleviated through forcing the love-object to gratify
oral cravings and, at the same time, dominating and controlling
them; and (2) the avoidance of castration anxiety by choosing a
love-object like one's self. Freud (1905d) in the *Three Essays* stated
that it is "only exceptionally that children are the exclusive sexual
object. They usually come to play that part when someone who is
cowardly or who has become impotent adopts them as a substitute,
or when an urgent instinct (one that will not allow of postpone-
ment) cannot at the moment get possession of any more appropri-

ate object. Even hunger does not permit of such cheapening—that is, variation in its object, as does the sexual instinct" (pp. 148–149). Freud remarked that the sexual abuse of children is more frequent among those who are in intimate contact with them (as, for example, schoolteachers), and he put forth the suggestion that those in whom the practice is exclusive may well be "insane" (p. 49). Socarides (1959) published a brief communication concentrating on only one facet of the problem, namely that the patient's paedophilia served as a defensive manoeuvre against introjective and projective anxieties of early childhood, helping to eliminate anxiety, guilt, and pain.

Ferenczi (1933) described the psychic consequences of sexual molestation of children by their parents. He noted interferences with the child's thinking and reality testing as well as with his autonomy and the formation of pathological defences. An identification with the sexual aggressor occurred, and the introjection of guilt by the child took place. Shengold (1974, 1979) describes "vertical splitting" in the victims and a "confusion and cloudiness that denote an alteration of consciousness affecting the feeling of identity and inhibiting thinking" (p. 112). Kramer (1983) has described the syndrome of "object-coercive doubting", a pathological defensive response to maternal incest. The contributions of Ferenczi, Shengold, and Kramer are of importance to an understanding of the paedophiliac, as many paedophiliacs have themselves undergone childhood sexual abuse.

Most recently Juda (see chapter four) has described a case of a homosexual paedophile whose paedophilia "did not develop out a drive-based castration-related, id/ego/superego model, but, rather, from the need . . . to attach himself to mirroring and idealizable objects in order to prevent his fragile and destructive archaic selfobjects (parental images) from fragmenting his self and object structure". The author concluded in this unusual presentation that "we can no longer assume that pedophilia is primarily or even usually an oedipally based, single-axis-oriented disorder".

While many explanations can be given as to the causation of a paedophile perversion, specific forms of perversion must be seen in relation to other forms. A comprehensive classification must correlate, integrate, and group many factors in a logical fashion.

Theoretical considerations:
a psychoanalytic classification and differentiating criteria

The perverse mechanism for the relief of unconscious conflict in these individuals exists at any level of libidinal fixation and ego development, from the most primitive to the more highly developed levels of organization. The underlying unconscious motivational drives are distinctly different, depending upon the level from which they arise. Oedipal paedophiliac activity arises from a phallic organization of development and must be differentiated from pre-oedipal paedophiliac perversion, which arises from pre-oedipal levels of development. We associate narcissistic neuroses and impulse disorders with the latter. The perverse symptom of paedophilia can operate at an anal level, especially when it represents a regression from genital oedipal-phase conflict. In the schizophrenic, the symptom may represent an archaic and primitive level of functioning, a frantic and chaotic attempt to construct object relations. There is a wide range of clinical forms of paedophiliac perverse behaviour, from those that derive from very archaic and primitive levels to those that are the product of more highly differentiated ones. Each individual case is hierarchically layered with dynamic mechanisms stemming from multiple points of fixation and regression. We can conclude that the clinical picture of the perverse paedophiliac activity itself does not necessarily correctly describe the origin of the particular mechanism responsible for it. This requires a study of the developmental stages through which the individual has passed, the level of fixation, the state of his object relations, and the status of his ego functions.

The classification itself has at its core the following concepts: (1) conscious and/or unconscious motivation; (2) the developmental stage from which the nuclear conflict arose; and (3) the degree of pathology of internalized object relations in the paedophiliac perverse patient. In the milder pre-oedipal type, the surface clinical picture of oedipal conflict may obscure the deeper and more important pre-oedipal ones, and regression does not involve severe impairment in object relations and other ego functions. In the more severe pre-oedipal type (Type II), pre-oedipal fixations are of prime importance, constantly dominating the psychic life of the individual in his search for identity and a cohesive self. Oedipal conflict and castration fear may defend against deeper fears, and pre-oedipal fantasies may defend against the emergence of oedipal material. There is always an interplay between the two.

It is my understanding that the true perversion is the pre-oedipal disorder and does not arise from oedipal conflict with a regression to earlier phases. Oedipal perversion is a different form of deviant sexual behaviour which occurs secondary to a temporary regression, does not represent a developmental arrest, and can be treated in the same way that we treat a neurosis (Schwartz, 1973).

In the clinical section that follows, I shall present two different types of paedophiliac perversion in patients who have undergone psychoanalytic treatment with me. The first patient, the case of Jenkins, is a pre-oedipal Type II sexual deviant whose fixation is in the practicing or differentiating phases of the separation–individuation process (Mahler, 1965, 1968, 1971, 1972); the second, the case of Randolph, whose fixation has been less damaging, occurred in all likelihood in the later phases of the separation–individuation process, the phase of rapprochement. Within the classification, I shall comment on differentiating criteria that separate, contrast, and clarify the two forms of clinical paedophilia. This grouping in an integrated fashion can reveal what can be expected in a well-conducted psychoanalysis of these patients: it can provide information as to the ultimate outcome regarding the removal of the perverse impulse, the establishment of heterosexual function, and the capacity of the individual to cathect a heterosexual love-object. Such a classification would shed light on the types of resistances to be met, describe transference manifestations, and connote the depth and frequency of regressive experiences and the capacity of the individual patient to use them therapeutically and recover from them. Within the classification we are able to define the basic nuclear conflict that will be affectively revived during therapy and the capacity of the individual ego to deal with it, specify the class of conflict to be met with (structural vs. object relations: Dorpat, 1976), and provide information as to the presence of areas of healthy-object relatedness which will serve as our therapeutic allies during the course of psychoanalysis. Further data collecting on other cases will undoubtedly lead to further clarification and refinement of the distinctly different paedophilias and thereby increase the efficacy of psychoanalytic treatment.

In my classification, it will be obvious that I rely heavily on the concepts of separation–individuation (Mahler, 1966), in the belief in a pre-oedipal fixation that is primary, and that I am in agreement with Greenacre's (1971) comprehensive summing-up of her extensive clinical research on perversion. She suggested that

> our more recent studies of early ego development would indicate that the fundamental disturbance is . . . that the defectively developed ego uses the pressure of the maturing libidinal phases for its own purposes in characteristic ways because of the extreme persistent narcissistic needs. . . . Probably in most perversions there is a prolongation of the introjective–projective stage in which there is incomplete separation of the "I" from the "Other" and an oscillation between the two. This is in association with a more than usually strong capacity for primary identification. [pp. 48–49]

The pre-oedipal forms of paedophiliac perversion

The pre-oedipal form is due to a fixation to the pre-oedipal phase of development from age 6 months to 3 years. It is unconsciously motivated and arises from anxiety. Severe gender-defined self-identity disturbance is present: for example, in the paedophiliac male there is a faulty and weak masculine identity. This disturbance in gender-defined self-identity is never absent from any well-structured perversion and may only become apparent when the patient's unconscious material is subjected to close analytic scrutiny. The persistence of the primary feminine identity is a consequence of the inability to traverse the separation–individuation phase and develop a separate and independent identity from the mother. Paedophiles of the pre-oedipal type are beset by anxieties of an incessant and intractable nature, leading to an overriding and almost continuous search for sexually perverse actions. There is a persistence of primitive and archaic mental mechanisms leading to an abundance of incorporative and projective anxieties. The anxiety that develops is due to fears of engulfment, ego dissolution, and loss of self and ego boundaries, self-fragmentation, and/or separation anxiety, "identity diffusion" (Erikson, 1950). The patients need the perverse acts to assure ego survival and transiently stabilize the sense of self. Consequently they must repeat the act frequently out of inner necessity to ward off intense anxiety.

The perverse symptom is ego-syntonic, as the nuclear conflicts—including fear of engulfment, loss of ego boundaries, disturbances of self-cohesion—have undergone a transformation through the mechanism of the repressive compromise, allowing the more acceptable part of the infantile sexuality to remain in consciousness via the Sachs mechanism (1923). Aggressive and destructive wishes towards the mother and a fear of her retaliation or incorporation by her, together with dreaded wishes and/or fears concerning merging with the mother, are warded off through substituting the body of a prepubertal child for the body of the mother. Aggressive and destructive urges are libidinized and lead to orgastic release, thus stabilizing the sense of self (Eissler, 1958; Lichtenstein, 1961; Socarides, 1985; Stolorow & Lachmann, 1980). Such a patient also achieves a "good" mother (father)–child relationship. There is a lessening of castration fear through identification with the partner and a warding-off of fears of disturbance in self-cohesion leading to death anxiety and severe hypochondriasis.

Subtypes of pre-oedipal paedophile perversions—pre-oedipal Type I and II—can be defined and differentiated by the degree of pathology of internalized object relations. The solution to this complex problem of separating the various types of pre-oedipal perversion has been facilitated by Kernberg's important work (1975) defining criteria for understanding borderline conditions and pathological narcissism. In utilizing this approach, the meaning of oedipal perversion as well as pre-oedipal Types I and II are clarified as well.

In the milder pre-oedipal form (Type I), illustrated in the case history of Randolph (see clinical section of this chapter), while the pre-oedipal fixation is aetiological, the clinical picture may be largely one of oedipal-phase conflict and regression and does not involve severe impairment in object relations or other ego functions. In the more severe pre-oedipal form (Type II), an earlier pre-oedipal fixation is of prime importance both aetiologically and clinically, constantly dominating the psychic life of the individual in his search for identity and a cohesive self. Pre-oedipal Type I paedophiliacs also may show some progression towards heterosexuality that failed at puberty and/or other behaviour—for example, transitory episodes of homosexuality, which these individuals often greatly fear and despise and which produce severe conflict in them. Oedipal conflicts and castration fears may defend against deeper fear, and pre-oedipal fantasies may defend against the emergence of oedipal material (Hoffer, 1954).

In the pre-oedipal Type II perverse paedophiles, there is usually an associated narcissistic personality disorder of various degrees of severity. The analysis of such patients leads me to conclude that their fixation lies in the practicing and differentiating subphase of the separation–individuation process. I owe to Kernberg (1980a) a scientific debt of gratitude for his division of the spectrum of narcissistic pathology into "most severe or lowest level, middle range, highest level of functioning" (p. 29). These ranges appear to be at least in part related to the "extent to which aggression has been integrated into the pathological grandiose self or, on the contrary, remains restricted to the underlying dissociated and/or repressed primitive object relations against which the pathological grandiose self represents the main defensive structure" (p. 29). In the case material of Jenkins (clinical section), we see a typical pre-oedipal Type II paedophile at a more severe or lowest level of functioning whose symptom picture is dominated by an unintegrated joyful aggression, a pathological grandiose self, severe splitting mechanisms, paranoia, and projective mechanisms.

While Randolph shows narcissistic symptoms of excessive degree of self-reference in interaction with others, excessive need to be loved and admired, an inflated concept of self with occasional feelings of inferiority, and a shallow emotional life, he presented an integration of a sort of his own conscious self-experience which differentiates him from the borderline personality organization patient. He also felt little empathy for others, and he tended to idealize those from whom he expected narcissistic supplies. He was restless and bored when there were no sources to feed his self-regard, and he devalued and consciously spoiled what he received from others.

Jenkins, in contrast, had the most severe degree of narcissistic pathology, and along with his pathological grandiosity there were overt borderline features: (1) generalized impulsivity; (2) lack of anxiety tolerance; (3) disposition to explosive and dissociated rage reactions; and (4) severe paranoid distortions in his interpersonal field. This individual engaged in "joyful types of cruelty" (Kernberg, 1980a), expressed a combination of paranoid and explosive personality traits, had rage attacks, and blamed others. We see in Jenkins dissociatively aggressively invested part-object relations directly manifest. This is accompanied by condensation of partial sexual drives, so that sadistically infiltrated polymorphous perverse fantasies and activities are strongly manifest. Furthermore, as noted by Kernberg, "when such primitive aggression directly infiltrates the pathological grandiose self, a particular ominous development occurs, characterological sadism" (p. 30). In this instance we find paedophile perverts who practise their perversion with direct sadistic pleasure and aggression. Fortunately, Jenkins did not suffer from the severest degree of malignant perversion that would be present in some borderline cases of paedophilia and schizo-paedophilia, but it was true that unwelcome and uncontrollable aggression emerged in the transference which unfortunately militated against the patient's intrapsychic change. In contrast, Randolph showed less severe narcissistic pathology, as the "grandiose self"—as described by Kernberg—"was free from direct expressed aggression and repressive mechanisms protected the patient against the underlying primitive object relations that condensed sexual and aggressive drive derivatives". Randolph was able to sublimate and integrate his aggression into adaptive ego functions (he attempted writing and also was incapable of working, while Jenkins was able to work with children in a sublimated fashion to ward off and make up for his archaic punishing superego).

Schizo-paedophilia, in contrast to both the pre-oedipal Types I and II paedophiliac perversions, may be explained by its relationship to autistic and symbiotic modes of adaptation. All schizo-perversions represent a coexistence of a sexual perversion and schizophrenia. These individuals' fixations are formed in the symbiotic phase, according to their symptoms part and parcel of a psychotic condition. Such a fixation at the autistic and/or symbiotic phase takes place in order to ward off the fear of dissolution of the self-representation through re-engulfment by the mother and somato-psychic fusion. This is in striking contrast to the fixation in the pre-oedipal form Type I which has taken place during the later phase of the separation–individuation process (with consequent separation anxiety as a major form of anxiety) and pre-oedipal Type II whose fixation in earlier subphases—for example, practising and differentiating—and whose major anxiety is that of fragmentation of the ego and threatened loss of self-cohesion.

The spectrum of pathology in individuals with pre-oedipal disorders can best be understood when examined from the vantage point of the *degree* of selfobject differentiation achieved. Each stage of selfobject fixation/differentiation, whether symbiotic, differentiating or practicing, or rapprochement, produces its unique clinical features, although overlapping of features may occur.

In pre-oedipal Type II paedophiliac perverts, I have found that selfobject differentiation is severely impaired and the self is only just emerging as autonomous and its cohesiveness greatly damaged by resultant "identity diffusion" (Erickson, 1950; Kernberg, 1975). The predominant anxiety in these patients is of fragmentation related to an imperilled self-representation (as in the case of Jenkins), in contrast to that of separation anxiety in pre-oedipal Type I patients (the case of Randolph). Fragmentation anxiety all but obscures the separation anxiety and "separation guilt" (Modell, 1965) arising from the unresolved mother–infant tie. A vitally important clinical finding is that fixation in the practicing and differentiation phases produces severe deficiencies in the self-representation, with overwhelming tendencies to grandiosity. Pathological grandiosity produces a clinical picture in which the perverse patient may appear more integrated at times, less conflicted, more at ease with himself, and less distressed, especially when he is in narcissistic balance, not challenged by external reality, and is able to practise his paedophiliac perversion without intrusion or threat of detection. Beneath this façade of normality, it is apparent that the patient is unable to discriminate between the realistic and fantasy aspects of himself, is incapable of participating in activities that do not protect his grandiosity, and avoids those that threaten it (especially true in the case of Randolph). He tends to withdraw from others and continually overvalues or devalues both himself and the social realities surrounding him. All activities, as in the case of Randolph, which are not in the service of enhancing his grandiosity are avoided, postponed, delayed, or not re-sponded to.

Disturbance in superego formation and freedom from internal conflict in pre-oedipal Type II cases

Since sufficient structuralization of the psychic apparatus has not taken place, these patients show a marked absence of internal conflict. Their behaviour is not regulated by a superego identified with the moral power of the parents (moral self-regulation) since the patients have not yet developed beyond the "first stage of superego formation" (Sandler, 1960). Instead, "they invoke and employ object representations to comfort, punish, control or quiet their activities in a manner similar to but [less reliable than] super-ego formation" (Dorpat, 1976, p. 871). The severe deficits in ego and superego formation create a crisis in their overall function, espe-cially if the fixation is in the practicing and differentiation phase. At that time, they are unable to carry out the acts of comforting, controlling, guiding, or approving that "individuals with a struc-tured superego and ego are able to do from themselves". This dilemma is temporarily resolved by using external objects (self-objects, including *sexual selfobjects, prepubertal children*) whose func-tion is to substitute for missing structures and the functions they perform.

Furthermore, the absence or presence of a defective superego—that is, an automatic self-regulatory conscious mechanism—creates not only the imperative desire and need for sexual congress with children but also serious therapeutic obstacles, as these patients may remain unaffected as regards alleviation/removal of their perverse practices with children through the transference relation-ship (the case of Jenkins).

Defences in a primitive stage of development with splitting predominating over repression in the pre-oedipal Type II cases (the case of Jenkins)

Defences of the pre-oedipal Type II patients are in the pre-stages of development (Stolorow & Lachmann, 1980), and splitting predominates over repression. In pre-oedipal Type I patients, in contrast, repression dominates with some splitting phenomena, but major defence mechanisms are introjection, projection, and identification. The pathological use of splitting is due to a fixation to or a defect in the developmental process, interfering with the sense of identity, and development of object constancy. While splitting may be found in the rapprochement subphase of the separation–individuation process (Mahler, 1971), there is a more primitive splitting occurring in the practicing and differentiating subphases. A "vertical splitting" (Kohut, 1972), which produces a side-by-side "dissociation of mental contents" that keeps primitive, archaic grandiose exhibitionistic impulses dissociated from reality functioning, was especially prevalent and marked in the case of Jenkins.

Splitting of a "horizontal" form (Kohut, 1972), which separates "the reality ego from unfulfilled narcissistic desires by virtue of repression" (p. 240), was present in the case of Randolph. The motive force behind splitting seems to be due to separate negatively and positively charged self- and object representations in order to protect the ego core from destructive aggression (Kernberg, 1975).

The pathological grandiose self

It remains to be seen whether the grandiose self—a term coined by Kohut in a different theoretical framework from Kernberg's—is a compensation for early experiences of severe oral deprivation, rage, and envy or simply a fixation on an "archaic normal primitive self" (Schwartz, 1973). It also remains to be seen whether the shifts between idealization and devaluation (including self-devaluation) are defences against rage, envy, paranoidal ideation, and guilt over aggression directed against frustrating parental images or are partly manifestations of absence and/or deficiency in the psychic structure that maintains a self-representation and the functional use of objects for sustaining an object relationship and response to its loss.

It should be noted that in both Randolph and Jenkins pathological grandiosity is present, although it is more severe in Jenkins.

*Selfobject differentiation in pre-oedipal Type II patients
contrasted with pre-oedipal Type I patients*

In pre-oedipal Type I patients, (1) the self is nearly separated from the object; (2) there is some splitting-off of aspects of the self- and object representations; and (3) the focus of *treatment* concerns itself with the integration of split-off aspects of self- and object representations (Kernberg, 1984b). The chief task with this type of patient is to ascertain the degree of his selfobject differentiation. The patient's gradually emerging autonomous self must be protected from engulfment by the mother (as illustrated in the case of Randolph). Further integration of the split-off aspects of the self- and object representations must be allowed to take place. The issue, from the point of view both of the nuclear pathology and of the treatment, is that of the non-integrated self versus the integrated self, for reality testing is nearly established in a quite firm manner. As regards defences in pre-oedipal Type I patients, they are not predominantly centred around splitting but around repression, introjection, and projection. The transference is from object to self. The self is the narcissistically chosen child with a minimum degree of grandiosity, and the patient does not have a well-structured pathological grandiose self. Regressive fragmentation is not as severe or as deep as in those patients who are fixated in the phase of differentiation or practicing (the case of Jenkins). Primitive defences are not usually called into play, nor are there frequent dramatic crises in the analytic sessions except on rare occasions involving bodily dissolution, regressive fragmentation, and regressive re-enactment of rapprochement-phase crises.

In pre-oedipal Type II perverts, fixation is in the earlier subphases. The earlier the fixation, the closer to borderline personality organization and the presence of severe ego weakness or defects (these are present to a minimal degree in pre-oedipal Type I patients). The clinical manifestation of characteristics found in this degree of selfobject differentiation are: (1) there is a gradually emerging autonomous self; (2) there is a splitting of "good" and "bad" objects; and (3) the focus of treatment is to promote a "holding environment" (Winnicott, 1965)—promoting an empathic context while permitting the patient to retain autonomy vis-à-vis the therapist. In treatment, temporal continuity is often lost, a distorted perception of others occurs, and very little empathy is shown by the patient. In short, relations are often chaotic and shallow. The key characteristics of these patients are (1) regression and/or split fixation to the subphase of differentiation; (2) splitting of good and bad self- and object representations; (3) the issue both pathologically and therapeutically is between true versus the false self (Winnicott, 1965); and (4) the major and characteristic anxiety of this type is the tendency for "identity diffusion" (Erikson, 1950; Kernberg, 1984b). The term "identity diffusion" may be equated with Kohut's term "impairment in self cohesion" or threats of fragmentation (markedly evident in the case of Jenkins). Characteristically, such patients with severely imperilled self-cohesion have a poorly integrated concept of self and significant others; chronic subjective feelings of emptiness; contradictory self-perceptions; contradictory behaviour that the patient cannot integrate; shallow, flat, or impoverished perception of others; and a pathological grandiose self that obscures the underlying identity diffusion—that is, inadequate cohesion. In effect, the pathological grandiose self plus splitting mechanism equals the diagnosis of this severe form of narcissistic personality disorder.

The pre-oedipal Type II paedophile is unable to achieve object constancy—that is, unable to maintain a representation of the good object, especially under the impact of being frustrated by it or where he is not mirrored, reflected, or admired by it.

From the foregoing it should follow that fixation in subphases antecedent to the rapprochement have certain particular consequences of a severe nature. For example, a pre-oedipal Type II paedophile pervert (1) engages in splitting rather than repression as a major defence mechanism; (2) does not suffer from guilt but may develop shame; (3) is subject to powerful regressions in contrast to pre-oedipal Type I patients; (4) searches for idealized selfobjects (prepubertal children) to represent his grandiose self and responds with bouts of aggression at period of regression if these needs are not met; (5) has part-object relations rather than whole-object relations (the child equals the mother for Jenkins); (6) suffers from the fragmented body image and is subject to feelings of dissolving and disappearing, in contrast to a much more stable body image in pre-oedipal Type I paedophiles; and (7) experiences grandiosity, omnipotence, and demands for flawlessness due to the infiltration of the ego ideal with these characteristics. It should be noted that pre-oedipal Type II patients appear to have a seriously defective or absent superego; their activities at best are held together by certain idealizations. When these idealizations fail or the idealized object (the prepubertal child) fails him, the patient is capable of engaging in further psychopathic behaviour and intense if not murderous aggression.[2]

Perverse sexual activity in pre-oedipal Type II patients

In pre-oedipal Type II perverts, the patient attempts to find a tranquil integrity of being through perverse acts, in a sense to settle a crisis of diffusion of the self through soothing experiences that he insistently and imperatively pursues without any concern for the demands of reality. A good example is provided in the case of Jenkins. The often insatiable and voracious sexual acts function as a substitute for action in the external world, helping to fill a void created by his inability to take part in life.

In contrast to pre-oedipal Type 1 paedophiles, the sexual acts of Type II cases do not function as a prophylactic device in response to a fear of object loss or fear of losing the object's love, nor are they due to sensitivity to approval or disapproval by the parents or parental surrogates so typical of rapprochement-phase conflict. Instead, these acts serve to diminish the defect in the self and supply the self with stimulation.

The sexual object (the child) is in effect similar to a transitional object (Winnicott, 1965) in that it must show readiness to comply, lend itself to manipulation, and be used, abused, discarded, cherished, symbolically identified with but must not intrude upon the paedophile (note in both cases, especially in Jenkins, the paedophile wishes no response from the child to his "seduction"). Unlike the sexual object in pre-oedipal Type I cases who may be "loved" according to the model of "narcissistic love" (Freud, 1914c), he must surrender himself to the paedophile's omnipotent control, must wish to provide him with something (vitality and "reality"), and must supply warmth and comfort to him.

In all paedophile perverts, the "deadness" of the internal world is ameliorated and the fragmented self is temporarily healed. Preliminary to sexual relations, these patients experience depletion and depression—archaic defences against sadism and aggression. They attempt to resolve this internal despair through restitution and restoration by giving pleasure to a real external object and to the self simultaneously (Khan, 1965).

Pre-oedipal Type II narcissistic patients develop anxiety and the need to engage in their perversion when their self-cohesion rendered fragile by developmental interferences, reinforced by the internal image of an omnipotent and flawless archaic grandiose self, encounters situations that make them acutely and painfully aware of the discrepancies between the actual self and wilful, grandiose self (an external conflict). This is experienced as a traumatic exposure with intense feelings of inferiority and feelings of rebuff, humiliation, self-fragmentation, and threat to self-cohesion. As one of the attempted solutions to this crisis, the patient attempts to restore self-cohesion by engaging in primitive perverse acts. In contrast, pre-oedipal Type 1 patients experience anxiety and guilt associated with separation due to the fear of the loss of the maternal object or separation from her (internalized conflict). The fear of engulfment by the mother leads them to perverse acts.

CLINICAL SECTION

The case of Jenkins:
pre-oedipal Type II paedophile perversion
(borderline personality disorder)

Jenkins was a pre-oedipal Type II paedophile at the most extreme range of narcissistic pathology. He posed a guarded prognosis because of the severity of his internalized object-relations pathology, insufficient and marked fragility of self-organization (self-cohesion) with tendencies towards fragmentation, severe narcissistic pathology, and ego deficits with an impairment of superego functions. His defences were in a primitive stage of

---

An expanded and revised version of this material may be found in chapter 18 of my book, *The Preoedipal Origin and Psychoanalytic Therapy of Sexual Perversions* (Socarides, 1988).

development, with splitting predominating over repression. Overt borderline features were present such as impulsivity, inability to tolerate anxiety, tendency towards explosive rage reactions, and paranoid distortions of reality. Most significantly, an early increase in primary and secondary aggression produced a hypertrophy of aggression which directly infiltrated his actions, threatening both object and self. Bouts of aggression could only be controlled through libidinization and had not been integrated into any existing superego structure. Part-object relations invested with aggression were acted out and relieved in sexual relations with prepubertal male children. The severity of his intrapsychic pathology was clearly manifest by the frequency of his paedophiliac practices, two or three times a week, even under conditions that could have easily led to his being apprehended by the authorities.

Jenkins was an intelligent man in his late twenties whose sexual life consisted of the seduction of prepubertal boys. Increasingly disturbing symptoms of anxiety, depression, and a fear of death, which he had first believed were unrelated to his perversion, led him to seek psychoanalytic help. He had recently been frightened by a near arrest for his paedophilia. Soft-spoken and apparently mild-mannered, he was intensely hostile and uncooperative, doing his best to discredit the analyst and frequently stating that the analyst must hate him for his perversion. His productions were often of a paranoid nature, and on a number of occasions he accused the analyst of having hypnotized him during the session without his knowledge. He felt he had a "vendetta against society". Why should he stop what he was doing, what had society ever done for him? Often he became jubilant upon reading in newspapers of the personal destruction produced by floods, civil wars, and earthquakes.

He was the second oldest of a large number of children in a disturbed, quarrelling, financially borderline family. He often went hungry and continuously felt mistreated, as far back as he could remember. His father was often cruel and vicious to his mother. He remembered his father's angry outbursts and his own wishes that he could protect what he later felt was a "cold and heartless woman". When the patient was 5 years old, he and the child above him in age were, because of economic hardship, placed in a orphanage on the pretext that the mother would return for them the next day. "I just waited and waited, the night turned into days, the days into weeks, the weeks to months and then to years." On occasional Sunday visits, he would beg his mother to allow him to return home, pledging that he would be no trouble to her. Since his placement in the orphanage, he had felt that there was no love in the world. At the age of approximately 7 or 8, he was terrified by a story of cannibalism among white mice, and he often played in his imagination with the fantasy that the mother eats the young who cannot take care of themselves. He often had fantasies of all the children in his family returning to the mother's womb, suppressing this when the fantasy of a frightful tearing apart of his mother began to intrude. At 8 years, he complained of some transitory visual hallucinations of a Christ-like figure approaching him. His brother, two years older than he, was often cruel to him, making him carry out delinquent activities, frightening him and then holding him close to his body and kissing him. At the age of 12, when told by his mother that she had wanted to "abort him", he felt "lucky and happy to be alive". Shortly thereafter, while attending a father–son dinner as a guest from the orphanage, he began to suffer from severe depression upon seeing a young boy engaged in an animated conversation with a loving father. He ceased imploring his mother to take him home at about 11 years of age but shortly thereafter developed fears of death, often attempting to approximate this condition by becoming immobile and holding his breath. However, he soon became terrified over his inability to maintain voluntary control over what he called his "experimental state of suspended animation". At age 12, he was seduced by various older boys, his brother, and by a counsellor in the orphanage, fellatio and mutual masturbation being practiced.

He responded to the growth of pubic hair[3] with disgust, shame, and a feeling that the appearance of pubic hair meant a step closer to death. Only adults had hair, and he wanted to remain a young boy. By 15, a sense of personal dissolution and fragmentation of his ego appeared. At these times he would gaze intently at himself in the mirror in order to help control the threatening loss of ego boundaries and self-cohesion. This very often failed. "Some sort of thought would run through my mind as I looked at my face. I'd look into my eyes, and then my mind would start to leave me. Maybe it has to do with death. I had the overwhelming feeling I'll vanish, break apart, dissolve, be no more. I can only stop it by calling my brother's name over and over again and then my body reconstituted." During anxiety attacks, he would feel torn apart and in danger of imminent loss of self. His thoughts would lack purpose: words would become meaningless, actions goal-less. This intense anxiety would cease upon carrying out sexual relations with a prepubertal boy.

His earliest memories were those of being uncared for, "not having enough to eat". His mother would always act as it she were "doing me a favour in giving me a piece of bread". The parents were frequently fighting, and he, like the other children, was left to his own devices. Between the age of 3 and 4 years, he witnessed parental intercourse, but he stated that "it had no effect on me" except that he pitied his mother and felt that his father was some- how treating her badly.

By age 4, he frequently told his mother that she would never have to worry, that he would "take care of her". However, at 5, the traumatic removal to the orphanage took place. His reaction was overwhelming loneliness and "coldness". He wanted his mother to come back and felt that she had deserted him. On the other hand, he began to feel that he had "to live", or otherwise "I might die". He regularly promised to be "good" on infrequent home visits if he were not returned to the orphanage. However, he was always returned to and stayed in the orphanage up to the age of 17.

At 6 years of age, he was "pushed around" by the older brother who often bounced him in his lap and considered him "cute". He was alternately hopeful of returning to his mother then despond- ent, depressed, and lonely when he was not. He felt tricked by the mother: "Waiting and waiting, I never gave up hope until I was seven. I would beg my mother not to send me back."

At age 6, he had his first sexual experience. An orphanage boy, aged 16 or 17, played with his genitals, and he felt "cold sensations around them". "I didn't realize what was going on." His first seducer was the monitor (an adult) in the print shop where he'd occasionally go to be comforted (organizing experience).

At age 8, he apparently suffered a febrile illness and saw the man on the wall, a Christ-like figure that appeared to him later on. Also at age 8, he was spanked by a headmistress of the orphanage in front of others and felt humiliated, but he learned "not to cry".

He remembered that at that time also his father came to the orphanage one day, and he had a memory of his walking away
slowly and felt abandoned. From 9 to 10 years, "we would occasionally watch, with other boys, chickens having their necks cut off
and dying in an agony pit at a local butcher shop".

At age 10, when he stopped asking his mother to take him back
he developed a period of depression, which lasted until the age of
13. At approximately the same time his mother told him that she
had once wanted to have him aborted, that she had only wanted
one child, and that he was the second. He stated that somehow or
other he managed to control a great deal of his depressive feelings:
"Maybe through sex I found a kind of adjustment. I began to realize
that there would always be sex around. If I wanted to badly
enough, I would entice and have sex with any kid I wanted to.
Sometimes I think of having sex with a boy during the day. Sometimes I feel depressed. Other times there would surge through me
a feeling of great strength and super-confidence, that I wouldn't
have to have sex with boys and that I could conquer worlds. I
would have the ability to do great things."

Narcissistic grandiose pathology was expressed in his dream
life. A frequent recurring dream up to the age of 20 was of flying.

Sexual psychopathology

Several months after the analysis began, the patient revealed
that "I have sex with kids so I won't die. It keeps me young, keeps
me youthful. Having sex with women means that you are a grown-
up already. Kids don't have sex with women, only grown-ups have
sex with women. If I don't grow up, I don't die." By incorporating
the child, he staves off threats to his own self-cohesion. Furthermore, having sex with children is better because woman are
"filthy". "They have menstruation, blood . . . blood on the sheets.
Kids are cleaner than women and men. They are in one whole
piece. I see a kid as being nice and clean, something about a woman
that's dirty. And women are designed so ugly and men are so
much more graceful. Men have beauty in their legs and arms."

His second sexual experience was with his brother, three years
older, and occurred between ages 9 and 10. Following this he slept

with an older boy in the same bunk from ages 12 to 13, with very little guilt. He began to kiss an older man, who was one of the counsellors in the orphanage, from 12 to 14. He was the first adult "who befriended me". At age 13, other boys began to laugh at his growing pubic hair, and he felt shame and wished the hair would disappear, as he equated it with growing old. Up to the age of 15, he was dominated by his brother, but shortly after that he became a leader, a "spell-binder", as he put it, a "prince", president of the club and leader of the boys' and girls' student activities. He was afraid of adults and decided that he would somehow through his grace, manner, and "charisma" be able to be everyone's best friend and leader. At age 17 he left the orphanage, attended a local college on a scholarship, and shortly thereafter received a bachelor's degree. His career choice was in the area of public health.

A crucial event in the patient's intrapsychic life reinforcing his narcissistic pathology occurred when he ceased asking his parents to be allowed to return home. The external world had failed to provide him with any positive response, and a "change" occurred leading to both grandiosity and splitting with the development of a "hollow self", with an external formidable, convincing, charming "false self" emerging. He became a "friend" to others in the orphanage (and later to the children he seduced), a role aimed at lessening his despair, pain, and need for love. He was, in a sense, a person without a centre, who appeared strong on the outside but who had given up all hope of love and identity. He now would begin to secure his needs through sexualization and through incorporation of external objects (younger boys). He no longer felt he could "join anyone"; instead, he must "impress them", overpower them with his personality, and prey upon them ("like the praying mantis") to keep himself alive, supply him with love, and defend him against threats of ego dissolution and death. Heightened narcissism and imperiousness became an essential part of his personality, but he usually managed to keep them under control, except for occasional aggressive outbursts. He adamantly stated that "a spirit of humanity" no longer remained inside him, and he attacked life and people—in a covert motivational state of vengeance, pain, and suffering. Reparative measures against his aggressive incorporative tendencies evolved in his choice of career—for example, counselling children and their parents—in order somehow to undo the damage he himself has perpetrated through his sexual abuse of children.

The patient was frequently sexually abused by others before he was 12 years old. But at age 12, he himself seduced another boy. This was a significant passage from passivity to activity. At that time, he would never allow anybody to insert his penis into his mouth, and he used to hate his brother for doing so. His first act of paedophilia in which he was the *instigator* occurred at the age of 13 or 14 on a day on which he was roaming through the "tremendous halls of the orphan asylum". He described with great poignancy the depressive anxiety that overwhelmed him on a day he did not have the bus fare and was being punished by being made to stay in the orphanage and not going home over the weekend. He felt he was in a "prison".

> "I had a terrible feeling, a feeling which is painful to me, a vacuum that I even now feel when I don't have a boy. It's hard to describe this feeling, that no purpose, that nowhere to go, that nothing to do. On that day I had that feeling. There was this kid sitting on the window. That was the first time I actually ever had sex with him. It was the same feeling that I had coming back over and over again today, purposelessness of life and with nothing to do, a complete blank, a vacuum. I was lost, no one to talk to, an awful feeling, a horror feeling. I don't know what it was. And then I saw that kid. Somehow or other, I seemed to know somebody else that 'used' the kid. He had sucked somebody off. Suddenly, when I saw the kid there I felt different. I didn't have the hollow feeling any more. I took him some place and had sex with him. I knew every nook and corner of the place. He was docile, a sexy kind of kid, like I knew he wouldn't refuse me [the child was 10 years old]."

On another occasion, at age 18, while playing a record of *La Bohème* he saw a child enter a courtyard of an apartment house where he was living.

> "Suddenly an impulse came to run down to look at this child. I knew just about where the kid would be at this time. I looked in the store. He was about eight or nine. I looked at him.

Something was gripping me inside. I kept looking at him. I felt like I was in love with him. I wanted to pick him up and hug him in my arms. He seemed untouchable and unattainable, beyond me—an awe about it—and yet just looking at him was not enough. Some sort of pain. It tore me inside and it made me very unhappy. . . . I was very lonely and sad that day, and as I looked at the courtyard the music had a sad beauty to it. The tenor sobs and is pouring out his heart—cold, lonely, and a face in the courtyard. Like something happened inside. I left the record, and it kept playing. I had to take a look at him. I stood in a position so our eyes would meet. His tan face, black hair, soft skin: I just wanted to hug him, to kiss him, hold him in my arms. I can't recall wanting my penis between his legs or any of those things. . . . He was carrying a quart of milk and there was something about his actions. He seemed like a very well disciplined child, like a good kid. . . . I feel I only woke up then . . . the renaissance of me. I began to develop a philosophy: 'If I am not for myself, who will be for me? And if not now, when?' "

Shortly thereafter the full-scale paedophiliac acts began to occur at regular intervals.

Jenkins's paedophiliac urges were precipitated by a specific kind of anxiety. He stated that it was

"a hollow feeling which tears me up and destroys me, incapacitates me by the fact that I can't do anything to stop it. Also I don't want to do anything else. Sometimes I might force myself to do some work and I fake it. I run around like a chicken with its head cut off. It makes me feel restless, unwanted, that there's nothing in me. I'm hollow. I'm glad it doesn't last more than a day usually. It's frightening. I think I have death on my mind. There is no purpose to my thought, to my work, or anything I might do. There is no goal, no sense of achievement. Things pile up on my desk and I can't deal with work. Everything is meaningless, including words. I was talking to my secretary the other day and all I heard was words. I couldn't feel it was important to her. When I'm in that kind of mood people have a tendency, it seems to me, to talk to me more. There is no direction, no meaning to things, no goal, no purpose, things don't matter, as if all the goals I had were gone. I can stand it for perhaps a day or less. The happiest moments are when I see a boy. Do you know that? The feeling of power when I see the boy. I decide I'm going to have sex with him. The sex itself is just a release, I feel very good about it all, powerful, *alive*. It's going to keep me living, and it's a challenge to keep me occupied. It tries my wits and ability, . . . The feeling is I want him, I want to hold him in my arms, control him, dominate him, make him do my bidding, that I'm all-powerful."

On numerous occasions the patient awakens in the morning and, instead of the hollow feeling, he has a feeling of numbness over his entire body, a feeling that he may be disappearing, like "I'm, losing myself, as if my body has a whiteness."

The perversion has a warding-off function, cancelling out threats to the survival of his ego and threats of ego dissolution and fragmentation. It has a compensatory function in that it makes up for the deprivations of childhood, provides him with a sense of power and control, and buttresses and reinforces his fragile self-representation. The child must be subservient to him and responsive in the sense that he allows himself to be used (the patient engages in intra-crural penetration) so that the patient can feel alive emotionally. He merges with the boy, secures love from the good mother (the good breast), and in his sexual excitement overcomes the deadness of his own internal world.

Jenkins suffered from a continuation of the primary feminine identification with resultant disturbances in his sense of masculinity. He had no father to identify with and was unable to traverse separation–individuation phases and felt tied to a depriving mother to whom he was unconsciously in bondage. He sought salvation from the mother, relief from unconscious femininity by incorporating masculinity from the male child, and most importantly relief from fears of fragmentation of his ego. Jenkins stated that when he had sex with a boy, usually for the first time, he ejaculated very quickly, but it was difficult to ejaculate the second time. "I find that if I get some sort of feeling that I'm part of the boy I can have an ejaculation." He merges with the boy in the sexual act. "I'm having sex with boys because I want to be a boy, part of him, a blend. I could feel it more than I can say. I'm a part of him and he's a part of me."

In a crucial session he remarked that he was seeing a movie in which there was a very beautiful girl on the screen. As he was watching the picture of the beautiful shape of her breasts, he imagined himself touching her breasts, but it "wasn't my hand, it was his hand" (he was actually afraid of a woman's breast). "I got a vicarious thrill out of it." It was only through an intermediary— the boy— that he could touch the breast of the mother. The boy was also a substitute for the good maternal breast. "The strong sensation of a breast in his hand. I could feel it. Also I can recall when I had difficulty in ejaculating with a kid, I imagine we are together and we are merged. I'm afraid of growing up, afraid of death, afraid of growing old. I must get comfort here on earth, and I'm afraid I'll die before I'll ever be happy."

As regards the paedophile object—the young boy—he stated that he wanted the boys to love him but he didn't want to love them. He said: "it sounds narcissistic, doesn't it? But I can't give love to a boy. I feel I become part of the boy through the sex act. I'm the boy because I treat him the way I would like to be treated. Though I don't think the boy enjoys it, goddamn it. If the boy enjoys it too much I don't. It's important. If the boy starts making sex advances to me I don't enjoy it. If he starts to enjoy it too much I don't like that [the patient laughs loudly]. You know, it's almost like having sex with a corpse—no responses—all I seem to want to do is to use his body—to satisfy my desire." The boy, like a transitional object, is used, abused, loved, and made impassive so as not to take over and "deprive" the patient.

On other occasions he compared his paedophilia to the devouring activities of animals of the jungle. He became satiated and relieved of his aggression by devouring his victims. "I like the smooth surface of the young boy's body, I don't like hair on it or pimples. I don't like to touch that. I can't stand it. It's like eating something, like candy. Often I would pretend I was eating people as a boy: I would give this one life and the other one death."

As regards heterosexual activities and his relation to women, he stated that he had only disgust for the feminine body. A woman was a filthy, angry, and distorted monstrosity. "Not in one piece like boys," as their breasts protrude. "An adolescent or younger boy is more feminine than any woman. There is no hair on him, the hair is ugly. Boys' bodies are V-shaped while women's are angular. Like a bag of shit tied in the middle." They disgust him. A woman had no genitals, only a dirty hole where menstrual blood could contaminate and kill him by penetrating the opening of his penis during intercourse. Rare attempts during his lifetime to carry out heterosexual relations would only put him into a "cold sweat". Adult homosexual relations, on the other hand, he found uninteresting, boring, and fearful.

The boy was part-object, not a full object, as the whole-object might harm him. If he had intercourse with a woman, the blood might get into the opening of his penis and he might get sick. It might coagulate and destroy him (the source of a partial delusion upon which he would never elaborate).

In another session he elaborated on the feeling that he could get anything he wanted from a boy, and that he had to control him. "I can't give or receive love, that's my main difficulty. But I must feel that I can do anything I want with him, not hurt him though, just having him in my power, just my penis between their legs, and I'd kiss them. It's a good feeling. My penis becomes anesthetized sometimes, though, and it's hard to have an ejaculation."

The equation boy = breast became readily apparent through the analysis. He was always afraid of breasts and did not know what to do with them. He had a strong wish to incorporate the maternal breast. This could only be attained through merging with the boy (breast), thereby making up for his deprivation. During the perverse act itself, he not only identified with the boy receiving love at the hands of the good other, but he had in his possession the good mother (good breast) to ward off her frightening configurations. It became. furthermore. obvious that he identified himself with the boy as a defence against destructive wishes towards more fortunate children.

The perversion was carried out when the patient found himself in a deep crisis: he had to satisfy his love needs and eliminate aggressive impulses that threatened to destroy him. This was accomplished by incorporation of the good love-object (the child, a *substitute* for the mother) within the self, thereby maintaining a relationship to objects and preserving the self through a fused relationship. At this point, without the child as the love-object he would develop severe fragmentation anxiety with fears of imminent ego dissolution. This introjection culminated in orgasm, and his primitive needs found a pathway for discharge through the genitals. Viewed in another way, the anxiety associated with the need for the mother and aggression towards her at least temporarily was successfully libidinized and overcome through projection and introjection. In the joining of object and self and in the control of the love-object, he overcame his sense of emptiness and abandonment. He avoided further regression into a somato-psychic fusion with the mother and loss of self in a threatened state of de-differentiation (regression to the symbiotic phase and possible psychosis).

The child-victim chosen for the paedophiliac act was an ideal image of himself, and the object relationship was a narcissistic one, from grandiose self to self. He had to have a particular personality, a "selfish, attractive, pampered, loved child". He could not tolerate fat, ugly, or stupid children. They had to be selfish, "i.e., able to look out for their own well-being". He was even proud of the way some boys took his money and called them "smart kids", in effect complimenting himself.

Splitting phenomenon in the case of Jenkins

In splitting, Jenkins underwent a "transformation" into two distinct personalities. This became apparent when the analyst asked him to call at a particular time in the evening in order to be informed of the time for his next appointment. In the next session the patient revealed:

"I called at 8:30 but couldn't make a complete transformation. I couldn't be 'A' or 'B'. Ordinarily my transformation would take place at 7:00 p.m., right after the meeting at the place of work. I had to call you at 8:30 so I had to hold off. I felt it right in the pit of my stomach. I was nauseous. I had a sort of dull headache. I was on the street and I was full of anxiety, and I had to keep waiting around until 8:30. I think I'm two different personalities. I was planning to have sex with a boy that night, and I knew that the only way to get rid of my anxiety was to have sex with a boy, but to have sex with a boy it is necessary to complete the transformation to 'B'. I could only call you as 'A', not as 'B'. 'B' was trying; 'A' has control over the transformation. I know all day that at 7:00 I would go through it and I needed the sex, and right away. I thought perhaps you wanted me to call as 'A' [projection mechanism, as I had no awareness of this complete splitting phenomenon]."

The patient was asked how his transformation took place:

"The transformation happened five minutes after my call to you as regards our appointment. There is no obligation and no responsibility when I make the change after the call. Before that I was angry at you. . . . In it, I change. I change, I become an entirely different person, in looks, too. I think I get a strange expression on my face. 'B' is the child, irresponsible and without anxiety. My anxiety increased in that 'A' was in the way. 'A' must be shut off completely, and all my awareness and responsibilities has to be shut off [splitting of the ego] and 'B' is unaware of the anxiety of 'A'. After sex I go back to 'A', and that is painful. My facial expression is blank when I'm in 'B'. Suppose I should meet anybody I know as 'A' when I am in 'B'. Then I would feel a terrible anxiety, as I would look and act differently. In sex, the kids only know me as 'B'—a different person, an easy-going and good-natured person."

In the splitting of the object, the boy represented that part of the split with which he was identified and who, in inner reality, was the harmless good mother. The other part of the split was the dreaded, destructive, hateful, castrated mother, who was unacceptable to him and whom he dreaded incorporating. The object, therefore, had to be idealized and could not produce anxiety and guilt. This split of both ego and object allowed him to carry out his activity without conflict by denying a portion of reality.

The perversion has two functions: a warding off of danger and a compensating one. The warding-off function cancels out dangers of castration and loss of object relations and threats of ego dissolution and fragmentation and other dangers. The compensatory function makes up for the deprivations of childhood, providing him with an omnipotent sense of power and control, and buttressing and reinforcing his fragile self-representation. It is an artificial means of self-esteem restoration.

The child had to be subservient to him, responsive in the sense that he allowed himself to be used so that the patient can feel alive emotionally. He merges with the boy, an acceptable substitute for the mother, secures love from the good mother (the good breast), and in his inner excitement overcomes the deadness of his own internal world. In identifying with the boy, his victim, he received what more fortunate children had had in their early childhoods. He also defended himself against envious destructive wishes towards more fortunate children.

The perversion was carried out when the patient found himself in a deep crisis: he had to satisfy his narcissistic needs, eliminate aggressive impulses, and overcome deep insecurities, threats of ego fragmentation, and aggressive impulses. This was accomplished by incorporation of the good love-object, a substitute for the mother, within the self, thereby maintaining a relationship to objects and preserving the self through a fused relationship. The child-object, although male, had strong feminine traits and appearance so that he represented, in part, both parents. The introjection of the child culminated in orgasm as his primitive needs found a pathway for discharge through the genitals. In the joining of object and self and in control of the love-object, he overcame his sense of emptiness and abandonment.

The equation boy = breast became apparent through the analysis. This was accomplished through substitution (the Sachs mechanism). He was always afraid of breasts, he related, didn't know what to do with them, and yet had a strong unconscious wish to incorporate the maternal breast. This could only be satisfied by merging with the boy (breast), thereby making up for his deprivation. During the perverse act itself, he had in his possession the good mother-breast without the frightening configuration of the adult female body. The pronounced death anxiety in the case was in reality a symbolic fear of death provoked by deficiencies in maternal caring, the resultant separation anxiety culminating in the fear of death (Hagglund, 1978).

The sexual-object choice in paedophilia must be smooth-skinned and must have no pubic hair and no breasts in order to erase all connections with the mother. He must be slightly feminine, not masculine, although possessing a penis in order to escape castration anxiety. His face must be of a particular type representing a part-object. The face = boy equation discovered by Almansi in voyeurs (1960) is as meaningful to these patients as the breast = boy equation. Furthermore, the object is not usually anally penetrated as it may be in adult homosexuality, and it must not respond. It is neither male nor female: it is hermaphroditic. The requirement that the child be immobile and non-reactive—in a sense, a "corpse," a dead child from which life is taken so that one may live—was an important finding in several of my pre-oedipal paedophile patients.

In paedophiles, however, the sexual-object choice undergoes further disguise: instead of an adult man there is a prepubertal boy, who stands for both self and mother. There is an identification with and incorporation of the masculinity of the boy in the sexual act and the unconscious enactment of the mother–child relationship (boy = maternal breast).

Jenkins was consumed with anxiety over death from an early age. It took various forms: cannibalistic fantasies, return to the womb fantasies, feeling "lucky to be alive", attempts at "suspended animation" and holding his breath, fears of growing up, his conviction that he was put in the orphanage in order to "live, not die," symptoms of ego dissolution and fragmentation expressed as "I'll vanish, break apart, dissolve, be no more", and, or course, his constant search for children whose bodies and qualities he incorporated in the sexual act in order to feel renewed. Renewal signifies rebirth, a flight from ageing and death.

Death anxiety arose from severe separation anxiety, a lack of libidinal satisfaction during early stages of psychosexual development as well as the overproduction of primary and secondary aggression. It was promptly relieved by seduction and merging with a prepubertal boy. Only a boy could be both idealized mother and rejuvenated self.

Course of the analysis

Jenkins' psychopathology was severe in its obligatoriness and harmful both to the sexual object and to himself. His assertion that he'd never hurt a boy "physically" was a source of some "pride". He did not possess a reliable enough observing ego to permit transference neurosis or transference manifestations to be analysed. His poor impulse control tended to be acted out in the transference, and there was a predominance of hostile, aggressive impulses. Superego reactions of shame and guilt and feeling contemptible were present on occasion but were projected onto the analyst. He was unable to maintain a working alliance except for short periods of time. The therapist was reacted to negatively on many occasions, although the patient was able to admit at times the extent of his desolation to him. A paranoid distrust of the analyst and of everyone else, intense pleasure in cruel fantasies, and the presence of a pathological grandiose self together with deficiencies in ego function and an infiltration of aggression into almost all of his activities, in the presence of severe ego deficits characteristic of pre-oedipal Type II narcissistic perverse patients, all militated against a successful outcome.

Beneath an apparent charm and gentleness, he felt that all people were "cockroaches". "Man is a pimple, he is rotten and he is worthless. He has done nothing to change the world and he never will. Everything he does is for sex." He left many sessions angry and despairing, wanting nothing from anyone, including the analyst. At times he expressed shame at having to be put in the orphanage, but he did not feel shame for his perversion. When he saw the analyst as his teacher, guide, or mentor, he felt somewhat fond of him and at these times tried to abstain from perverse activities without much success. He was quick to feel that the analyst might be "making fun" of him.

Knowledge of the unconscious meaning of his need for boys led him for brief periods to attempt cessation of his paedophilia. "The analysis gives me some sort of strength today, but it now gives me anxiety when I feel the drive to have sex with a boy—like a kind of an insight into myself that it was a wrong, not right, idea, that I shouldn't do it. I didn't have to do it today. I don't have anything to take its place, however. It's a fulfilment. I somehow feel that if I do it, the anxiety will go away." The mechanism behind his perversion that would gradually empower him to have some degree of control over his dangerous sexual activities if he so desired was often met with taunts and accusations of hypocrisy. "I'd sooner love dogs or cats than human beings. They are certainly more worthy of my love. I don't want to change, because I don't want to change myself or society. That's why I don't want to stop." On other occasions he said, "I know that I don't want to stop. It's not that I can't. You're daring me, aren't you?" He was filled with hatred, loathing, and bitterness. Quietening down later in the session he managed to say, "I don't want to stop right *now*. I like you, you're the only sensible person I've ever talked to. You talk sense and you make sense. You could make me stop. You could do it. I'd like to. I wouldn't stop for anyone else."

Despite some evidence of a growing positive transference, the patient was frequently paranoid, mistrustful, and accusatory. His hatred for humanity, his despair, and his need for relief from threats of fragmentation, the necessity to ward off a break from reality, were too intense for him to continue therapy. He terminated treatment after approximately one year. Psychoanalytic treatment, however, was not without value, for it seemed to me he learned to understand in part some of the unconscious meaning enacted in his perverse activities, the mechanisms responsible for his perversion, and he was able to share his grief and fear, rage and despair, with an understanding human being.

It was important for me to realize that while Jenkins suffered the most severe degree of sexual pathology at the extreme end of narcissistic pathology, I later encountered other paedophiliacs in my psychoanalytic work whose level of fixation was not at differentiating and practising subphases and who did not present ego problems on the magnitude encountered in this unfortunate patient. In such instances, enriched by psychoanalytic insights that frequently only come from the study of the most serious cases, I was able to expect a more favourable outcome.

The case of Randolph: pre-oedipal Type I paedophile perversion

That paedophile symptoms may occur in an individual fixed at a higher level of development than in the case of Jenkins is evident in the following case illustration. Randolph's psychopathology arises from rapprochement subphases, with some evidence that there is a fixation at the practising subphase of the separation–individuation process. He has extreme fears, and he desires to merge with the pre-oedipal mother. His psychopathology included (1) fears of dissolution of the self-representation; (2) fluidity of ego boundaries with impairment of body-ego; (3) introjective or projective anxieties; (4) fluctuating states of object relations; (5) threatened loss of self-cohesion; (6) oedipal and pre-oedipal castration fears; (7) a continuation of the primary feminine identification with the mother; and (8) archaic aggressiveness which is expressed in violent, sadistic fantasies or masochistic acts and fantasies.

Throughout this patient's life history there was a continual interplay of four major themes that dominated his life, now one, now another gaining ascendancy in the clinical picture: (1) a powerful primary feminine identification, which he attempted to repudiate; (2) regressive episodes with dread/wish of maternal engulfment and ego dissolution; (3) pathological perceptions and altered body-ego experiences; and (4) perverse fantasies largely around paedophilia and homosexuality.

This patient, unlike Jenkins, was unable to stabilize himself through the formation of a well-structured perversion and was constantly in danger of regressive experiences and fears of engulfment. The alternation of slipping from one perverse fantasy to another was vividly evident throughout the analysis. Regressive productions were subliminally evident in the patient's daily activities and erupted dramatically into consciousness in the protective atmosphere of the analytic setting and under the influence of the transference.

The presence of the "little man" phenomenon was a further corroboration of separation–individuation theory when applied to perversions. It is due to the presence of an ego separate from the rest of the ego and has been described by Kramer (1983) and Volkan (1995). At the end of the third year, according to Kramer, it separates from the rest of the ego and passes through different stages of libidinal development, aspects of which attach themselves to the "little man". Its function is to make the *mother equivalent* available to the rest of the ego from which separation would never be required. This isolated segment, however, interferes with the development of a properly integrated ego and impairs the function of synthesis. It led to a weak, helpless, impoverished, and limited ego, even though the "little man" is evidence of "possessing great power".

My patient, furthermore, was prone to experience sensations of a change in the organization and sense of unity of the body ego in size, configuration, and spatial orientation—that is, altered body-ego experiences. I consider these phenomena to be regressive re-enactments of a fear and dread of engulfment by a mother and/or wishes to be penetrated by the father. They derive from faulty selfobject differentiation, a fixation in the earlier phases of separation–individuation. Altered body-ego experiences in perversions are attempts to obtain instinctual gratification through someone else's ego, suggesting an ego defect in these patients. Pain is used to stimulate skin sensation and to cause the reinvestment of the body-ego boundaries. A frequent finding is that there is a feeling that objects and people are actively inside one.

As perverse fantasies/acts were for the most part unacceptable to his conscious ego, especially those of homosexuality and paedophilia, he was unable to neutralize his anxieties from which he sought salvation. They found expression through his perceptual apparatus, through visual, auditory, and tactile spheres—that is, through altered body experiences (Socarides, 1988, chapter 21; Woodbury, 1966). Pathological perceptions were experienced as reality and responded to accordingly—for example, "I feel my arm is being cut off!" They constituted an externalization of conflict symbolically expressed in faulty perceptions.

Randolph was a 24-year-old college dropout and aspiring writer, from a prominent family, referred by a retiring psychoanalyst who had treated him for two years without an improvement in his symptomology. Unlike Jenkins, Randolph did not have the severity of degree of narcissistic pathology of a borderline quality as had the former patient. His character structure was more of a pre-oedipal Type I pervert with fixation as the rapprochement phase, short of the ability to achieve object constancy. Splitting and paranoid projection, although present, were mild compared to pre-oedipal Type II paedophiles. His major mechanism of defence was repression rather than splitting, although splitting occurred occasionally during the sessions. Furthermore, he had achieved a degree of development of superego structure and felt extreme guilt, shame, and inferiority for his paedophile impulses. He struggled mightily against his paedophile impulses as well as against homosexual, transvestite, and exhibitionistic impulses. Anxieties unneutralized by overt perverse behaviour left him incapable of functioning for years, except at a marginal level.

Paedophile impulses and practices began at the age of 10 or 11 years and in earnest after 13. In contrast to Jenkins, he fought against them and felt great shame and distress over them ("how could I contribute so to the destruction of other human beings!"). Anxieties were of such intensity that they caused impairment in all areas of function: group membership, affectivity, work, socialization, intellectual activities, intentionality.

He fled therapy after one-and-a-half years following a near-homosexual experience that he found frightening, and he quickly married a childhood girlfriend. On rare occasions he had been capable of heterosexual intercourse, using paedophile fantasies to achieve erection. He divorced a few months later due to his inability to function, with an increase of anxieties, and returned to treatment for another year and a half. During this period he married once again and was able to function marginally heterosexually. These marriages were a forced attempt to overcome the perverse fantasies and establish heterosexuality.

Unlike Jenkins, who chronically engaged in paedophile activities, my patient experienced his conflicts through pathological perceptions and body-ego disturbances—for example, pains in his leg, changes in the shape and size of various parts of his body. He suffered from dreams of being enveloped by the maternal body, sensations that he was being swallowed up, falling into space, being crushed and overwhelmed, being eaten by spiders, and so forth. In addition to these dreams and fantasies of being "swallowed up", he attempted to fend off these unacceptable wishes through the perceptual apparatus and experienced pathological body-ego sensations. Internal dangers were experienced as external visual perceptions.

Perverse activities themselves were prohibited by the ego opposed to them. These infantile fantasies remained isolates within the unconscious and were not absorbed into his perverse symptomatology.

He had rare tic-like movements and made sounds that expressed various fears, dreads, and satisfactions. Although castra-

tion anxiety was also in evidence, there were significant disturbances in his ego functions which could only be explained as due to
a pre-oedipal fixation.

He suffered from a gender-defined self-identity disturbance,
with a continuation of his primary feminine identification with his
mother and his wish and/or dread of maternal re-engulfment.

He maintained the tie to his mother through the "little man"
phenomenon in which the connection to the mother was assured
through the transitional object, the "little man". He feared the dark
until age 14.

Early history

Since 5 to 7 years of age, he imaged that a little man might be
perched on top of the drapes, slowly coming down them. At
approximately the same age he was petrified of certain animals—
for example, a bear—which would appear in the dark. The bear
was quite tall and would draw back the curtains and "look at me".
It was a large, frightening animal, obviously on its hind legs. "My
mother told me I had seen the big bad wolf. I dreamt about the big
bad wolf, but it stopped after she told me that story."

In his childhood years he felt that there were wolves under his
bed which might bite him on the ankle so that he would stay away
from the edge and sometimes lean over to see if he could see them.

This patient did not experience the wretched economic life and
family pathology of Jenkins. Yet his early life was replete with
separations and illnesses. The patient experienced abandonment
and separation anxiety due to the multiple and chronic comings
and goings of both mother and father, as the father was a business
executive attached to a foreign bank. Although he was born in the
United States, within one year the family had moved to a city in
Europe and then to other major capitals around the world. This
required the periodic absence of the mother and of the father, with
severe sense of object loss. In addition, there was an early weaning
from the breast, a tonsillectomy at age 2½ years, followed by
measles; whooping cough at 4½ years; and the presence of a phobic
fear of wolves at 5½. This later led to obsessive symptoms, all in an
attempt to control rage and fears.

In contrast to Jenkins, there were more neurotic symptoms in Randolph. Separation anxiety as a major anxiety, in comparison to fragmentation anxiety present in Jenkins, was striking. In Randolph, the loss of the object, severe illnesses, and severe separation anxiety played a greater role in subsequent psychopathology, whereas in Jenkins the loss of the object and the presence of severe aggressiveness, even before he was sent to the orphanage, amounted to a threatened destruction of both self and object and an inability to achieve developmental steps in selfobject differentiation. The fixation in Jenkins was more at the practising and differentiation phase, while in Randolph it was more at rapprochement. Randolph fought against paedophile, transvestite, and exhibitionist impulses and desires. Jenkins, on the other hand, because of the severity of his aggression, split both object and subject to ward off the destruction of object and self, and fears of ego fragmentation of the self; a structured perversion resulted in order to successfully alleviate the overwhelming threats to his ego. However, Randolph's inability to form a well-structured perversion left him prey to the development of multiple perverse fantasies, severe alteration in body-ego experience, and pathological perceptions.

In Randolph, the prepubertal boy was of a certain type who represented the idealized, sustained, competent male self as well as the powerful feminine self in identification with the pre-oedipal mother. He also escaped oedipal guilt by turning to a male rather than to a female. He would, furthermore, achieve victory over his older brothers (by two and four years), who would often hold him down when he was a child, rendering him helpless.

He often spoke in the sessions about "becoming a man". Maybe the defects in his personality had stopped him from ever becoming one. "I wish that my father was more aggressive in character." When he went to a college function, he took up smoking a pipe. His grandfather once said, "I'd hoped you'd follow in your father's footsteps." His father always under-tips, and this annoys the patient. When speaking of the emotions of love, he states: "Half the time I go through emotions of being a son with a mother and father, but I don't love them. I don't have any strong feeling of love or great affection."

Unlike Jenkins, Randolph was brought up in an "aristocratic" household. There were constant feelings of loss—a pattern of constant shifts and changes of scene and environment, and loss of one parent or the other for various periods of time. Although Randolph was born in the United States, when he was a year old the family had moved to Europe and the mother took care of him herself, except she frequently went out to dinners and luncheons secondary to her husband's job. When she did that, a rather timid German housemaid took care of him for the first year. At the end of his first year, his father went away for one month. "Me and mother slept in my room, and she took care of me while the maid went to the beach with the older boys." He had a small room next to the mother and father's and a crib for naps on a sort of balcony outside the bedroom where she would watch him. The mother stated in a letter to his former analyst that at that time he was a "happy, healthy baby with a good appetite . . . who started out as a sunny, happy, and a very healthy baby and a great chatterer". In the middle of the second year, however, the maternal grandmother became seriously ill and was not expected to live. The mother left the patient with a Swiss maid while, with the other two boys, she went to America for four to six weeks (this was a second major separation and loss of the object). A third separation occurred a few months into his third year. Because of a new appointment given to her husband, the mother again went to Europe to find a new home in a foreign capital. This necessitated at least two trips, with one maid staying with the children. This was a separation of three to four weeks, and at this time the maid moved the patient's crib to a room on another floor, further isolating him.

An additional separation occurred at age 2½ years. All the boys were shipped with a maid to a mountain spot near Geneva for two to three weeks while the mother went to Paris to make arrangements for the move (a fifth separation). when he was 2¾ years old, the family moved to the United States, and on board the ship the patient became severely ill with bronchitis and the doctor ordered a trained nurse to stay with him. The patient recalled that he was very unhappy about a nurse being there—"I don't want the lady to stay"—and as a result the mother was with him a great deal and the "lady did not stay at night".

A nephew, age 22 years, was taken into the family when the patient was 2½ years old in order to especially take care of Randolph. He stayed with the family until the patient was 3 years of age, at which point they moved to the house in the Paris suburbs and Randolph had his own room for the first time. The male cousin stayed in a room next to Randolph until he left in early summer.

When Randolph was 3½, the patient's mother began an incessant travel schedule to international conferences with her husband. It was "expected of her" and she "enjoyed it", she stated in a letter. There were plenty of social demands on her. At 3½, Randolph had his tonsils removed, as did the other two boys, ages 5 and 7. The husband came for a short time during this period. Also at this age, all three boys had measles. Following the measles Randolph contracted whooping cough and was quite ill. The paediatrician advised taking him out of the damp Paris climate to the mountains. One of the maids took all three boys for a school holiday and left Randolph at a chalet, where he stayed for about two months with his nurse (this constituted a further abandonment and a major separation and feelings of desertion). Both wife and husband went to visit him separately during that period, and when they went to bring him back he cried, because, according to the mother "I had changed the way I fixed my hair and I didn't look like the photograph he had of me." He recalls today that he did not recognize his mother and felt dissociated from her when she returned to see him.

An additional traumatic separation occurred when the patient was 4 years old. The father and mother had to come to the United States for important business, and the mother also had to receive X-ray treatment. The boys, however, were sent with a maid to Montana for Christmas; the parents joined them at New Year's, and they all came back to Paris together.

Also at age 4, he was at a bilingual school, where he felt quite liked. At age 5, everyone came to America together; the two older boys went to camp, while the patient and his parents had a cottage nearby. By this age, however, the fear of the wolf and the bear had started, and he tried to handle it the best way he could. He was clinging to his mother, but phobias and later obsessions began and severe separation anxiety was manifest.

At age 6, a further abandonment occurred. The husband and wife went to another assignment for some meetings, leaving him with a Norwegian girl and his brothers. While the other boys went to camp later on, the patient and his mother and one of the maids spent their time rather happily at a resort. The husband came home from abroad one weekend. With the coming of World War II, the father stayed with a governmental service in England for two years, and the patient, his two brothers, and his mother returned to the United States. Significantly, the father was absent for those two years when the patient was age 6 to age 8.

He recalled that he cried easily up to age 10 or 11. He would also jump up and down on rocks to see how many times he could do that without "paying"—in effect, a compulsion. He frantically tried to keep up a "front", but underneath he felt frightened, inadequate, without strength. He did not know the reason why.

Beginning at around age 11 or 12, he started stealing money from his parents. In addition, his brothers would make him cry, and he was very attached to his mother. He felt quite isolated from his brothers, and when he first went to school he experienced severe separation anxiety.

He recalled a dream around age 6: "I hated the dream. It was the first time I recalled hating to go to sleep afterwards. A dream of being powerless to move and a kind of *humming sound* like a power station, like large things closing in on me. Struggle to wake up. Sometime I woke up in a sweat." His associations were that on a recent evening he had written a letter to himself in the future: "September in the rain. I was writing to tell myself what the world would be like in the future." He usually had this dream while falling asleep or waking up in a semi-nightmare. Sometime he experienced the following phenomenon: "Something jumping on my back or my being flung up in the air. I would fight like mad." He also had a vague impression of something "light-coloured, a force coming at" him, coming into the room. Sometimes it came through the top of the window and a very large bird, a vulture, would swoop down.

He recalled that when he was 8 years old his father came back from the war. "When I saw my father's bed, I was disbelieving that father was going to come back to us."

At 5 to 6 years he developed compulsions and obsessions about stepping on cracks, and so on. "It I stepped on a crack with one foot, I had to equalize it by stepping on the right. If rounding a building, I had to do the same thing on the opposite side of the building to equalize it." He recalls that he felt rebuffed by his mother severely at age 11 or 12. "Around eleven or twelve I walked up to my mother's room, knocked on the door, and woke her up. I can't remember whether she had already had Meniere's syndrome or not. It was one of the few times she lost her temper. She was practically *growling*, told me to get back to my room. I was greatly distressed. I was afraid of the sound she made, perhaps like the sounds I don't like in the dream. A sense of rebuff. I looked and saw that her light was on" (narcissistic mortification). As he related this, he developed a lump in his throat and a fear that he would be unable to swallow. When he saw her cry on that occasion, and also one other time at age 8 or 9, he was struck with disbelief and fear that his mother could be "weak". This represented a fear of being weak himself due to his primary feminine identification with her. Her anger towards him for interrupting her while he was in the room also made him feel abandoned and separate.

This patient did rather poorly in school, finding it difficult to complete assignments on time and resenting authority. He always felt he missed his mother and was only happy when he was near her. He entered college but failed to get past the second year because of his inability to study and his worry over paedophile, homosexual, and transvestite wishes, along with pathological perceptions that would assail him especially when going to sleep. A year before entering treatment, he had the conviction that Chicago was going to be atomized by an atom bomb and this belief, arising from some newspaper stories of the force of atomic energy and mention of the hydrogen bomb, led him to a semi-delusional belief that something might occur of that nature. Although he said that he did not quite believe it, it forced him to leave Chicago a few days early.

Sexual psychopathology

Paedophilia.   At age 11 or 12, he had his initial contact with a younger boy (two to three years younger) and the boy's brother, who lived next door. He went into the bathroom with the boy, and they looked at each other. "I just got a physical sensation, and now as I say this I feel as if my hands are injected with novocaine and they're larger" (alterations in body-ego). He also stated that he felt a slight amount of sexual excitement when this happened. This occurred at least five times with this boy over the next two or three years. Beside mutual masturbation with the young boy, he liked to assume the man's position in intercourse and rub his penis between the boy's thighs. He stated that maybe this was an attempt to imitate intercourse one might have with a woman, with him being the man. He not only wanted physical touching but wished to see the "leg and shape of the leg—the leg would have to approach the feminine in appearance. Occasionally the back of the hand or the face were important. . . . The face is the primary source of attraction. Any element of being masculine—that is, rugged in appearance—is not exciting. Blond hair is more attractive than dark. The leg between the calf and the thigh is important and also a trim ankle" (his mother has trim ankles, he states). "A certain facial expression on the boy's face has special importance and is exciting. There are certain expressions and certain kinds of faces that appeal to me, a kind of look, a faint smile, with a slight element of superiority. And yet a young face—the faintness of an element of scorn, pride, and general impression of self-sufficiency—is important to me" (narcissistic object choice with superiority and grandiosity). "I dislike almost all pictures of children, especially if they are drooling. I feel embarrassed to admit all this. I feel that any sign of strong emotion immediately turns me off. I prefer the term 'a self-contained individual', 'an individual with a dry sense of humour'. I guess that is what I'd like to be. In effect, I'm portraying myself—contained, smooth voice, unemotional in demeanour, and with a manner of self-sufficiency and self control. There is something about the total formlessness of the face." He also does not wish the child to react in an emotional way, because he does not want to be the recipient of any emotions (similar to Jenkins).

After puberty, aged 14, he began to feel increasingly guilty and bewildered by the fact that his acts continued—for example, twice at age 14 and once at 16. Sexual relations with an 11-year-old boy involved mutual examination and masturbation. The second incident occurred in his own home, when a boy of his own age came to visit.

He became increasingly disturbed: "Any time I see a small boy I'm overwhelmed with a sense of guilt that I've tampered with another individual in society."

BMA Library

BMA House, Tavistock Square, London WC1H 9JP

British Medical Association

BMA House

Tavistock Square

London

WC1H 9JP

BMA

He reports the following dream of paedophilia:

"Walking down a row of houses, I turn into a dark alley. A boy is in the alley and he follows me. I couldn't remember what he said but I saw what the general tenor suggested. After the sex exposure I like to expose myself and see myself nude and see him nude, he followed me into the house. He started to undress himself again. I did not respond, as if I had no feeling at all, as if there was a feeling of nothingness."

He continues:

"All my fantasies at the start for a couple of years were accompanied with masturbation with girls, and at some point [age 11 to 12] very gradually they began to shift over. The first recollection of anything with sex overtones was same sex with the two boys who lived next door. We would go to the bathroom, engage in exposure, look and take all our clothing off, and put it back on again. At that age I was beginning to brighten up when anyone showed affection towards me. One time, while playing in the neighbourhood, Hardy was standing at my door giving me some kind of medal. He made the motion of kissing my cheek. It embarrassed me and I blushed, but I *felt very good.* At age twelve I played strip poker with Joe who was fourteen. I remember being very suddenly interested in him and his penis being so large. Someone mentioned masturbating to me. The first time I masturbated was around that time with Derek. It was initiated by me, going into the garage, into the cellar where there would be mutual masturbation. I'd also place my penis between his legs. I don't remember whether that went on for more than one summer. There are still times during the present when I miss that, look back at the whole thing with pleasure. But it is also important to me that I don't do the seducing that much. I get to know some people and the boy will come to me and make it evident what he wants—what I look at most is the legs, abdomen and body. I don't often think of masturbating the boy now. I look at the face, the hair is usually blond, the legs long and slim. The legs are feminine. Sometimes in my fantasy I will rub my hands over the legs and abdomen. It is very important that there be *no hair*—somehow the presence of hair makes it unattractive and even *repulsive*. Sometimes in this fantasy I am masturbating, I want to stop and say, No, no, no; and I try to slip the fantasy into that of a girl . . . .

"There's something about the line of the leg, extremely graceful looking and exciting, the calf below the knee. The first boy was someone I was attracted to. He was small, not really feminine, youthful for our group, very vital. He seemed younger than most people in my class in the eighth or ninth grade. However, at ten or eleven there was sex with the W. brothers. We would go into the bathroom, take our clothes off, and look at each other. A curious feeling at the same time. Although I was interested in girls at that time I lost interest in girls. At the private school at sixteen I started to have an interest in younger boys and I started to have the feeling of bewilderment at all of this."

Similar to Jenkins, he is relieved of any feeling of depression by thoughts of having sex with a boy. He reported in one session that after a weekend of being with a woman as friends, he was walking home and felt very fatalistic, that soon one would be dead in the world anyway, but his spirits lifted when he saw a boy. But he did not approach him. Paedophilia was a defence against death and ageing, narcissistic damage, and deterioration.

The patient's paedophilia and transvestite and exhibitionistic wishes assert themselves when he feels a great despair and lack of willingness to go one with life. He stays up all night, reversing his sleep cycle, feels superior to others, and is able to be alert and think only when others are asleep. However, he is assailed with all kinds of horrifying dreams of engulfment, alterations in body-ego, and pathological perceptions.

In a session when he thought of his homosexual encounters, he had the fantasy of animals reaching out towards his penis. He felt anger and intrusion. Then he had the sensation that somebody is "sawing my leg off, sawing my right leg off" (pathological perception).

Homosexual feelings have left him with much anxiety, rage, and a wish to engage in self-castration. He also notes that because of his attractiveness, his natural good looks, he has been approached by men quite frequently, since the age of 11 or 12. "When

I go down to these buildings I'd be approached by one man or another. It has become exasperating." Sometimes he wishes to be a woman, wishes to hurt himself, to have his penis cut off, to be a hermaphrodite. But for him the worst thing of all is to become a homosexual and lose his complete identity as a man.

His first adult homosexual experience occurred when he was a sophomore in college. He had been drinking, and a man was singing with him on the subway. After an hour of talking with the man he'd met, "I took off my clothes and went to bed with him. I did not like the physical contact and vetoed immediately the idea of being kissed. All I wanted was to be masturbated and that's all I indicated I was interested in. He wanted to suck my penis, and the whole business of so much passion just didn't click." There have been a total of about six homosexual experiences: one with two men, three with two others, beginning several years ago. "In each case I wanted the orgasm itself produced by somebody else. I have distaste for the man's body. It has a smell I don't like either or to any great extent the penis. The main pleasure in masturbation is *exposure*—that is, the taking off of clothing. I am interested in the other man's nakedness, presenting myself naked to the man is what excites me."

In contrast, the attraction of the young prepubertal body of a boy was the attraction of the feminine, but the object is a girl with a penis.

"In masturbation the image was of a woman's figure when I was much younger. Then I became confused. There was fear attached to the image of a woman, but not with a boy or the blankness of a boy. The blankness is where the genitals would be. Each time the idea of naked girl in active intercourse is not exciting, even though the girl might be. At the point, though, of having intercourse, I begin to veer away. This has permitted me in fantasy often making surprising and compelling efforts at erection, sometimes with a boy, a woman, a man in fantasy. The boy in the fantasy is actually cut out before the climax and the woman in the fantasy put in. First the idea of a naked girl without intercourse, and, as the intercourse occurs, the boy supplants the girl, and when orgasm occurs the boy is cut out and the woman put in" [this attempts to save him from anxiety].

Of importance seems to be early memories of his mother looking threatening, savage, and smiling an extremely diabolical smile. "A little wave of fear would go through me." Another fantasy was reported following the last one: "Some girl I don't know who, instead of being a fantasy of embracing a girl, I was standing behind myself watching. I feel red spots on my hand at the end, and it became disfigured and also became grotesque. This happened to the girl too, and I think she becomes like a witch." At other times he has fantasies of his mother's face turning into a frightening mask. He recalls that at age 7 or 8 his mother kissed him goodnight and she put her tongue out. His lips kissed her tongue; it startled and frightened him. On another occasion he reports the fantasy of accidentally sitting on a razor, that he would cut off his penis or injure his face, his cheek, or his eye, cutting his eye.

At other times the patient has vivid dreams of "things" on his arm which look like very large dark-green moles moving up his arm. He also notices this on his leg. This has happened when he had guilty feelings for approaching a woman. If she acquiesces, he has a fear of imminent disaster. The ensuring drop in self-esteem is expressed bodily in a hypochondriacal fear of being affected with a melanoma.

Fear of maternal re-engulfment.   In one session he reported the following fantasy:

"Falling off a roof, the bodies in a courtyard. I feel floating now. I observe that someone falls on my body, a woman, tearing me apart with her teeth. I'm not sure whether there are children or not. One leg comes off. She called for me—I saw what was happening—to come down. The woman was tearing apart the children [the devouring, enveloping, destructive mother, the wish/dread to be eaten by the mother, although it would mean his own self-destruction]."

He reported a dream of engulfment:

"*Some men who in retrospect might represent the actor Dean Jagger go somewhere down below, a path into the mouth of a cave or a gully. Something is living in there, a huge spider, a tarantula ten feet long.*

Everybody grows apprehensive. Then I am in the middle of this. The tarantula comes along yelling and this thing gets a hold of me—jaws chopping."

Sounds are very important to his dreams. A bear who is standing on his hind legs is the father of the primal scene emitting sounds of sexual intercourse, which he wishes for and fears to be part of . It also represents his wish to be devoured and merge with the mother.

At the border of sleep he has the following dream or a fantasy— he cannot tell which:

"I take some kind of injection, treating myself for something. Then I go to Dr K., ashamed to tell her that I have treated myself. Also afraid that her treatment and mine may not mix well. While she examines me (she has given me a rectal exam) I hear a sound like a dissonant piano chord—somehow con- nected with my skeletal structure. In this dream I see an ana- tomical view of myself, my body structure is coming apart. That same time I turned around in a dream and Sam is there display- ing a statue. I turn away, then turn back. The statue represents death. The same night I dream I'm in a French music hall, first sitting in a box at the left side. A group of chorus girls are dancing to the music that I have composed. The stage is being cleared in preparation for a play I have written. Suddenly I see a piano on a platform obstructing the stage. A man is playing wild music faster and faster. Very disturbing. He dies."

Regressive wishes to merge with the mother occurred in almost every session. A recurrent fantasy was particularly disturbing. "I am in a room or a house and instead of going into the house I find myself inside a passageway which got tighter and tighter, and I kept being wedged in." His associations led to his understanding that this represented his wish/dread to return to the womb, with a fear of death, a wish to die, a wish to deny life, but also a wish to go back to the beginning, to be reborn. He recalls that he was told that the process of birth by his mother was a comparatively easy one, his being the third child, even though she was 41 years old.

"I was not planned. There was some oversight as they hadn't planned for me. Maybe the only reason I'm here could be I'm here by accident, but I'm here. I've always had the feeling my mother had a great dominance over me by allowing herself to have a small son at that age. In giving herself that pleasure I feel it had a great effect on me. *If the general aspects of my life had been handled another way, or if my father could have been more assertive and masculine, I wouldn't be this way."*

His dream life and fantasy represents fear of engulfment, his wish and dread of being devoured, lost in space—anxiety and guilt in association with selfobject differentiation—for example, a recurrent dream that he places back to 3 years of age, lasting up to age 13: *"There's a steady kind of buzzing and a buzzing around where things are closing in on me. Not necessarily living things—for example, elephants, a great weight moving in on me, and I'd be unable to move."* In addition to this mass approaching there is a whirring sound that is present (Isakower phenomenon). *"It sounds like an electric planet pulsating, a feeling of pressure and a light colour closing in on me."* The following are dreams and fantasies of his unconscious dreads and wishes for maternal re-engulfment.

He dreams of being in a tunnel, and he comes to a chamber in the centre and there is a strange object there whirring like a big top, making a terrible, horrible sound. A dream of engulfment is represented in following fantasy: *"I'm falling down a well or something of this sort. Splashing into water and a huge cover descends over me that seals me off.* Also I dreamt of *a huge large spider coming after me."* On another occasion he dreams: *"I'm living in a flytrap, an indescribable, awful other place. I'm downstairs. My mother is there, something about a letter containing some money. At one point a man comes down with his trousers torn away and he's in a rage and I have some thought about my mother's presence as a comfort. She's arranging the aspects of my life."* He dreams: *"There was a huge dome proceeding underground, all of a sudden thinking about getting into the dome. I looked into the dome and there was the president* [grandiosity]. *Then trying some means of transportation."* At other times he has fantasies of a heavy grey-domed terrace overlooking the night sky and a steep cliff to the side of it, and he is terrified that he may fall over the side and be lost in space.

Another dream concerns his having difficulty breathing, at which time he asks someone to help him. *"There is an office with a woman in it, a female doctor somewhere in her forties. I don't remember her face but she is quite a comedian. Horseplay and laughing. She removes a bullet from me like a clothespin covered with plastic. She warned me that it might be painful but there is no pain. She located the bullet and she took it out and we look at it."* His associations were that he frequently imagines being shot like that, like this wouldn't happen to him but it does. He also remarks that perhaps he is being relieved of his penis, the possession of which has been so traumatic for him.

"Being somewhere with a series of things closing in on me, something of the size of elephants, like big. Don't know if it's alive or not. Usually accompanied by a noise. If you've ever heard the note of an organ—vibrations in the floor. More than you can just hear—the room vibrates to it, a sort of buzzing sound. It gets closer, the humming was within me. I also feel unable to move. I want to take flight and I can't. I can't move. A sort of fatalistic feeling about it.

At times he dreams of violence, not only to himself but that he has committed violence towards others. At one point he dreams of killing a man.

"I committed a murder. I don't recall how I did so. I killed a man and I don't recall the actual circumstances. I have to dispose of the body and dump it into the bathtub in the living-room. In the dream I have read somewhere that one uses quicklime or liquid cement to get rid of the body. What I had was liquid cement. Now maybe I had to disrobe the body. I put the body into the bathtub. I would disrobe the body and the contractions of cement would break it up into small pieces and therefore I would dispose of it. I realized it could not harden. Then three maids came in and they would see it. I can't recall how any of them looked. One of them was about to move towards the tub, and I stopped her. I wondered if perhaps I would be able to conceal this. How long could I live with my conscience? Probably quite a while.

The dream was quite real but it seemed to him that his disposing of the body is the disposing of himself, and the finding of the body reconstitutes himself.

At other times, he stated, he is afraid of everything:

"So afraid of the night and what it brings that I want to blot out the day or both, night and day. Instead of feeling emotion at some level, my intellect takes away the awareness of the emotion, passes it out so that I don't feel it but I know I've been afraid. I have an inclination to stop seeing people altogether. I have a daydream that a convenient way of looking at things is just not to think about anything, not to think about reality. I suppose the nullification of others at night-time is what is important, for me to get away from everything, I guess to stay alive. It makes me feel weak, but maybe that's why I walk around at night, in order to feel strong."

Oedipal paedophilia

It is important to differentiate oedipal paedophilia[4] from the pre-oedipal form. When perverse symptoms arise from the oedipal phase of development, the pathological behaviour is slightly deviant, transitory, and not well-structured, and failure to engage in the perverse act does not lead to intolerable anxiety. The oedipal form arises from a *structural conflict* between major structures of ego, id, and superego—that is, between the subject's aggressive, sexual, and other wishes and his own prohibitions or ideals. The nuclear conflict consists of renunciation of love for mother and corresponding conflict in the female. It must be differentiated from the pre-oedipal, which arises from pre-oedipal levels of development, with which we associate narcissistic neurosis and borderline conditions. The clinical picture of the oedipal paedophile is largely one of *paedophile behaviour* in which oedipal-phase conflicts predominate and in which there is a turning to a prepubescent child for sexual gratification. The regression does not imply a disturbance in object relations nor a disturbance in ego functions. In the oedipal form, object relations are from self to object, in contrast to pre-oedipal forms, in which object relations are mildly to moderately to severely impaired and consist of object to self.

The developmental history of the oedipal paedophile and his attainment of a degree of object constancy makes him more favourable for therapy. In pre-oedipal forms, fixations may be moderate to severe and are located in the earlier phases of the separation–individuation process. In the more severe paedophiliacs, those in which primitive aggressive wishes predominate in association with a high degree of narcissistic pathology, fixation will be considerably more intense and originate in early phases of separation–individuation fixations, bordering on the symbiotic phase. While the oedipal paedophile has a structural conflict, the pre-oedipal paedophile has an object-relations conflict—that is, anxiety and guilt in association with the failure of developmental, selfobject differentiation.

As regards therapy, transference in oedipal paedophiles may be quite ideal, as in neurotics. A careful assessment of the ego functions is necessary in any case that appears to present itself for therapy. Reality testing and impulse control are intact. Thinking is unimpaired; self-concept and ego boundaries are essentially unimpaired. Conflicts are internalized, affect is appropriate, and aggression is essentially well-defended against. These ego functions are severely impaired in the pre-oedipal forms. As noted earlier, oedipal perverse symptoms may be treated similarly to the neurosis and may be termed perverse paedophile behaviour. Such perverse behaviour appears secondarily to a temporary regression and does not represent a primary fixation or developmental failure with consequent gender-defined sexual-identity disturbance—a finding in all pre-oedipal perversions.

It is imperative, therefore, for any investigator and the legal system to determine the type of paedophilia one is dealing with. Long prison-term confinements may be cruel and unnecessary for those individuals who are non-predatory—that is, non-obligatory—but who have temporarily and incidentally engaged in an act of paedophilia. In my opinion, these patients are suitable for psychoanalytic therapy. What is required is a careful clinical evaluation and developmental history to differentiate between these two forms.

Schizo-paedophilia:
the co-existence of schizophrenia and paedophilia

Schizo-paedophilia, a term coined by this author (Socarides, 1988), connotes those individuals with a paedophile perversion who are also schizophrenic. Their fixation point is in the symbiotic phase (Mahler). Of overriding importance is the treatment of the schizophrenic decompensation, with its associated delusions, hallucinations, and ideas of reference, and other secondary symptoms of schizophrenia. Improvement requires a return to a compensated state of schizophrenic adaptation, but paedophile symptoms may remain unaltered alongside the *primary* symptoms of schizophrenia. Paranoia and paranoid symptomatology are striking features in such cases.

In the history of schizo-paedophile individuals, the emergence of their psychotic symptoms, and the enactment of their perversion, bears striking similarity to the pre-oedipal perverse individual, Type II (those with narcissistic/borderline pathology). For example, there is an intense fixation to the mother, severe separation and fragmentation anxiety, very pronounced feminine identification, severe difficulties in relating to the opposite sex from earliest years, and perverse sexual interests beginning in childhood. Such manifestations should, however, be viewed against a backdrop of the degree of ego pathology present, which one finds is strikingly dissimilar to that found in pre-oedipal, Type II perverse individuals. The patients' overt psychotic symptoms obviously mitigate against confusing the two.

The differences between schizo-perversion and pre-oedipal perversion (non-schizophrenic), were brilliantly defined by Bak (1971) in his paper "Object Relations in Schizophrenia and Perversion." He noted: (1) Perverse conflicts and their delusional elaborations are "consequences of the schizophrenic process rather than its cause" (p. 239). (2) In pre-oedipal paedophilia, object relations are maintained despite a "fused body image, a fused genital representation", in contrast to perverse activity in a schizophrenic where they are maintained. (3) Perverse impulses as well as other sexual impulses are a frantic attempt to create object relations in schizophrenia. (4) Perverse impulses, so often seen in paranoid schizophrenics, are not "aetiological"; their conflicts and their delusional elaborations are "consequences of a schizophrenic process rather than of cognitive origin" (p. 242). (5) Paranoid delusions with perverse contact of a paedophile nature often occur in schizophrenics; the reason is, however, that an object relation may be highly pathological and yet nevertheless be preserved. The delusions are an attempt to maintain object relations in the face of (a) severe regression; (b) attempted destruction of object relations; (c) the presence of primary defect or deficiency in the autonomous functions of the ego; and (d) the inability to maintain a protective stimulus barrier. If the regression is severe, the delusional content contains a less experiential basis, and a systematized delusion, similar to that found in paranoia, cannot be formed or maintained.

Schizo-paedophilia may be explained by its relationship to autistic or symbiotic modes of adaptation. There is a fixation at the autistic and/or symbiotic phase of the separation–individuation phase of development in order to ward off the fear of dissolution of the self-representation through re-engulfment by the mother, as well as threats of a soma-psychic fusion. This is in striking contrast to the fixation in pre-oedipal forms that has taken place in later phases of the separation–individuation process—for example, practising and differentiating. It is of vital importance to correctly diagnose schizo-paedophiles from the other forms of this perversion, for in these cases the combination of an inability to neutralize aggression during paedophile enactments, fuelled by delusional thinking of a paranoid nature as well as real fears of possible detention and imprisonment, sets the stage for an ensuing tragedy.

Notes

1. Well-structured perversions are the relatively pronounced cases in which the perverse development is clear and definite. In these patients, non-engagement in perverse practices induces severe anxiety. Because the perverse acts are usually the only avenue for the attainment of sexual gratification and are obligatory for the alleviation of intense anxieties, and because the intensity of the need for such gratification is relatively pronounced, I refer to such cases as the "well-structured perversion".

2. In some instances, the threat of the paedophile being identified to the authorities by a child victim leads to the murder of the victim, who would otherwise be spared after the sexual act—for example, a boy aged 10, the son of

a Rabbi, was thrown off the roof of a playground building because his assailant was the playground assistant, who was known to all (*New York Post*, 10 May 1995).

Even more tragic and horrendous was the killing of sixteen prepubertal children and the maiming of thirteen others (ages 5–6 years) as well as the teacher who tried to defend them, in Dunblane, Scotland, in March 1996, by a 43-year-old brooding loner, Thomas Hamilton, who then took his own life. Hamilton abused his sons, cruised young boys, and photographed very young children. People were referring to him as a pervert, he complained. He was dismissed as a boy-scout leader in 1974 because of complaints that he was overly "familiar" with his charges. It was also reported that he had abused a child. He had been rejected as a member by a gun club a few weeks earlier but was allowed access to a gun. A licence was granted as he did not appear to the authorities as being "mentally ill" and had no previous criminal record (*New York Times*, 15 January 1996).

The combination of defective superego, murderous rage, narcissistic injury, and frustration of sublimated paedophile activities in a paedophile individual may well have led to one of the most heart-breaking paedophile tragedies of the century.

3. The repudiation of the appearance of one's own pubic hair is a frequent finding in the history of paedophiliacs, fetishists, and homosexuals with a strong feminine identification. It represents no longer being the "loved child" and constitutes a threatened fresh disruption with the primary feminine identification with the mother, which has been soothing during the latency period. Fears of separation and separateness from the mother, as well as castration fears of the oedipal period, are reawakened.

4. Limitations of space preclude case illustrations of both oedipal and schizo-paedophilia. Both conditions are, however, recognizable on clinical examination—by their history. association, symptomatology, type of conflict, and attainment or lack of development of ego functions.

CHAPTER TWO

Dogman:
a prepsychotic paedophile

Vamık D. Volkan & William F. Greer

Much has been written over the past several decades in the psychoanalytic literature about childhood sexual abuse and its pathogenic influence on the mental development of its victim. In contrast, despite the prevalence across many historical eras and cultures of paedophilia, there has been a paucity of published case reports of the psychodynamics of its perpetrators by psychoanalytic investigators. Not only are non-exclusive and exclusive paedophilic sexual deviants relatively common throughout much of the world, transient sexual impulses towards infants in those responsible for their routine care are even more common. Depending upon these individuals' levels of superego development, such impulses may or may not be enacted. As Socarides (1988) has aptly pointed out, however, paedophilic fantasies and behaviour are, in and of themselves, an insufficient basis on which to arrive at a diagnosis of what he refers to as "true paedophilia". He defines the true paedophile as an individual "who must engage in sexual relations with a prepubertal child (before the development of secondary sex characteristics) in order to achieve sexual gratification and to obtain relief from unconscious conflicts" (p. 448). This deviant sexual practice must, moreover, be the exclusive source of orgastic release for the individual, and abstinence must induce severe anxiety. While the patient's paedophilic activities we examine in this chapter fail to reach the threshold for true paedophilia as defined by Socarides, we nonetheless believe that his case affords insight into the inner psychological world of the pre-oedipal type to be described below. Indeed, his dynamics correspond closely with those of the case he reported in his book on the pre-oedipal origins of the sexual deviations (Socarides, 1988).

Psychoanalysts have recognized for years that the same symptomatic phenomenology may have very different aetiologies depending upon the level of identity integration and structural development achieved by the individual who exhibits it. They endeavour, therefore, to understand not only different symptomatic expressions, but clinical forms of the same expression, from the mildest to the most severe. Paedophilia, which can range from transient paedophilic behaviour to the exclusive well-structured form seen in "true paedophilia" (Socarides, 1988), is no exception. Based upon the work of earlier contributors (Gillespie, 1956; Greenacre, 1968, 1971) on the origins of the sexual deviations as well as his own extensive clinical psychoanalytic experience with such patients, Socarides (1988) developed a unitary theory of their cause and a comprehensive classification system organized around three basic concepts: (1) the role of conscious and/or unconscious motivation; (2) the developmental stage at which the individual is arrested or fixated; (3) the extent of the pathology of internalized object relations. On the basis of these criteria, he identified, differentiated, and defined five forms of sexual deviation. The most relevant here are the oedipal and pre-oedipal forms. The oedipal form involves a failure to master castration anxiety associated with the positive oedipal wishes and fantasies. The pre-oedipal form involves a failure to negotiate the symbiotic and/or separation–individuation phases of early childhood development. This failure to adequately separate results in a wish for and dread of symbiotic fusion and creates the anxiety out of which the deviation arises. Incompletely separated, these individual are unable to develop a gender-defined self-identity. In essence, the symptom is the outcome of an object-relations conflict rather than a structural conflict. Within these two types of psychic structures (the oedipal and pre-oedipal) in which sexual deviations may occur, Socarides identified a latent form in which the individual may or may not be conscious of wishes of a deviant nature and may or may not act upon such wishes if they enter conscious awareness.

The patient whose case we present in this chapter was treated by Greer, who consulted regularly with Volkan over the course of the patient's five-year psychoanalytic psychotherapy. We called him "Dogman" because he often wore a dog costume at company functions and, at times, behaved like one. His attempt to change his body image did not progress as far as a transsexual's—that is, he did not seek surgery to become a dog. During his treatment he had transient psychotic episodes. While disruptive to the therapeutic alliance and evocative of countertransference reactions, these episodes did, however, permit us to see what was underneath his multiple defences, most of which were organized around introjective and projective moves. Deutsch (1942) might have called him an "as if" personality, and Winnicott (1960) might refer to him as having a false self. In Socarides's (1988) diagnostic schema, Dogman would be classified as a latent pre-oedipal paedophile since he abstained from such activities except when under severe stress, the stress in this instance being the birth of his son. Under the threat of the eruption of infanticidal rage at his envied son, who received the maternal care of which he had been profoundly deprived as a child, he shifted from the latent to the overt form of the deviation. He did, moreover, like many of these individuals, masturbate frequently to fantasies about women that were of an overtly aggressive and sadistic nature.

The syndrome exhibited by people like Dogman which is rooted in massive psychic trauma in childhood has been referred to as soul murder by Shengold (1988). Our patient's soul was indeed "murdered" in his infancy and early childhood, an experience we believe that formed the core of his "infantile psychotic self", a term coined by Volkan (1995). Since this concept informs our understanding of Dogman's incestuous paedophilic activities and other symptomatic expressions, we will briefly expand upon it before we proceed further.

In early life, ego deficiencies caused by genetic (biological), physiological, psychological, and environmental factors lead to conflict in object relations. Conversely, unworkable early conflicts in object relations preclude the evolution of self- and object representations and the development of associated ego functions to mature levels. Under these circumstances the "infantile psychotic self" is created and is saturated with "bad" affects associated with the aggressive drive. In adult language we refer to such affects with terms such as "emptiness", "helpless rage", or "anaclitic depression". In contrast to a "normal" and ordinary infantile self-representation, the infantile psychotic self does not evolve and reach a more mature level at which the differentiation of self-images from object images and one object representation from another become stable, and at which "bad" affects mentioned above are tamed.

Volkan (1995) described various fates of an infantile psychotic self ranging from its shrinking and disappearing as the child develops a new core saturated with libidinal affects to its dominating the personality from infancy on and causing childhood schizophrenia. In some individuals who develop an infantile psychotic self and who later also develop a healthier infantile self, the latter *partially* encapsulates (D. Rosenfeld, 1992; H. Rosenfeld, 1965; Volkan, 1976) the former. Furthermore, the healthier self, as it goes through its developmental track, becomes the "spokesperson" for the infantile psychotic self, which, as we have already stated, does not develop. The healthier self, through fantasies, re-enactments, and actions, attempts to promote a fit between external reality and the infantile psychotic self in order to maintain a sense of reality. Some such fantasies, re-enactments, and actions (such as Dogman's paedophilic fantasies and actions) are also in the service of providing pleasurable affects for the infantile psychotic self and replacing "bad" affects of this core with "good" ones. Unfortunately such fantasies and symptoms do not accomplish this end permanently and are therefore destined to endlessly repeat themselves. Through psychosomatic manifestations, assaults on his wife, fantasies of violence against women while masturbating, clowning, lying, and inhibitions (e.g. he never learned to drive a car until his fourth year of treatment), Dogman tried to create a fit between his infantile psychotic self and the external world. Through sexual orgasms (paedophilic acts and masturbation), he also attempted to infuse his infantile psychotic self with pleasure (libido).

We believe that pre-oedipal paedophiles like Dogman seek to achieve not only symbiotic fusion with the mother's image through their sexual-object choice in order to achieve "the reassuring and reaffirming function of the self-representation" (Socarides, 1988, p. 17), but, in addition, a new symbiotic core saturated with libidinal affects. As previously stated, however, they fail in their effort to change the nature of their infantile psychotic core and are doomed to repeat their fantasies, actions, and symptoms.

Life history

The patient, whom we call Joseph, was in his late thirties when he sought treatment because of a facial tic and concern over a bad marriage. What Joseph referred to as facial tics were recurring facial grimaces that made him look like a snarling dog. He also sniffed the air involuntarily, like a dog trying to catch a scent wafting by. He had been unhappily married for about 20 years and at times felt that it was impossible to live with his wife because of her constant jealous accusations of infidelity. On occasion he lost his temper and assaulted her when she interpreted some insignificant detail of behaviour or conversation as evidence of her allegations. It was one of these altercations, during which he had struck his wife in the face with his fist and then tried to throttle her, that instigated his search for help. He was afraid that he might lose her or perhaps even maim or kill her. These fears exacerbated his tics, over which he had become extremely self-conscious. He recalled having similar tics that had lasted a year or so when he was in his latency.

Joseph was college-educated and a successful plant manager with a local food-processing company. The company's logo depicted a funny-looking dog, which Joseph had volunteered to represent in the company's frequent public-relations events. By wearing a dog costume, he became the company's official clown. This role suited Joseph perfectly because of his penchant for

Adapted from V. D. Volkan, *The Infantile Psychotic Self and Its Fates*, pp. 175–203 (Northvale, NJ: Jason Aronson, 1995). Reprinted by permission.

clownish antics around his staff and friends. He revelled in the thought that he was another Bob Hope. He did, indeed, have a wry, pungent wit, which he often used both to express and to conceal his anger. Before official appearances he would frolic about the plant in his dog costume, snarling and hiking up his leg, pretending to urinate on the amused employees. From the beginning of his treatment there were indications in his tics and sniffing behaviour that Joseph might have unconsciously identified with a dog, and that he voluntarily accepted "becoming" a dog in serving his company.

Besides becoming a dog, he frequently lied about himself and his background. For instance, he once told his young son a story about his exploits as a professional boxer because he thought it might make him proud of his father. In casual conversations he would insinuate information about himself to impress others. He often daydreamed of himself as an invincible, omnipotent, superman-like hero. On the other hand, he "forced" others to take care of him. A good example of this was that he never learned to drive a car. His wife drove him to work and picked him up at the end of the day. While on official business, dressed in the dog costume, he would be driven by a chauffeur in the company's limousine.

When Joseph's son (who was in his late teens when Joseph began his treatment) was 3 years old, Joseph sucked the little boy's penis. He had never told this to anyone before for fear of the legal consequences. He enjoyed films about graphic violence directed towards women, films that he purchased through the mail. He routinely masturbated as he viewed them, fantasizing raping and beating women. Except for his wife, he had never raped a woman, nor did he ever have intercourse with a child. Greer, his therapist, whom I [V.D.V.] supervised, has considered rightly that Dogman was not suitable for psychoanalysis proper. He knew that the classic technique needed to be modified. Joseph was offered and accepted psychoanalytic psychotherapy.

After being seen face-to-face for a couple of months, Dogman was treated on the couch. With patients like Dogman, who grossly distort the therapist's representation from the beginning of treatment, Volkan (1986) suggests that, at least initially, they be seen face-to-face in order to establish a *reality base*. Such an initial and direct face-to-face experience with the therapist is useful when the patient later develops a full-blown transference psychosis and looks for memories and realistic perceptions of the therapist to fall back on in order to tolerate it. The ground rules of psychotherapy were simply and directly explicated to the patient, including instructions in free association. No psychotropic medication was prescribed for Dogman's mental condition. His treatment lasted for five years, during which his infantile psychotic self was modified. For reasons we will describe, however, he did not reach a mutually agreed-upon therapeutic termination.

The early environment

Joseph was born into a poor Catholic family in a small industrial town. His father, a factory worker, was an alcoholic. He deserted the family when Joseph was 2 or 3 years old, and Joseph's mother had to look after him and his sister, who was five years older, by herself. Apparently the mother had required intermittent psychiatric hospitalization since Joseph's birth and was thought to be a schizophrenic. When she was away, a widowed maternal grandmother took care of the children. If the grandmother was unavailable, they were placed temporarily in an orphanage.

Aside from an ineffable feeling that there was no warmth in the house, Joseph had few conscious memories of his early childhood. To this day we do not know if there had been a real dog in Joseph's early environment. He did have one when he started his treatment, and at times he seemed to identify with it. For example, when his wife was harsh with the dog, Joseph felt its pain and would become enraged.

When Joseph was 3 years old, his mother had one more hospitalization. As he was later told, she was diagnosed as suffering from an inoperable brain tumour but not from schizophrenia, although she may have had both. Joseph retained three memories of her after she returned home: one of her lying ill on a sofa, throwing up in a bucket; another of his rousing her from sleep to tell her the house was on fire (he and his sister had "accidentally" set the house on fire by playing with matches); and still another of her falling down the steps as he rushed into her arms to hug her.

She died when he was 6 years old. With the exception of one incident that occurred in the funeral procession, he recalled little of this time. The memory he did recall clearly was riding in a car with his sister and an aunt on the way to the cemetery to inter his mother. His aunt inadvertently sat on his mother's picture, which his sister had brought along, and shattered the glass. It is possible that this is a screen memory reflecting the little boy's perception of death and psychic damage. After the mother's death, the children returned to the Catholic orphanage, with which they were already familiar.

While in the orphanage, Joseph contracted streptococcal meningitis, from which he nearly died. He remained in a hospital for months and slowly recuperated from the illness. The neurologist who cared for him evidently became very fond of him, intimating that he might adopt him, and Joseph recalled being utterly crestfallen when he did not. It is difficult to tell how much of this was a wish and how much reality, but in any event he was sent back to the orphanage, where he remained until his maternal grandmother took him and his sister to live with her on a permanent basis.

The grandmother was an impecunious, alcoholic woman who had been widowed for years. Unable to adequately care for the children, she perpetuated their neglect. With almost no guidance or discipline, the children were forced to look after themselves. When not in school, Joseph spent most of his time on the streets with children similarly dispossessed. He started to smoke when he was 7 because he thought it manly. He was inclined to play with younger children because he thought he could acquit himself more advantageously in their games and squabbles. He recalls being perpetually scared, as a child, of his own aggression and that of the other boys. He consciously worried that if he got into a fight with one of them, either he or the other boy might be seriously injured or perhaps even killed. Indeed, so uncertain was he of his capacity to control his murderous rage that he developed inhibitions against activities that either challenged his competence (i.e., might humiliate him) or were imbued with aggressive symbolism (as reflected in his inability to drive a car).

Joseph's sister and grandmother used to dress him up in girl's clothes and parade him around the neighbourhood. Although acutely humiliated by this, he rarely complained. They stopped this practice, however, as he got older. One good friend occasionally rescued him from these women. This friend regularly invited him over for dinner and to other family activities. Joseph recalls being on his best behaviour around these people for fear they would not ask him back again. Around this time he was molested by men who offered him rides. There was no actual intercourse, but they fondled his genitals and kissed him. Aroused by their seductions, Joseph participated.

Although he had inadequate support for his overall psychological development, Joseph received guidance for his intellectual growth. His early psychic deficits and object-relations conflicts remained part of him, but he grew up in respect to intellectual relationships, as exemplified by his being an excellent student in parochial school. He remembered the Catholic nuns who taught him as harsh, stern women, singularly insensitive to children. They sometimes threatened the children with corporal punishment for the most minor infraction of the rules. Joseph often recalled one incident that particularly injured his pride: a nun chastised him in front of class for wearing the same pair of frayed and dirty trousers to school each day. She then threw a donated pair at him as a replacement and directed him to put them on. He could see that they were too large and baggy, but despite his feeble protests she insisted that he wear them. He was flooded with a sense of humiliation and shame at this treatment. The school, however, was probably the most stable institution in his life.

Adolescence

The neglect that characterized his childhood continued into his adolescence. There was virtually no warmth, support, or discipline given by the grandmother. She often was too drunk to talk to him, so he would retire to his room or go out on the streets to hang out with his friends. She once asked him to scrub her back as she bathed. He was so repulsed by the sight of her shrivelled breasts and state of decrepitude that he excused himself and fled the house. His relationship with his sister was not much of an improvement. She would invite him on her dates, during which he was privy to her lovemaking with boys. He was convinced that she must be the "town pump", given the steady stream of boys that courted her. To escape all of this, he frequented his maternal aunt's home. Unfortunately, she, too, was an alcoholic, and she allowed him to fondle her breasts when she was intoxicated. He would get so aroused by this that he would rush into a bedroom and masturbate.

Joseph recalled almost nothing about his father until after his mother's death. Although his father lived nearby, he rarely visited his children. Joseph poignantly recalled the many times his father arranged to see him, only to fail to appear at the appointed time. He would sit on the front steps in anticipation of his arrival, expecting every car that turned the corner to be his. His anticipation would turn into acute disappointment when it became apparent that he was not going to come. When Joseph eventually saw his father, there were never any explanations or apologies, only more empty promises, and he grew to despise the man for his unconscionable treatment.

On the rare occasions when he did keep his promise to visit, his father would take his son to a tavern he frequented. When intoxicated, the father would provoke fights with other patrons. When in a more sanguine mood, he would ask Joseph, who was a talented vocalist, to sing ethnic ballads, to the pleasure of the father's friends. Other than this rather narcissistic exploitation of his son, he gave him little warmth or kindness.

When Joseph was in his early adolescence, his father married a divorcee with a daughter about Joseph's age. He invited Joseph to move in with them, an invitation Joseph accepted with misgivings. In his perception, there was little warmth or affection from either of his parents. On weekends his father would routinely drink heavily, becoming aggressive towards anyone who crossed him. Joseph silently rankled at all of this until he could no longer contain his rage. His stepmother instructed him to mow the lawn one afternoon when he was engaged in something else, and he hurled obscenities at her. When his father was advised of this that evening, he went berserk and chased his son around the house. Terrified, Joseph took refuge in the tool shed and locked the door, but his father tore the door from its hinges and assaulted him. Joseph told his recently married sister about the incident, and she promptly moved him in with her. It was there that the patient committed his first paedophilic act.

Joseph's regularly baby-sat for a couple in her apartment building who had a toddler of about 3 years, and sometimes she left her brother in the care of this child while she ran errands. On one such occasion, Joseph noticed that the child seemed to get excited when he bounced her on his knee. This, in turn, excited him, and he began to fondle the child's genitals. He repeated this on several other occasions.

Adulthood

After graduating from high school, Joseph joined the military. While stationed overseas he met a native who was to become his future wife. The courtship was brief, and he soon proposed marriage. His fiancée could hardly speak a word of English, was poorly educated, and had no job skills. Nevertheless, they married within a year and lived with her parents until he was transferred back to the United States. By this time his wife was pregnant with his first and only child. After his son's birth he became envious of the attention his wife lavished on the child. His incestuous paedophilic activity occurred on an occasion reminiscent of the first such incident. Asked by his wife to care for the toddler, he became flooded with sexual fantasies. When he changed the child's diapers, he became so excited at the sight of the toddler's penis that he impulsively sucked it. He described the experience as something close to a state of beatitude. Afterward he loathed himself for this act and vowed never to do it again. He kept his vow with his son but constantly worried that the child might have been damaged by this deed. A year later, however, he molested a little girl who had been left with his wife to baby-sit. The fact that his wife was a foreigner whose skin colour was different from his symbolized to Joseph, as we learned in his psychotherapy, that she would be a different woman from his mother and grandmother. He later became disappointed with her and thought of his marriage as horrible.

Joseph was able to attend college with the money he received from the military and became employed after graduation. His father had died twelve years before he started treatment. He had no close relationship with his sister or, for that matter, anyone other than his wife, whom he beat occasionally.

Treatment

The first year

Joseph presented himself as if he were two entirely different men. One was a competent and respected plant manager, perceived by his associates and those who reported to him as a normal man, especially when he did not act like a clown. The other was a frightened, bewildered, paranoid, helpless, enraged infant/child suspended in a time warp. The first Joseph had to manage the second and change the external environment to respond to the latter's internal needs, mainly through various actions (e.g. wife abuse, paedophilia, and clowning).

Joseph's abject dependence on his wife was immediately evident. She drove him to the therapist's office and then went shopping, returning in fifty minutes to fetch him. As Joseph was driven to and from his sessions, it was not unusual for him to fantasize that something dreadful, or even fatal, would happen to his wife. Hearing an ambulance siren would make him extremely anxious that his wife might die at any moment from some inexplicable cause. He would then think that he was responsible for her misfortune and should turn himself in to the police. It occurred to the therapist that perhaps his childhood fantasy of being culpable for his mother's illness and death was being relived.

At his workplace thousands of food cans were found to be contaminated and had to be destroyed. Joseph oversaw this operation, but the company's failure to produce perfect food led to his notion that thousands of penises and much faecal material, symbolized by the contaminated cans, were being thrown at him. His thinking almost felt real, and the therapist thought he might be delusional. The people he supervised did not know this part of his inner world, and he continued to perform as a good supervisor.

Joseph became aware of a need to prepare and rehearse material for his sessions en route to the therapist's office in order to appear profound and witty. He recalled that when young, he had behaved in the same way to please his one good friend and his friend's family, without whom he would have had no one to pay attention to him. If Greer was silent behind the couch, Joseph would fantasize that he had slipped out of the room. "If I don't keep my act going . . . the whole edifice will collapse," he said. Boyer (1967) and Volkan (1986) speak of the noisy *phase* in the treatment of already regressed patients. In treatment, individuals like Dogman will not tolerate the therapist's silence at first. Silence increases the intensity of such patients' fantasies and may bring them to a delusional level. Thus, until a firmer therapeutic alliance is established, the therapist makes noncommittal sounds. It is important that the therapist does not interfere with whatever relationship the patient works out with him. Joseph said, "If I do not walk the straight and narrow, I will be abandoned." He was also sensitive to any sign of illness in the therapist. The meaning of this was readily available to Joseph, who spoke of his mother's vomiting spells.

He referred to world-destruction fantasies, but they were not on a delusional level. Destruction of the world meant the destruction of both Joseph and his therapist. He was concerned that his world-destruction fantasies might be threatening to the therapist, and that Greer "might get scared and run out the door". Then he stated, "I scared my mother to death." Joseph recalled his childhood wish to push his mother down the stairs when he rushed into her arms to hug her. The therapist told Joseph that he was aware of his patient's caution about being openly hostile with others. Danger lurked everywhere. Joseph's clownish antics and buffoonery were related to his desperate need to engage others, but in his paranoid orientation to life, the spectre of loss hung over him like the proverbial sword of Damocles.

In the second half of the first year of Joseph's treatment, the therapist was included in the patient's introjective–projective cycle, which was contaminated with feelings of helplessness and murderous rage. If Greer made a false move, Joseph threatened to attack him with the penknife he carried with him for protection. On the other hand, he wanted to protect Greer from harm. For example, if Joseph heard a noise as he waited for the session to begin, it provoked fantasies of Greer being attacked and brutally assaulted by an enraged patient, a displaced representation of Joseph. Then he fantasized that he would rush into the office, save Greer, and earn his eternal gratitude. A dream narrated at this time conveyed the magnitude of aggression and helplessness with which Joseph was struggling. "I had a gun", he said, "with which I was randomly shooting people on the street. I also had a hand-grenade, but it made no 'bang' when I threw it. I woke up terrified." Some persons who actually commit a murder or a series of murders have psychological backgrounds similar to Joseph's. To his credit, Greer was able to tolerate the derivatives of aggression Joseph was bringing to sessions. He also knew that the therapeutic relationship he was involved in with Joseph might be the patient's only hope to modify his psychic organization.

As he grew more anxious about being abandoned by his therapist, Joseph reported fantasies of being greeted by him with thunderous applause. Joseph readily saw his grand entrance as a famous personage as a defence against his irrepressible fear of going absolutely unnoticed. In turn, the therapist readily joined Joseph in exploring the connections between what he was bringing to his treatment and his childhood experiences. In other words, transference interpretations and their association to the patient's childhood history were offered. After a while the therapist noted, however, that such interpretations were not effective and understood that they served to escape the intensity of affects that Joseph induced in himself and in the therapist. The therapist and his supervisor noted that a patient like Dogman does not use transference and/or genetic (psychological) interpretations at this phase of the treatment to initiate psychic change.

The following illustrates a more effective response made by the therapist. When Joseph began coming to his sessions in a rather dishevelled and unhygienic condition, the therapist noted that he was involved in another re-enactment but said nothing about it. Joseph had become the reincarnation of a neglected child needing physical care from a mother figure. This time, instead of interpreting the transference and its genetic connections, Greer allowed the re-enactment to continue. Joseph came to his sessions without a bath or a shave for weeks. Greer tolerated this behaviour, but ultimately explained to the patient that he believed his actions demonstrated how Joseph needed to be cared for. He added, "You have given me a first-hand experience of your need and of how important it is for you that someone, in this case me, know this." Soon after this, Joseph stopped coming to his sessions so unkempt, but for a long time he continued trying to find out if the therapist loved him. If the cheque he wrote to Greer was not cashed promptly, Joseph fantasized that Greer did not need his money, that his love could not be bought, and that Greer would abandon him. That Greer did not abandon Joseph made him a new object (Giovacchini, 1972; Loewald, 1960; Volkan, 1976). The newness of the therapist's representation is based on the therapeutic reactivation of early developmental paths. In order to follow this path, the patient needs to make therapeutically regressive moves.

The second year

As the close of the first year of treatment approached and passed, Joseph's intensely sadomasochistic relationship with his wife underwent some changes. His sexual attraction towards her waned along with their ritualized daily intercourse, which had nothing to do with an adult love relationship. It was another re-enactment so that Joseph would have the illusion that he could daily find a mothering person to change the "bad" affects in the early mother–child unit into pleasurable ones. Because he occasionally raped his wife, the daily intercourse was also in the service of discharging his rage. A libidinal child-mother (husband-wife) fused representation could not be maintained.

The waning of interest in his wife was accompanied by increased interest in a pubescent girl across the street, whom the couple had befriended after their son went away to school. Joseph, overcome by erotic fantasies about this girl, became overtly seductive with her, and she readily reciprocated. When his wife was out of the room the girl would sit on Joseph's lap and tickle him, much to their mutual delight. She would brush against him with her exposed thighs, and pause over his hand. Joseph began reporting memories of being intensely aroused by his sister's sexual activities with her boyfriends when he had accompanied them on dates. He told Greer of his boyhood fantasy of his sister performing fellatio on him. He also remembered the incredibly intense excitement he felt when he had fondled his drunken aunt's breasts and how he rushed into the next room to masturbate to relieve his tension. As he put it, "Lust has no scruples." Meanwhile, he became "afraid of everybody and everything". He thought he would feel safer if he went incognito, so he purchased a pair of dark glasses that he wore everywhere. In his fantasies they were like mirrors, reflecting and deflecting images of dangerous others. Joseph was attempting to slow down the introjective–projective cycle.

Although a therapist may find it easy not to interfere prematurely with a patient's re-enactments (e.g. Joseph turning himself into an unkempt child), it is obviously more difficult not to respond when a re-enactment is hurtful to an innocent party, such as a child. The therapist and his supervisor decided that if the therapist remained in the therapeutic position, he might, in the long run, be more helpful in the modification of Joseph's paedophilic and related activities. The therapist decided that he should at least try an interpretation to see if it would stop the patient's behaviour with the young girl. In essence, what Greer told Joseph was that he was defending against memories of being deprived of early maternal care. He was seeking a child with whom to have a mother–child oneness, through which he would feed, get fed, and be blissfully gratified. In his unconscious fantasies, he was both mother and child in this relationship.

Rather than working with this interpretation, Joseph chided the therapist for what he perceived to be efforts to transform his heinous deeds into psychoanalytic excuses. He became involved about this time in a new action and arrived for a session mildly intoxicated. Greer voiced his hunch that Joseph was behaving in a provocative manner to get his therapist to punish him for his paedophilic and similar activities, and that his representation in his patient's mind was that of someone who either prematurely forgave or punished, with neither being a useful reaction in the long run. He added that he preferred to continue as Joseph's therapist and asked Joseph to join him in exploring the deeper motives of his actions.

In the next hour Joseph disclosed that he was having fantasies of sucking Greer's penis and connected this with his sucking his son's penis. Paedophilic activities were thus in a sense brought into their sessions. Greer felt that Joseph's fantasies about him were connected with both a wish for closeness and an expression of aggression and thought that he should deal first with his patient's need for closeness and leave the exploration of aggression for a later time. With Greer's help, Joseph further understood that as a child he had hungered for a good relationship. Now both therapist and patient could speak more comfortably about how Joseph, in his paedophilic experience with his son, was attempting to create his own mother–child interaction, control it, and make it pleasurable. In reversing roles, Joseph made the infant a nurturing mother, a nurturing penis/nipple, fused with it, and sought a pleasurable experience.

Not long after speaking of his childhood "hunger" and lack of a nurturing environment, Joseph reported excruciating abdominal pain and bloody stools. Concerned that he might be developing a peptic ulcer, he arranged a consultation with an internist, who confirmed his suspicions. Conservative treatment was initiated, and his symptoms remitted. They were to wax and wane over the next several years in conjunction with the therapeutic work. (A study focusing on the psychosomatic aspects of this patient has been published elsewhere: Volkan, 1992.)

After Joseph received physical help for his peptic ulcer, his mood changed. The aggressive aspects of his early mother–child experiences surfaced once more. Joseph noticed that he was more irritable and given to rages towards his wife; jealousy was all the provocation he needed. At work, heretofore the clown prince, he found himself more sardonic with his co-workers. His banter and repartee were used more to hurt than to entertain. This change of mood was ushered in with the remark: "I am like a lump of ice that has started to melt."

Towards the latter part of the second year of treatment, a new symptom emerged. Joseph observed with jocularity that when angry with others, he would cast a dirty look at them. He played with fantasies, which were like delusions at times, in which this look would annihilate its recipient. These fantasies were particularly active on his way to the therapist's office. He would stare at drivers that offended him, visualizing their cars swerving off the road into the woods. These images were almost invariably accompanied by memories of being in his mother's funeral procession with his sister and the aunt, who had sat on his mother's picture.

Once when he heard an ambulance siren, he suddenly felt the urge to assault his wife, who, it will be recalled, chauffeured him. The therapist commented that perhaps the siren reminded him of the dying mother whose death had deprived him of his childhood.

He confided that he had felt flawed and damaged as far back as he could remember. Half seriously, he said, "All I want is a Mommy and a Daddy to grow up with and leave me an estate in the Bahamas. What I need", he continued, "is a primal-scream therapist." Greer, moved, simply replied that he could hear Joseph's pain. Greer felt as if he were a nurturing mother, who, despite her child's having a painful temper tantrum, still could maintain the child's welfare in mind.

The transference began to include symbolic anal elements; for example, Joseph worried that the grease from his hair tonic might soil the therapist's couch. If so, he was to be told so that he could bring in Handy Wipes to clean up the mess. Joseph also became aware that he averted his gaze from the therapist as he entered his office in order to protect the therapist from his dirty looks. A little later, Greer saw him scanning his desk as he went towards the couch. Inquiries into this behaviour revealed only that he was worried that something was different about this piece of furniture (there was not). The therapist thought of the desk as an extension of himself and as symbolic of the dying mother, so he mused aloud that perhaps Joseph was anxious that his destructive fury (anal sadism) might have given the therapist a brain tumour. The patient then sheepishly admitted that he made faces at the therapist as he lay on the couch, gloating at the thought that he could humiliate him with impunity. He understood this behaviour as an expression of the enraged feelings he had when he was "too weak and too small to voice them". In another session Joseph became aware of clenching his teeth when he spoke, eliciting fantasies of himself as a vicious dog. Within weeks the sniffing "tic", so prominent when he first came into treatment, reappeared. All this time Joseph struggled with his paedophilic fantasies and impulses towards the girl across the street, who was now in mid-adolescence, more curvaceous and sensual, arousing him whenever they were to-gether. His fantasies ranged from passionate trysts on romantic isles to raping her. The sight of her with boys her own age evoked

jealous rage. He acted the part of the spurned lover bent on re-
venge. His conversations with her were marked by tart barbs that
hurt her feelings. His wife, at last, sensed his affection for the girl
and ordered her out.

At times the therapist found Joseph's activities with the girl
across the street repugnant, but he kept his feelings to himself and
told him only what was in the service of protecting the therapeutic
relationship and alliance. He warned, however, that in the real
world, his activities with underage girls might get him into legal
difficulties and make it impossible for him to continue his treatment. "Would you let me suggest to you that you put these impulses into words and thus allow me to protect the continuity of
our relationship?" the therapist asked.

In the next session Joseph reported a fantasy in which he had
sucked the girl's breast, sucking so voraciously that he sucked out
all her fluids, killing her. The therapist told him that he was
continuing to remember his childhood in his fantasies about this
girl, and that fantasies could be better analysed than actions because actions would actually change the external world. Joseph was
clearly driven to recreate a mother–child experience, but because in
reality his experience with his mother had been replete with frustrations, his experience with the girl eventually allowed his aggression (the wish to "kill" her) to surface. The therapist interpreted that
his first flagrantly paedophilic activities and then his fantasies
about the girl were his major resistance to owning his angry,
hungry, helpless, and humiliated core (his infantile psychotic self).
He further explained to him that, as a child, he had been subjected
to many humiliating events and was recalling them by sexualizing
them and by re-enactments. Although trying to change his helplessness and humiliation through experiencing sexual pleasure might
provide temporary release from tension, it took real courage to
allow himself to verbalize these impulses and feelings. Joseph
responded well and spoke of how he had been sexually abused as
a teenager, being kissed and fondled without actual intercourse.
This theme was further expanded in a dream in which he saw his
son as a statue with a knife stuck in it. His associations brought
feelings about his own sexual abuse and his jealous rage at the sight
of his infant son at his wife's breast. In turn, he had sucked his son's

penis in order to kill him. By now, both meanings of his paedophilic activities—the wish to have a nurturing mother and the wish to kill the "bad" mother—were understood.

Joseph ceased his paedophilic activity and his involvement with the young girl. This was accompanied by an increased rage towards his therapist; he spontaneously revealed that as a child, even after his mother's death, he used to have fantasies of killing her. He seemed to be owning and expressing the "bad" affects of his infantile psychotic self instead of using paedophilic and related actions as a defence against them.

The third year

Not long after the beginning of the third year of treatment, Joseph told the therapist that it was his birthday and that his wife had forgotten it and his son had sent him a smoked salmon. He was incensed with both of them for their perceived thoughtlessness. How dare his son send him such a gift, which he derisively referred to as a penis in a box. He added: "I suppose he sent it to remind me that I had oral sex with him." He suddenly fantasized being in a catatonic state, intuitively understanding this as a defence against his rage.

Joseph became obsessed with motorists once more as he was being driven to his appointments by his wife. More overtly aggressive now, he made obscene gestures to them, bellowed oaths, and shook his fist. All of this made him quite anxious, however, because he feared that some enraged driver might shoot him. The therapist explained that being enraged and frightened in a car was what he remembered being in the funeral procession as a boy. He then connected this with the patient's inhibition against driving, which represented a defence against his conscious fantasy that he had killed his mother.

In the early part of his third year of treatment, amorous fantasies about women with whom he worked preoccupied him constantly. Every morning when he arrived at the plant he sought them out and, under the guise of humour, made inappropriate professions of love to them. His suggestive remarks and overtures were good-naturedly received by some, but they offended others.

If the women failed to respond as he wished them to, he felt acutely rejected and humiliated. Then violent criminals of current notoriety would come to mind—criminals with whom he identified

An incident occurred at a picnic for the company employees and their families, where Joseph wore his dog costume. About to be overcome by heat, he retired to the back of the air-conditioned limousine where he could remove the full-head mask without being seen by the children. Some of his acquaintances opened the door as he rested. Several children saw him. He thought that the children who knew of him in costume as a real dog would know now that he was an impostor. This thought was accompanied by an image of himself in the back of the car at the funeral procession. What was inferred from this incident was that his efforts to be both mother and child happily engaged with each other were unmasked and that the "killer" (of his mother) was exposed.

As a dog/clown, Joseph wished to change the horrible affects that saturated the fused child–mother representation in his infantile psychotic self. Beneath the pleasure-giving dog/ clown, there was a dog, a sense of self as being less than a human infant. When saturated with "bad" affects, the dog would be vicious. We recall how a nun made him wear large baggy trousers and how his grandmother insisted on parading him about dressed as a girl. These incidents may have played a role in his unconscious choice of a dog symbol to represent his fragile core's psychic tissue. As a dog, he invited love and nurturing but also expressed snarling aggression. Through his humorous antics and acerbic wit, he could express his enormous aggression yet maintain object ties. Furthermore, by being a dog/clown, he could reach up (Boyer, 1961; Volkan, 1976) and try to establish a relationship with the representation of his father. It should be recalled that his father used Joseph to entertain his friends in a bar. As an entertainer he received his drunken father's approval while still hating him. This understanding of different meanings of the dog symbol was interpreted at appropriate times.

After the dog was unmasked, Joseph came to his sessions anxiously searching for the therapist's car. Even if he saw it, he expected to come to his office and find him gone (as were his other caregivers and his father). He felt agitated on the couch, saying he needed a pill to calm himself. He then paused reflectively for a moment and with insight said, "A pill is a nipple, isn't it? And a nipple is better than a penis." With mock hostility he enjoined the therapist to speak to him and threatened to kill him. "You know, my anger has no stages. Either I am in control or I am not." His aggressive thoughts and fantasies became more explicit and graphic with each session. His dreams were full of scenes of murder, rape, and paranoid fears of attack. Reanimated infantile rage led to verbalized fantasies of mutual fellatio between him and the therapist.

An already regressed patient, Joseph was experiencing a therapeutic regression. His infantile psychotic self, flooded with unneutralized aggression and other unnamable affects, as well as his wish and dread to fuse with the mother/analyst representation, was being presented to the therapist without the benefit of defensive buffers. As this process continued, the therapist noted that Joseph was able to keep the therapist's new object representation more effectively within himself. When his fellatio and other homosexual fantasies about Greer peaked, Joseph dreamed of a police officer arresting an aggressive man and forcing him to submit to anal intercourse. Through this dream, which recalled his sexual abuse by men, Joseph also provided associations indicating that he was anally taking in the therapist's representation (his words) and keeping it. Through such an identification he was learning to control his rage. In the dream, the aggressive man represented Joseph's enraged infantile self, but the policeman was also Joseph, containing such an infant self.

The fourth year

Most of the issues Joseph dealt with in the latter part of the third year of his treatment were also present in the first part of the fourth year. As an infant and a child, he had little experience with what can be termed *trust*, so his therapeutic experiences with Greer's representation could not readily be made trustworthy and so maintained. Any frustration with Greer would push him, once more, to re-enact old ways that ranged from more paedophilic thoughts, to desire for the teenage girl across the street, to physical abuse of his wife. At times he felt paralyzed in his attempt to get out from under the influence of his infantile psychotic core and expressed his frustration with Greer by saying: "If you get a package with the salutation 'Dear Shit' on it, you will know where it came from."

In the second part of the fourth year, Greer returned from his vacation to find Joseph flooded with paedophilic dreams. Rather than engaging in actual paedophilic involvement or related activities or being flooded with fantasies about them, he now seemed better able to control his actions and fantasies, as they were transposed into his dreams. The other actions continued, however. During his therapist's vacation, Joseph often had grabbed at his wife's breast in his sleep so aggressively that she would be forced to awaken him to keep from being injured.

As his therapeutic regression became more noticeable and "hot", everything seemed to be centred around his relationship with Greer. When Greer was a minute late for their appointment, Joseph felt ignored, forgotten, and mistreated. If Greer parked his car in a space other than the one in which he ordinarily parked, Joseph felt that it was done intentionally to make him anxious. He feared that Greer would find an excuse to terminate his treatment if he became too aggressive with him. Joseph dreamed of being with a woman who put a leash around his neck and treated him like a dog. She represented the mother/analyst to whom he was connected with an umbilical cord (the leash). His main fear was that his new object relationship with Greer might be modelled after the first one. Greer interpreted this fear.

As Joseph's transference relationship became more and more intense, there were indications of improvement in his life in the external world. His relationship with others, especially with men, became more mature at his workplace. He reported a rebirth fantasy in which he would go to a nearby bridge, remove his clothes, and make it appear as though he had jumped over the side and drowned, a suicide victim, but he would dress in other clothes and vanish, never to be heard from again. Thus he would be separated from his wife. He wished to be reborn again, to be away from his non-nurturing mother and to have a hope of being better parented in his new life. This was a portentous fantasy, as later developments clearly showed.

In their sessions Greer began perceiving Joseph as more like a neurotic individual than one bewildered by object-relations conflict. He certainly had not worked through such conflicts completely, but he could more genuinely and more readily connect their appearance in the transference and extra-transference relationships to their genetic (psychological) causes. He could now work with his dreams as a neurotic might. In one dream *he was hungry and went to the refrigerator to get something to eat, but the refrigerator suddenly turned into a coffin. He did not open it and kept repeating, "I just want lunch."* Intuitively he understood this sequence of images to mean that he was going to have to face the fact that as a child, he could not get the necessary narcissistic supplies from his dead mother. Notwithstanding this, he persisted in his unconscious search for a nurturing mother in his relationships and in his dreams. For example, he dreamed *of performing fellatio on a small boy whose penis grew larger and larger as he sucked, until it was nearly the size of an adult's.* The therapist addressed the progressive aspect of this dream, telling Joseph that he was seeking a nurturing mother whose breasts he could suckle in order to become more independent and free to grow up as a man.

As he often did, Joseph recalled and re-examined his paedophilic experience with his son and his wish and his dream of performing fellatio on his therapist. He then thought of ferocious dogs and the pleasure he derived from needling the women at work. Greer pointed out the terrible dilemma that the patient had to face as a result of his untamed aggression towards the very objects he needed badly. The ferocious dogs represented Joseph's oral sadism, which he could now own not by re-enactment but by dealing with it in the psychological realm. There followed a dream in which *Joseph kissed a little girl whose mouth had a strange taste that reminded him at once of sour milk.* The therapist explained that it was his rage, along with his mother's unavailability, that soured the milk and motivated his interminable search for a good mother.

As the fourth year of treatment came to a close, the patient's relationship with the young girl had receded into the background. She came to his house one day and announced that she was a lesbian. Joseph became extremely agitated and had to go to bed with his wife and perform cunnilingus on her. But in his next session he asked rhetorically whether he was so deprived of love that he could accept anything as the genuine article. Not long after this, instead of being involved in an action, he dreamed of the girl.

She came into his yard, removed her blouse, and was forced to perform fellatio on him against her will. Joseph knew that the dream represented his losing his mother and other caregivers and that in order to deny his deprivation, he took what was being withheld.

After Greer cancelled one appointment, Joseph dreamed of a woman at work who had a child every other year (a super-mother) and whose last name implied that she prepared meals for others. In the dream *she wore a T-shirt through which he could see her protuberant nipples. He tenderly embraced her "instead of sucking her breasts"*, he sobbed. The dream was initiated by the cancellation of an appointment; an improvement in his condition could now be expected inasmuch as he could now cry and accept the loss of the nurturing experience in his infancy and childhood.

The fifth year

As the fifth year of Joseph's treatment commenced, he was in considerable emotional turmoil, attempting to mourn over his childhood developmental losses and to modify and/or dissolve his infantile psychotic self. He was also changing some of the defences his previous uninvaded part had employed to keep his infantile psychotic self in check. In the past Joseph had avoided learning how to drive a car. A car was an aggressive tool, and thus he avoided the possibility of killing someone (his mother). Furthermore, an important memory of his childhood was riding in his mother's funeral procession and his aunt's crushing of his mother's photograph. The car was like a childhood *linking object* (Volkan, 1981) for him and represented a link to his mother as well as the fragmentation of her image. Without telling Greer, Joseph began to take driving lessons, and soon after this he began to drive. He feared at first that he might hit and kill a child, but when he understood that he really wanted to kill the helpless, aggressive infant within, he drove more freely.

Once Joseph became more independent and no longer needed to be driven to work or to sessions, his wife got a job. This drastically disturbed the balance at home. Joseph perceived that his wife possessed many of the same character traits as his mother, but she tolerated Joseph's physical and verbal abuse without leaving him.

He would hit her on the head in a conscious and unconscious attempt to create another brain-damaged woman. She was part of an external environment he created to meet his internal demands.

Joseph wished now to be free of all of his symptoms. As he improved, his wife became more paranoid. Joseph was no longer after little girls, but his wife continued to accuse him. One day his wife wondered what he and his therapist were doing during their sessions. She asked, "Do you suck each other's dicks?" The question made Joseph uncomfortable because he actually had such fantasies. That night he had a dream in which *a piece of cylindrical faecal material came out of his mouth and then turned into a cobra.* Joseph once more was able to examine his earliest infant–mother relationship and the associated "bad" feelings as well as unconscious fantasies. His associations to the dream indicated that in sucking his son's penis and later fantasizing taking in the therapist's, he was in search of his mother's "good nipple". The reality was, however, that she had frustrated him. In consequence, he had projected his infantile rage on the nipple/penis and turned it into a faecal cobra/penis. It was internalized as such and was assimilated into his infantile psychotic self. He now wanted to spit it out.

After working on this dream, Joseph improved even more. He knew that, at least in part, his wife stood for the non-nurturing, brain-damaged, ineffective mother representation. In turn, he knew that his wife had played such a role and that their marriage had been a stormy, pathological one. He had no realistic hope that she would change and meet him at his improved level. He attempted to discuss these issues with his wife and asked for a divorce. Both of them agreed that this might be the best solution. The idea of actually separating from his wife/mother representation made Joseph anxious, however. By separating physically and intrapsychically from a "bad" mother, he might be utterly alone. He was having fantasies about making a woman at work his future wife. She was, in fact, a healthier and a more appropriate choice than his present wife. At the peak of Joseph's considerations, Greer took a two-week vacation, which he had planned earlier. The patient reacted to this with a psychosis-like episode in which he lived out a version of his rebirth fantasy.

Joseph disappeared from his home in confusion and lived on the streets, as he had done as a child and an adolescent. When the therapist returned from vacation, he received a call from Joseph's wife, who informed him that her husband had failed to return from work the previous afternoon and that she was extremely frightened for his safety. She had already notified the police, who advised her that it was too soon to declare him a missing person. During the fourth day of Joseph's disappearance, Greer received a call from Joseph, who disclosed his whereabouts. Joseph had been told by the director of the shelter where he was staying that he should admit himself to a hospital, and he came to Greer's office later that day to discuss the issue. The therapist, unaware of the countertransference being induced in him at this time (to be discussed later) and not noticing the progressive aspect of what Joseph had done, concurred with the advice. On a conscious level the therapist was feeling uncomfortable, because while everything was going so well, his patient appeared to be disorganized. This embarrassed the therapist, and he became concerned about what the shelter director or other professionals would think of his reputation.

Joseph quickly admitted himself to a local psychiatric hospital, where he remained for thirty days. This, to a great extent, crystallized in his mind that whatever experiences he had with Greer would not change his fate, and that in the long run any caregiver, such as the neurologist he grew fond of after his meningitis, would reject him. The neurologist had saved his life but did not adopt him. Greer saved Joseph from his psychological prison, but now he was rejecting him and sending him to be cared for by others. At this time, neither the therapist nor his patient realized that Joseph's seemingly psychosis-like behaviour was a re-enactment of his rebirth wish and that, indeed, it had a progressive aspect. With the help of the supervisor, who later learned what was going on, the therapist came to understand his reactions. The therapist was the anxious, enraged, and bewildered child whose mother had disappeared, and Joseph was that mother. In turn, Greer "rejected" his patient.

Upon discharge from the hospital, the patient returned to his sessions. The first hours were devoted to an account of his activities while in his psychosis-like state. He had lost his identity temporarily and found himself at a nearby resort, where he sat on a bench next to a prostitute, whom he initially perceived as an idealized woman. She told him that she had resorted to prostitution to raise money to care for her infant daughter. After they made love in a motel, Joseph found himself acting very maternal towards the woman. He soothed and comforted her, offering to send her money to help her care for her infant. Her story about being a destitute mother too proud to accept charity moved him to tears. Greer understood this as an enactment of the patient's search for an idealized mother–child fusion during his therapist's absence. Obviously the patient was still having difficulty verbalizing this search.

But the therapist sensed that Joseph's latest psychotic-like episode was different from his previous ones, because this time he was able to keep or to restore quickly his observing and working egos and be curious about his experience, connecting it with his childhood losses and his rebirth fantasies. He was aware, perhaps for the first time at a truly affective level, of his emotional hunger. He sensed what he called an empty feeling in his stomach as he devoured a birthday cake at a fellow employee's birthday party. Several days later he experienced another episode of a bleeding duodenal ulcer, which was treated by his doctor. Soon, however, we felt that the developmental path from somatization to verbalization of affects had been opened in Joseph. He seemed to be flooded with unnamable "bad" feelings, reporting that they were the cause of the "hole" in his stomach. As Herbert Rosenfeld (1985) states, in patients like Joseph "psychotic aspects . . . may leak out in psychosomatic symptoms" (p. 381). Through his psychotic-like behaviour and psychosomatic reactions, Joseph's infantile psychotic self was dislodged, and he could reframe and re-symbolize it and get a better hold on it.

A memorable dream followed this episode: Joseph saw himself holding a baby that looked like an underdeveloped foetus with a swollen stomach. They were in a kitchen with a black woman who was wearing make-up. The black woman asked Joseph not to talk to the baby. Joseph, angry at the woman for this directive, told her that she was no longer needed in the kitchen and she could leave, which she did. Joseph looked at the baby and knew that this underdeveloped infant was himself. A thought came to his mind that at last he had seen how he looked as a baby (his infantile psychotic self). The baby looked almost dead. Joseph knew that when the baby died he would bury him. In reality, Joseph had heard that the funeral director had put a great deal of make-up on his dead mother. "The black woman is my mother, the corpse," he declared with confidence. He realized that now he might be ready to genuinely separate from her representation intrapsychically and ultimately free himself from his fusion with her representation. He could now talk to the baby, own and separate it from the rest of his personality, and repress (bury) it.

Flight from treatment

Belatedly, after the patient's hospitalization, the therapist understood that Joseph's recent regression into a psychosis-like episode and his development of a psychosomatic symptom were in the service of progression. It was like a disorganization that occurs during adolescence, followed by a new reorganization of the personality (Blos, 1979). In actual treatment, therapeutic movement phases do not always take place in the neat and orderly fashion that is described by theoretical formulations. Many therapeutic regressions occur and are followed by progressions. By going two steps up and one step down, and by repeating this process, the patient slowly improves. Joseph exhibited a drastic therapeutic regression that ushered in the recapture of his infantile psychotic self. We were impressed with Joseph's intrapsychic improvement, but he faced what proved to be, for him, two untenable dilemmas. The first one pertained to his wish to crystallize in the external world the intrapsychic separation from his mother's representation by divorcing his wife. The second one involved new complications in the transference–countertransference axis.

The first dilemma was that Joseph wanted a divorce, but anxieties about being on his own without the support of a "mother" were paramount in his thoughts. These anxieties about being able to function competently by himself evinced themselves in a dream in which *he was walking on water* (a narcissistic defence), *supported by an unseen canoe*. The therapist empathized with Joseph's anxieties as he strove to move in a progressive direction. The therapist cautioned Joseph that despite his wishes to resolve his infantile anxieties, this was a process that could not be hurried because he continued to depend on a mother representation (the canoe that probably also represented Greer) from which he drew strength. The therapist emphasized that they needed to do more therapeutic work.

Joseph was convinced that the real proof of his being well would be tried in the complications of divorce proceedings. He understood why he had married his wife in the first place and what kept them in this relationship. As he separated his "brain-damaged" mother representation from his wife, he developed empathy for his wife and her unhappy task. He urged her to consult a therapist, which she did for a short while. There was, however, no change in her paranoia and, moreover, no motivation to change as far as he could ascertain. In the end, however, Joseph could not bring himself to divorce her, and he felt that further therapy would only keep his worries about this torturous and conflicted issue indefinitely and painfully open.

The second dilemma was that the therapist, unconsciously responding to the patient's projection of the "hungry" infant representation onto him, had concurred with the advice of the shelter's director that Joseph should admit himself to a psychiatric hospital. This led to the therapist becoming identified in Joseph's fantasies with the neurologist who had saved his life when he was a boy but who later abandoned him. After an unexpected and unplanned encounter with Greer's wife and adopted daughter at his office, therapeutic matters became even more complicated. Because the child belonged to a different race, Joseph knew immediately that the therapist's daughter was adopted. Joseph then spoke of his wish to be adopted by the therapist's family and felt frustrated. This request and Greer's assent to his hospitalization kept Joseph from leaving the hospital altogether after his month's stay; he continued to be very much involved with the hospital's treatment programme for recently discharged patients after he resumed work with Greer. This programme, for all practical purposes, was undermining the intrapsychic work Greer and Joseph were attempting to do in order to work through the recent complications in the transference–countertransference. It was as if, disappointed with the mother/neurologist/therapist, Joseph had gone to an orphanage. Thus, in his mind, his therapist had become similar to object representations towards which Joseph felt murderous rage. At the same time, Joseph wanted the therapist to remain as a nurturing mother. To protect the "good" therapist from his rage, Joseph escaped from treatment and remained married to his wife.

It has been a little over a year since Joseph left treatment, and Greer and I assume that he functions with high-level borderline personality organization. We suspect that he still keeps his wife as a "bad" object representation, while Greer's representation, which Joseph keeps at a physical distance so that he cannot be contaminated with his "badness", remains a "good" one. Evidence of this formulation is our knowledge that Greer still preoccupies Joseph's mind. Less than a year after Joseph prematurely ended the treatment, he called Greer "to say hello and explain why I walked out on you". He then proceeded to say that he knew that he had used something the therapist had said as a pretext to terminate his sessions abruptly. His complaint was that the therapist's interventions had become repetitious, which they had not. The implication is that Joseph needed a reason to distance himself from Greer to keep him as a "good" cushion to fall back on in the future. Joseph sent Greer a poem that captured with poignant clarity the torturous inner world about which he seemed to have great insight now and into which both men had travelled in order to make drastic modifications in Joseph's infantile psychotic self. Joseph is being encouraged to return to treatment and finish the therapeutic task.

CHAPTER THREE

Juvenile paedophilia: the psychodynamics of an adolescent sex offender

Brett Kahr

Sexual-arousal disorder in children and adolescents

Most of the psychoanalytic understanding of paedophilia has derived from intensive clinical work with adult patients; however, we now recognize, quite shockingly, that approximately one-third of all sexual crimes against children will be perpetrated by other youngsters (National Children's Home, 1992). The early pioneers of child psychiatry and sexology certainly appreciated that small boys and girls do actually display signs of perverse sexual behaviour. Sigmund Freud (1905), of course, had long ago suggested that even newborn infants reveal symptoms of perverse sexuality, as evidenced by their penchant for deriving pleasure from different sorts of bodily stimulation. However, in spite of the frequent references to childhood sexuality in both its normal and perverse forms (cf. Kern, 1973), the vast majority of psychoanalysts have neglected to devote ample attention to the study of perverse sexual activity in children. Exceptionally, some cases do exist in the literature. In 1959—the same year in which Charles Socarides published his landmark paper on the psychodynamics of adult paedophilia—Melitta Sperling, a specialist in the treatment of psychosomatic disorders in children, produced her little-known paper, "A Study of Deviate Sexual Behavior in Children by the Method of Simultaneous Analysis of Mother and Child." Regrettably, this report has received virtually no attention in the psychoanalytic literature, in spite of its brilliance and sharp awareness that sexual offending begins during the first years of life, and that one can and should intervene at an early stage in order to prevent the development of further perverse psychopathological manifestations.

In her chapter, Sperling presented three cases of young, sexually deviant children. A 6½-year-old girl called Rhoda entered treatment with Melitta Sperling after staff at her school had observed the girl in the toilet, with her underpants taken down, inspecting and touching the genitals of other young female pupils. Rhoda had enticed her classmates to engage in this activity by bribing them with sweets, purchased with money stolen from her mother's purse. In addition to her exhibitionistic and touching behaviour, Rhoda would sometimes hit the other girls on their naked bodies, thus revealing an early intermixing of erotic and sadistic strivings. Sperling treated Rhoda's mother, and it soon emerged that Rhoda's mother often engaged in physical fights with her own mother, and neither mother or daughter would be wearing any clothes!

Sperling's second case, an 8½-year-old boy called Jerry, also entered treatment after pressure from his school. Jerry had already used extremely obscene language in the presence of adults, and he had also begun to attack younger girls at school, pinching them, and inserting his fingers into their anuses. Once, he even stabbed another child in the back with a pencil. Significantly, Jerry feared injections, so much so that he had to discontinue his treatment sessions with an allergist. Sperling eventually discovered that Jerry's father would often bite his son on the buttocks, pinch him, squeeze him, and "practically to stick his nose in Jerry's anus" (Sperling, 1959, p. 230), suggesting a highly inappropriate eroticization of the relationship between father and son. In view of Jerry's fears of injections, and of his penchant for inserting fingers and pencils into the bodies of younger children, one cannot help but wonder whether Jerry's father had also inserted his penis into his son's rectum, though Sperling did not comment on this possibility.

The third case, a 9-year-old girl called Judy, used to enter her mother's bed and would pet and kiss the mother's vulva. Judy would then ask the mother to reciprocate. Judy's mother had evidently become aroused by the sensation of her daughter's tongue, because when she and Judy would bathe together, the mother would hallucinate that her daughter Judy possessed a penis between her legs.

On the basis of her clinical material, Sperling (1959) concluded that "deviate sexual behavior in children is dynamically a disturbance of the superego resulting from the internalization of certain unconscious parental attitudes" (p. 238). Furthermore, Sperling noted that it would be essential to transform the unconscious perverse needs of the parents in order to minimize the acting-out behaviour in the children; and this would best be accomplished by treating both the child and the mother in simultaneous analysis. Sperling's work deserves further detailed consideration as an inspiration to those who wish to recognize the very earliest warning signs of sexual offending in later life (cf. Winnicott, 1960).

More recently, Donald Campbell (1997), a former Chairman of the Portman Clinic, has written an important study on the fantasy life of an adolescent boy with paedophile tendencies, as well as work on the assessment of young sexual abusers (Campbell, 1994; cf. Hodges, Lanyado, & Andreou, 1994; Hurry, 1990; Lanyado, Hodges, Bentovim, Andreou, & Williams, 1995). Campbell (1994) has appreciated that the average sexual offender will commit approximately 380 crimes against children during a paedophile career; therefore, clinicians must strive to work with younger offenders in order to prevent them from becoming invariant paedophiles. Campbell's work with a patient called "George" documents very vividly the way in which a sexually abused child will repeat his own experience of victimization by targeting younger and more helpless victims who can be abused in almost exactly the same manner.

In recent years, the literature on the incidence and prevalence, the epidemiology, the aetiology, and the treatment of young sexual offenders has begun to mushroom considerably, as more and more workers have at last developed an appreciation for the importance of early intervention (e.g. van Dam, 2001; Vizard, Monck, & Misch, 1995). Eileen Vizard, a Consultant Child and Adolescent Psychiatrist in the British National Health Service and Clinical Director of the Young Abusers Project, has lamented that none of the major diagnostic manuals actually includes an official psychiatric term for juvenile paedophilia, and she and her colleagues have suggested that we refer to such cases as "Sexual Arousal Disorder of Childhood" (Vizard, Wynick, Hawkes, Woods, & Jenkins, 1996, p. 262; cf. Vizard, Hawkes, Wynick, Woods, & Jenkins, 1994). Vizard and colleagues have recommended that by naming this unpalatable form of behaviour in children, we will have made a first step towards its recognition and ultimately towards prevention and treatment.

In 1987, Vizard established the East London Community Team Programme for the treatment of sex offenders, with the aid of psychiatric and probation-service colleagues (Mezey, Vizard, Hawkes, & Austin, 1991). Vizard and her associates had provided detailed psychiatric and psychosocial assessments of sex offenders, as well as therapeutic group work, in which offender patients could discuss their own victimization experiences, their sexual attraction to children, and their tendencies to deny the seriousness of their offences. As the work expanded, Vizard began to concentrate more extensively in the field of forensic child psychiatry and forensic child psychotherapy (cf. Kahr, 1996), and she recognized the increasing importance of intervening before the sexual offending patterns had become ossified within the personality structure of the perpetrator. Patients referred to the East London Community Team Programme ranged in age from 21 years to over 60 years. In an effort to reach a younger population, Vizard founded the Young Abusers Project at the Tavistock Clinic in London, in 1992, co-sponsored initially by the Department of Health, the National Children's Home, and the National Society for the Prevention of Cruelty to Children, in order to treat younger sex offenders below the age of 22 years.

The Young Abusers Project has now provided in-depth psychiatric, psychological, and social work assessments to several hundred individuals between the ages of 6 and 21 years, all of whom have committed serious sexual offences against younger children, or who have shown the tendency to do so, as evidenced by highly inappropriate sexualized behaviours at home or in school. Although most of the referrals continue to be abusive boys, the Young

Abusers Project has in fact assessed a small number of abusive girls as well. The Young Abusers Project operates on a philosophy that combines psychoanalytic thinking and treatment strategies with child-protection principles, in an effort to provide a safety net in which young offenders can talk about their substantial difficulties. Staff at the Young Abusers Project maintain a strong appreciation for the importance of preventative work, striving to assess and treat children at increasingly younger ages, before they have begun their careers as potentially invariant adult paedophiles.

Patients undergoing the assessment and treatment programme at the Young Abusers Project must be referred by a professional agency, invariably a consultant child psychiatrist, a social worker from a local social services department, or a probation officer in certain instances. The vast majority of the referrals to the project will already have performed penetrative acts involving the insertion of the offender's genitals into either the vagina, mouth, or anus of another child. Many will have performed comparable penetrations on more than one occasion. Victims can be younger siblings or cousins, or they may be fellow schoolmates or neighbours. Alternatively, the victims of the sexual assaults might be complete strangers, targeted by the young offender. Not all the patients referred to the Young Abusers Project will have actually engaged in a penetrative act with their penises; some perpetrators will use fingers or other objects. Nevertheless, we regard the penetration of the anal region as a very disturbing indication of psychopathology, rather than as a mere expression of childhood play and curiosity, especially when a marked age difference exists between the perpetrator and the victim. Many of the 14-, 15-, or 16-year-old patients will have violated the bodies of younger children of 2, 3, 4, or 5 years of age. We simply cannot rationalize such breaches of bodily boundaries across a generational gap as mere examples of adolescent sexual investigations.

After extensive team discussions of the case at hand, a pair of specialist social workers will interview each prospective referral in two meetings, each lasting for approximately two hours. On these occasions, the young person will have an opportunity to tell the full details of the offending behaviour that has brought him or her to the attention of the professional network. The social work specialists then advise on suitability for treatment, whereupon a percentage will be referred for group psychotherapy or for individual psychoanalytically orientated psychotherapy. I worked for the Young Abusers Project as a psychotherapist from 1994 until 1998, and during that relatively short period of time I had the opportunity to work psychotherapeutically with some six adolescent sex-offending boys between the ages of 16 and 21 years of age. Although my clinical experience cannot be described as vast, some general principles have emerged that bear recounting, especially in view of the sheer paucity of psychoanalytically informed writings in this field.

To my great surprise, all six boys with whom I have worked sat down in a chair at their first meeting with me, and promptly spread their legs wide open, displaying their crotches in a very protuberant fashion. I felt confident that the young patients did so very unconsciously, but it struck me as quite extraordinary that each of the young offenders should do so in quite such an overt manner. I realized that none of my other patients, irrespective of their baseline diagnostic categories, had ever splayed their legs in a session. We might perhaps regard this unique form of presentation as pathognomic of adolescent sex-offending behaviour. In this way, the young men succeed in communicating to the psychotherapist straight away that they have little capacity to talk or to think, but that they use their genitalia as a means of expressing powerful emotions. Not surprisingly, as treatment progresses, and the boys begin to learn about the language of emotions, the rate of leg-splaying behaviour begins to decrease, albeit very slowly. One of the boys used to bring a mobile telephone with him to psychotherapy sessions, and he would place the phone noticeably between his two spread legs, so that the telephone would resemble a part-object penis. As one uses a telephone primarily for the purpose of talking and communicating, this patient managed to concretize in rather a dramatic fashion exactly how he would speak with a phone-penis placed at his groin. This boy used very few words, but he had raped two 7-year-old girls with his penis. Thus, the penis does the talking for these boys, and psychotherapy helps them to rectify the situation so that they can begin to speak with their voices rather than with their genitals.

Virtually every single boy referred to the Young Abusers Project has suffered from some form of violation in early life. Many have themselves been victims of sexual abuse at the hands of a natural parent, or a step-parent, or a foster-parent, or some other relative. Others have experienced tremendous deprivation during the early years of life. In the psychotherapeutic relationship, all of the patients will find some means of concretizing the early abusive experiences in the transference, and many will actually barge into the consulting-room, before the psychotherapist has opened the door, providing archaic evidence of the need to "break and enter".

Clinical material: the case of "Z"

The referral

I began to work with "Z", a 16-year-old male sexual offender, in the latter months of 1995. Z had committed several acts of sexual misconduct, including the disrobing of prepubescent girls, and additionally he had in fact perpetrated full penetrative intercourse on three young girls, all aged 5 years. The local department of social services assigned to care for Z had enormous worries about the aggressive behaviour of this young person.

Z first came to the attention of the social services authority as a small boy, because his mother had put him up for adoption during his eighth year, claiming that she could not care for him adequately, noting that she might beat him to a pulp if she had to continue living with her son. During this previous year, Z's father had died from a heart attack, and no doubt the sudden loss of the father proved highly unsettling for Z, for his mother, and for Z's six siblings. Z then progressed from one foster-care home to another, becoming increasingly violent towards both children and adults, hitting and screaming with great frequency. At the age of 14, Z had attempted to strip a mentally handicapped 10-year-old girl of her dress and brassiere, and he had also removed his own trousers and underpants in the presence of another 10-year-old girl in a toilet, urging her to take her clothing off as well. Later that year, he progressed to penetrative vaginal intercourse with three different 5-year-old girls whom he had abducted from a local playground. Naturally, the authorities became increasingly vexed by this troubled and troubling teenager, and, quite understandably, they sought the help of a specialist unit.

The psychiatric assessment

Z first presented to the Young Abusers Project in the latter part of 1994, for both psychiatric and psychological evaluations. Z's designated social worker approached the project in the hope that we would offer our expert opinion on three particular issues and concerns:

1. A determination of the risk that Z posed to other people in the local community, especially young children, as a result of his physical violence and his sexually abusive behaviour.

2. A recommendation about the suitability of his current foster-care placement.

3. A recommendation for treatment options should the Young Abusers Project be able to demonstrate that Z did indeed suffer from a potentially treatable psychiatric condition.

In order to arrive at an evaluation of Z's mental state, my colleagues drew upon the vast file of documentation from social services, the police, reports from previous child psychiatrists and child psychologists who had evaluated Z over the years, and so on. My psychiatric and social work colleagues from the Young Abusers Project also arranged for Z to be interviewed in depth jointly by a probation officer and by a child psychiatrist on our staff team. Subsequently, a clinical psychologist employed by the Young Abusers Project performed a full evaluation of Z's cognitive capacities.

Z arrived at the offices of the Young Abusers Project near Christmas in 1994. The staff who first assessed Z became anxious almost instantly, unprepared to meet such a tall and broad-shouldered teenager, standing more than six and a half feet in height and weighing roughly 250 pounds, with huge musculature. Additionally, we must mention that Z comes from a Black African background, his parents having emigrated from Nigeria some twenty years previously.

Z proved extremely paranoid and uncooperative during the two formal psychiatric interviews, and he showed evidence of his deeply entrenched violent tendencies during the very first encounter by throwing a chair across the room. The probation officer and the child psychiatrist maintained their composure, and in spite of Z's violent outburst, my colleagues persevered with their psychiatric examination, and they continued to ask Z questions about his abusive behaviour towards younger children.

Surprisingly, Z spoke rather rapidly and rather freely about his penchant for molesting prepubescent girls, and he talked at length about how he had inserted his "hard cock" into the "ginas" of the little girls, and how this had aroused him. He also confessed for the first time that both he and a male school friend had targeted young girls together, and that, on more than one occasion, Z and his chum would have enforced intercourse with two different girls and, during the middle of the rape, Z and his friend would switch positions, penetrating both girls in turn. Hitherto, the social services did not know about these additional crimes.

In spite of his violent outburst during the psychiatric interviews, Z did admit that he wished to be helped by the Young Abusers Project, and that he spent a lot of his time worrying about being arrested by the police. Z told my colleagues that he dreaded spending his grown-up years in prison. Afterwards, Z became extremely sullen and depressed, refusing to lift up his head. Z thus revealed his capacity for feeling shameful affects, which might ultimately be mobilized in psychotherapeutic treatment.

Later that month, Z underwent a full battery of psychological testing. During this interview with our staff clinical psychologist, Z proved much less willing to engage, and he refused to draw any pictures for the Draw-A-Person Test or for the House–Tree–Person Test, even though the psychologist had asked him to do so. He did, however, respond grudgingly to some of the projective tests, notably the Thematic Apperception Test cards, although he complained that he had difficulties concentrating, claiming that he needed to "clear my head". Towards the end of the testing situation, Z became overtly tearful. Overall, Z performed rather poorly on the Wechsler Intelligence Scale for Children–Revised (WISC–R), receiving an overall intelligence quotient score of 52, which placed him in the 0.1 percentile of people his age, indicative of a moderate learning disability.

During the administration of the Comprehension Sub-Test of the WISC–R, the psychologist asked Z what he would do if he happened to walk past a stamped envelope. Quite tellingly, Z responded that he would "leave it on the floor, walk past it". This communication, in particular, seemed highly indicative of both Z's internal world and of the tremendous neglect and deprivation that he experienced throughout his childhood. I suspect that he very much identified with the stamped envelope lying on the floor, unposted, as this mirrors his earlier experiences of having been abandoned by his mother at a young age, and then passed on from one foster home to another in succession, providing him with no continuity or security during his crucial early developmental years.

After the completion of this extensive evaluation, the consultant child and adolescent psychiatrist at the Young Abusers Project formulated the following conclusions. The psychiatrist remarked that on the basis of his sexually abusive behaviour, Z displayed all the indications of the DSM-IV diagnosis for "Pedophilia" (302.20), but in view of the fact that Z had not yet reached his sixteenth birthday at the time of the report (a necessary condition for receiving such a diagnosis), our staff psychiatrist indicated that Z suffered instead from the DSM-IV category of "Conduct Disorder, Solitary Aggressive Type" (312.00). Furthermore, the psychiatrist noted that Z suffered from "Mental Retardation" (318.00), although at the present time it still remains unclear to what extent such learning disabilities resulted from any primary organic deficit, or to what extent they became manifest as a result of prolonged psychological traumatization (e.g. Sinason, 1992). The consultant child and adolescent psychiatrist summarized Z's case thus: "Bringing these diagnostic features together, therefore, Z could be described as a young man with a background of psychosocial deprivation and learning difficulty. His history of generally aggressive behaviour towards peers has now developed into a particular form, that of sexually abusive behaviour towards young females. This pattern is likely to persist and may develop into a permanent personality disorder, particularly if Z's current and to some extent self-acknowledged difficulties are not addressed appropriately."

My colleagues concluded that Z posed a genuine risk to young children, especially young females; and they also expressed concern about his capacity for angry or aggressive behaviour or ideation towards older women, reminding us that in view of Z's substantial physical size of six and a half feet, he possessed the capacity to perpetrate actual bodily harm against adults as well as against children. The Young Abusers Project recommended that Z should not ever be left alone with any children under any circumstances whatsoever. Colleagues also expressed concern about the viability of Z's current foster-care placement, in view of the fact that Z's foster mother had a 5-year-old son of her own, and that the presence of a 5-year-old child might prove too distracting for an accomplished child-molester such as Z. The psychiatrist expressed a thought that a supervised residential-care facility might be more appropriate for such a disturbed and disturbing boy, rather than a private foster-care home in the community. Finally, the psychiatrist recommended that psychotherapeutic treatment would be of great value to Z, bearing in mind, however, that any treatment would cause Z to become aware of deeper layers of aggressive affect.

Z's very committed social worker discussed the implications of the psychiatric and psychological reports with senior staff at the social services department, all of whom agreed that Z did indeed pose a severe risk to children in the local community, and that the Young Abusers Project should be called upon to provide psychotherapeutic treatment for Z The social worker then asked Z for his views on the matter, whereupon Z replied that he did want to talk to somebody, but that he would prefer to speak to a Black psychotherapist. At this time, the Young Abusers Project employed three psychotherapists, including myself, all Caucasian; therefore, it would be impossible to supply Z with a Black clinician.

The psychotherapy assessment

Z had to wait approximately nine months until I could see him for our preliminary psychotherapy assessment sessions. The Young Abusers Project would not, of course, begin treatment until we had assurances that the local social services department could provide funding for the work on an ongoing basis and, of equal importance, that a professional escort could be engaged to transport Z to and from his psychotherapy sessions. It would not be feasible or helpful for Z to travel to my office on his own, as the risk of acting out against children en route would be too great. We all assumed that psychotherapeutic treatment would stir up many anxieties for this

fragile young person, and that he would need a responsible parental figure to contain some of his fears before and after sessions. In
this respect, the Young Abusers Project subscribes not only to the
basic tenets of psychoanalytically orientated psychotherapy, but
also harbours an appreciation for the basic principles of child
protection. Thus, our treatment of offending adolescents resembles
the work of the child psychotherapist in many ways.

After discussing the case at length with my team colleagues, we
all agreed that I would meet with Z for two psychotherapy assessment sessions, in order to determine his suitability for ongoing
psychoanalytically informed work. In view of the large distance
that Z would have to travel, as he lived outside London, it would
not be possible to offer more than one 50-minute session per week.

Z arrived on time for his first psychotherapy assessment session in the latter part of 1995, escorted by his loyal social worker.
I opened to door to my office at the appropriate moment, and I
introduced myself simply and efficiently to Z and to his social
worker. Silently, I gestured for Z to enter the consulting-room, and
I asked the social worker to remain in the adjacent waiting area.
The Young Abusers Project relies on the escort not only for transportation purposes, but also to provide an additional sense of
security for both the patient and the psychotherapist. All of our
patients know full well that their escorts will be waiting for them
on the other side of the door, and I have come to appreciate the
ways in which this knowledge reduces the temptation for the
patients to become more violent than necessary during treatment
sessions.

I then closed the door to the consulting-room, and I sat in my
chair behind the couch. Z sat in another chair on the other side of
the room, directly across the way from my own seat. I now had an
opportunity to observe his physical presence. He filled the leather
chair fully, with his large frame. Z sat with his legs splayed wide
open, in characteristic paedophile fashion. I realized that I had
never before worked with such a physically large and intimidating
patient, and in my mind, I became preoccupied with stereotypes of
violent, young Black men. I remained silent, eager to learn how he
would respond to this unusual, yet long-awaited situation. Z did
not speak at all; instead, he began to look all around the consulting-

room, soaking in every detail, and staring relentlessly at the couch, at the bookshelves, and at the Persian carpet. After he had absorbed the room visually, Z then turned his head towards the ceiling and peered first at the upper-right-hand corner of the ceiling and then at the upper-left-hand corner. He continued to do this for many minutes, staring anxiously, as though searching for something. It suddenly occurred to me that during Z's last visit to the Young Abusers Project, he would have met with my psychiatric and probation service colleagues in a specialist video suite, where his psychiatric assessment would have been filmed, for both child-protection purposes and for the project's ongoing research work. I suspect that he had anxieties about being photographed. But I also realized that he might be nervous because I had *no* video cameras in my psychotherapy-room.

Five minutes had elapsed, and neither of us had spoken out loud, but although Z had not verbalized any anxieties at this point, he had certainly communicated extensive anxieties through his scoptophilic behaviour, thus prompting my first interpretation. I looked at Z, and told him that I could see how important it might be for him to scan the room with his eyes, noting that he had never been in my room before, nor had he ever met me before, and therefore, it would be important for him to see what sort of a room he had entered. I then commented that he seemed particularly concerned with the corners of my ceiling, as though he had been searching for a video camera, since his last visit to our project would have taken place in a specialist video suite. I underscored that Z might be pleased that I had no video camera in my room, but that he might also be worried, in case the presence of a video camera made him feel safer so that other grown-ups could see what he did at every moment. This intervention seemed to speak to Z, and after I had mentioned the missing video camera, he smiled, and he began to talk to me.

Promptly, Z told me that he did not want to speak to me, because he had very bad memories of the probation-service colleague, Mr X, who had co-facilitated the initial psychiatric interview some months previously. Z decried that "Mr X treated me like some sort of an idiot. He made me show him what I did to those girls by using some dolls. He asked me if I knew the names of private parts, as though I didn't. He was a real idiot." I responded to this outburst of denigration by mentioning that I knew that various professional colleagues had diagnosed Z as suffering from mental handicap and learning disability at several points during his life, and that perhaps he worried that I too would treat him as a stupid person who did not understand what grown-up people had to say. Z smiled, once again, as if to indicate that I had succeeded in alleviating at least a very small modicum of anxiety.

Z then began to stare at a delicate nineteenth-century engraving that hangs in a frame over my analytic couch. The engraving depicts a group of travellers heading on a journey. Z continued to gawk at the picture, and then he blurted out: "I bet that painting was done in 1979." I wondered why on earth Z mistook this very old picture for a work of art from 1979. Concretely, I reasoned that even a person with absolutely no training in art history would be able to sense the value and age of this engraving. But I then realized that 1979 represented, in fact, the very year of Z's birth. I then shared this insight with Z, and I commented: "I wonder whether you chose 1979 as the date, because that is the year in which you were born. And this drawing hanging over the couch depicts a group of travellers going on a journey. Perhaps you have a wish to go on a journey here with me, starting over at the very beginning. And you must be wondering what sort of journey it will be." The patient looked somewhat more mystified, but he responded by telling me that his father had once bought him a set of drums, and he liked to play on these drums. I found myself wondering whether Z's comment about the drum set represented some unconscious acknowledgment or validation of my interpretation about the nineteenth-century engraving, as though I had given him a present of a kind in the form of rudimentary psychological understanding.

As the first assessment session drew to a close, I reminded Z that he had come here, in part, because both his social worker and the staff at the Young Abusers Project had recommended that he do so, but also, in part, because he himself had asked for help. Z grunted, "Yeah, that's right." I told him that I had learned of his request for a Black psychotherapist, and that he may have felt disappointed to meet with a Caucasian man instead. He nodded his head in agreement, but verbally he told me that it did not matter. I explained to Z that he and I had an important decision to make regarding whether he would come back to see me every week to discuss his problems and his difficulties. Unhesitatingly, he nodded that he wanted to return. I reminded the patient that he and I would meet at precisely the same time, one week hence, and that he might want to use the intervening week to think carefully about what it might be like to see me on a regular basis.

The following week, Z returned for the second of his psycho-therapy assessment sessions, accompanied by his social worker once again. He spoke prosaically about his week, painting a rather gloomy picture of his desolate life. Z explained how he would spend all day in bed, watching one television programme after another on his satellite system. He reeled off the names of each programme, their starting times, as well as the names of the central characters. Z reported this information in a bleak, telegraphic style that communicated both the emptiness of his external world as well as the profound schizoid defences that he had erected against his overpoweringly violent internal world. I linked the list of television programmes to what I imagined to be the patient's wish to enter psychotherapy, suggesting that Z wished to tell me how routine his life had become, and how frightened he had become to venture out of the bedroom in his foster-mother's house. I wondered whether he wanted to enter into psychotherapy in order to address these issues. He nodded softly.

Towards the end of the second psychotherapy assessment session, I explained to Z that I saw no reason why he could not work with me in psychotherapy, and that I would agree to meet with him at a regular weekly time, and that this would be an ongoing arrangement over a long period. I also sketched out the clinical calendar, informing Z that there would be regular breaks in the psychotherapy at Christmas, Easter, and during the summer. Additionally, I reminded him that his local social services department had agreed to pay his fees, and I told him the amount. I also clarified my relationship to the Young Abusers Project, informing him that I work as a psychotherapist for the project, and that I would not be communicating directly with Z's own social worker, but that the social worker from the Young Abusers Project might

do so from time to time, especially if any of the grown-ups involved in Z's care had great worries about his safety, or about the
safety of other children.

Just before the 50-minute hour ended, Z glanced at a very green
and leafy plant that sits on a table against the wall of my consulting-room. This particular plant has blossomed very well over the
years, and it has sprouted many different shoots, which trail to the
floor. Z turned to me and asked: "Who waters that plant?" I did not
respond directly, whereupon Z remarked: "Plants should be wa-
tered five times a week." It struck me as rather extraordinary that
a handicapped and uneducated young person should be able to
have a sense that in intensive psychoanalytic treatment, the patient
attends five times per week. Although Z knows little or nothing at
all about the practice of psychotherapy, I suspect that he knows
that most working adults go to their offices from Monday to
Friday, inclusive, and I suppose Z had begun to wonder why I
could see him on only one day each week, instead of five. I interpreted this to Z, but he smirked and admonished me in his Mid-
lands Black patois: "What you talking about, man? I speaking of
your plants." Regardless of his denial of the wish to meet with me
every day, I understood Z's commentary about the frequency of
watering as a very hopeful sign, suggesting that Z possessed the
capacity to internalize some good psychical nourishment. We arranged to begin regular sessions at the start of the following term.

The first trimester of treatment

Z did not reveal an enormous amount of information about his
violent tendencies, or about his abuse of small girls, during the two
psychotherapy assessment meetings. I suspect that he feared to talk
at length in case I might refuse to offer him a treatment vacancy.
However, once the psychotherapy had begun in earnest, Z quickly
unleashed a torrent of violence and abusiveness, offering me a
glimpse into his very tortured mind.

Z spent the majority of his early sessions telling me that although I might imagine that he spent all day at home, he really had
an "intergalactic" career as a World Federation boxer, and that
after his sessions, he would dash off to Gatwick Airport and begin

a week of gruelling training sessions and fights overseas. He told me that he fought in Borneo, in Chicago, in New York, in Paris, and in many cities besides. Z boasted that Mike Tyson, the famous boxer (and convicted rapist), was his special mentor and that Mr Tyson had arranged exciting fights in which Z could demonstrate his skills and techniques. It did not surprise me that Z, a young Black sex offender, should identify with Mike Tyson, an older Black man who has had the perverse capacity to transform his own aggressive libido into a career structure that has brought him considerable fame and wealth. Above all, I regarded Z's deeply entrenched "intergalactic" fantasy world as a desperate attempt to fly away from his extremely arid life in England, and as a means of informing me of the extent of his violence.

Although Z devoted most of his sessions to fantastic tales of international boxing tournaments, he would often slide into a more overtly infantile mode of communication, and at times he would leave his chair, pluck a book from my shelves, and curl up his massive, hulking body into a little ball. Then he would open one of my clinical textbooks and pretend that he had taken a copy of *Goldilocks and the Three Bears*, whereupon he would then tell me the story of Goldilocks, in an extremely girlish, high-pitched voice, revealing a very frightened and timid child within his gargantuan frame. The internal terror became extremely clear as Z modified the story of Goldilocks to include a scene whereby the three bears come home from the forest and tear Goldilocks to shreds, using their sharp teeth and claws. I became frequently confused as to whether I had a menacing late-adolescent boy with me in the room, or a petrified 3-year-old child. In fact, both aspects of Z's character structure appeared in the course of each session, though not in such a structured manner that one would regard him as a case of Dissociative Identity Disorder.

Z did not speak a single overt word about his family life, either about his family of origin, or about his foster-mother. I had the impression that he found it too dangerous to talk about real people in the consulting-room, and so he focused his attentions on fictional characters or out-of-reach characters instead, such as Goldilocks and Mike Tyson. Z also regaled me with a series of credible imitations of personalities from very unsophisticated television soap operas and films, and he particularly enjoyed mimicking the comical American actor Jim Carrey in the film *The Mask*, in which Carrey repeats the words "Somebody stop me!" with particular dramatic flourish. Z would often lapse into his Jim Carrey voice, shouting "Somebody stop me!" several times throughout the session. I interpreted that perhaps Z hoped that I would be able to stop him from feeling so angry and so violent, and also from feeling so sad inside.

On another occasion, Z jumped up onto the window-sill of my consulting-room, which overlooks the main high street. He managed to open up the top of the window, and he shouted outside in a very loud and pained voice: "Help! Help! Please help! This horrible man is keeping me here against my will! Help! Help!" Naturally, I felt very panicky at this point, and rather worried that some passer-by would telephone the police. But I then realized that Z wanted me to feel as frightened as he had always felt. In a very soft and calm voice, I suggested that although Z had shouted "Help!" out of the window, he really wanted to ensure that I knew how much he wanted help from me, and that he must have wondered whether I would be able to help him with his feelings. To my surprise and relief, this verbal intervention succeeded in calming Z considerably, and he then removed himself from the window-sill and sat himself in the chair once again.

Towards the end of the first trimester of treatment, Z's long-standing social worker retired, and for three weeks different untrained escorts had to bring him to his sessions, pending the appointment of a new social worker. Z found this loss very difficult indeed, and his violent behaviours in the session increased dramatically during this time. Such data absolutely reinforces the necessity for a stable external environment during the treatment of a forensic patient such as Z. Eventually, a new social worker began to work with Z, and as the weeks wore on Z became somewhat more contained. I spoke about the ways in which the change of social worker had mirrored the inconsistency of the many different homes in which he had lived over the years, with a veritable succession of foster-mothers. I also verbalized anxiety about what sort of constant figure I would be, and whether he would arrive next week to find a different psychotherapist sitting in my chair. Z simply sniggered with derision.

As our first break approached, Z became increasingly anxious, and he devoted much of his session time to a detailed, yet fictitious, recitation of his aeroplane itinerary. He would boast: "Next week, I is goin' to the Bahamas to fight Big John Smith, and then I is goin' to board a plane to Florida to fight him again, and then I is goin' on a plane to Spain to fight El Caballero." I commented on Z's frequent references to plane flights, and I wondered whether he had begun to have fantasies of whether I might be going on a plane over the forthcoming holiday break, and that perhaps he had also begun to have anxieties about whether I would return. Z simply called me a "fucking fool", and told me that I had lied to him, and that really I had never boarded a plane in my life! He found the thought of me disappearing too unbearable, very reminiscent of the father who had died suddenly from heart disease during Z's latency years.

The second trimester of treatment

Z did in fact survive the first break in treatment, and he returned promptly for the start of his second term of psychotherapy. But as the fourth, fifth, and sixth months of our psychotherapeutic encounter unfolded, Z became increasingly violent, both verbally and physically, in the course of his sessions. It may be that Z now felt safer to unmask the really treacherous areas of his mind, knowing that I still wanted to work with him, and that I did, in fact, bother to return after the first holiday period. Z routinely scowled and sneered and smirked at virtually every single comment that I would make, deriding all of my interpretations with considerable contempt. The psychotic and fantasmatic nature of his internal world became increasingly rich. Z not only spoke about his special relationship with the aggressive Black rapist Mike Tyson, but Z also claimed that he had begun to have secret meetings with another Black hero, also accused of sexual crimes—namely, the pop star Michael Jackson.

Z told me that he had now given up his career as a World Federation boxing champion, so that he could earn a huge salary as head of security for Michael Jackson. He provided me with untold details of Michael Jackson's putative timetable, and, rather creatively, Z informed me of all the secret measures that he would have to adopt in order to keep Mr Jackson safe at his many concert appearances. Z informed me that he had employed a gang of security officers who had sworn complete and utter allegiance to him, and that these men would kill anybody who tried to hurt either Michael Jackson or Z himself.

This gang of security officers became a particularly menacing constellation in his mind as the weeks unfolded. Z actually frightened me when he told me that on the previous evening, he and his gang of security officers had loaded their silenced revolvers and had gone cruising through the streets of London, looking for White men to abduct. They found one White man who wore glasses (as I do), and they tied him up and threw him into the boot of their car. Z claimed that he and his men then drove the kidnap victim to an abandoned warehouse near a wharf and systematically tortured him, by blinding him with a knife and then carving lines on his chest until he bled to death. Afterwards, Z claimed that he and the gang cut the man up into a million pieces and threw the remains of his body into the river Thames.

Throughout most of the subsequent session, Z had remained quite sullen and silent. But then, towards the end of the session, he stuck his hand into the pocket of his trousers and then removed his hand very quickly, shaping his fingers like a handgun. He glanced at me with a maniacal expression, and he aimed his fingers at me, and shouted "Pow", pretending to shoot me. Naturally, I did become very frightened at this point, but I tried not to show it. Z leered at me, and he told me that unless I played my cards right, I would also end up like the abducted White man, diced into many pieces, and floating in the river. The Goldilocks voice of the first trimester had disappeared, and I now had an extremely good indication of the deeply disturbed, violent nature of this young sex offender.

After pretending to shoot me with his fingers, Z told me that his gang of security officers had instructions to pick him up at Heathrow Airport and to drive him in a limousine to Michael Jackson's mansion in London, prior to a concert performance at Wembley Stadium. In recounting this fantasized story, Z committed a very revealing parapraxis. Consciously, Z had intended to say, "My men are gonna meet me at Heathrow, and drive me to Mr

Jackson's mansion." But instead, Z actually said: "My men are gonna *beat* me at Heathrow and drive me to Mr Jackson's mansion." Fortified by Freud's observations that slips of the tongue often reveal unconscious wishes, I interpreted that although Z enjoyed telling me about how he and his gang would spend their time killing people, his slip of the tongue indicated just how frightened Z had become of this gang that he had created, and that perhaps he really worried whether his own aggressive wishes would result in somebody beating him up. I also wondered aloud whether he even feared that I or a member of the Young Abusers Project staff would beat him up as well.

This interchange between the two of us proved transformational. Z now began to develop a deeper appreciation that his wish to terrorize resulted from his own fear and from his own experience of having been terrorized. I also became more secure in my work with this dangerous young man once I realized that he found me more frightening than I found him. As soon as I made my intervention, Z curled up into a big ball once again and grabbed a box of tissues, and he then began to eat one of the tissues in a moment of acute anxiety. Z then placed two of the stark-white tissues over his black face, which I understood as his wish to identify with me and with my whiteness, and as an expression, perhaps, of his deep desire for me to rescue him from inside the awfulness of his aggressive interior.

Tragically, Z's new social worker resigned from her post at the end of the second trimester. She complained to the social worker at the Young Abusers Project that she found her work with Z too challenging, and that she had received a job offer to work with younger children. Although the staff at the Young Abusers Project had made every effort in our initial negotiations with Z's social services department to ensure continuity of escorting, this could not be promised, and so Z's external world now matched his internal world, with extreme unreliability prevailing. Z began to ask me anxiously, at the end of every single meeting, "When's the next session?" I told him that our next session would be at the same time, next Tuesday, as always, but that in view of the changes of social workers, perhaps he had begun to find it difficult to believe that his psychotherapist would actually show up for work. Devastatingly, Z did not attend for his last session before the next holiday break. I received a message late in the day from the manager of the local social services department, informing me that although she had tried valiantly find a temporary escort, nothing could be arranged. Our social worker fired off a stern letter of protest to the social services department, reminding them that they had a contractual obligation to provide a reliable escort for this disturbed patient. I myself sent a "holding" letter to Z expressing my regret that an escort could not be found to bring him to his last session before the break, and that I would, as agreed, plan to see him at the appointed time, three weeks hence, after the Easter break.

The third trimester of treatment

Z returned from his break looking very depressed and very forlorn. He told me that he wanted to jump off a cliff, then stab himself with a knife, and then hang himself with a rope, and then swallow a whole bottle of poison. Never before, or since, have I heard a patient report such dramatic suicidal ideation. I linked this depressive outburst with the fact that he did not see me before the Easter break, and that although he had received a letter from me, he must have felt very abandoned by all the adults looking after him. Amazingly, Z then picked up a heavy clinical textbook from my bookshelf and proffered the book to me, whispering, "With this book, I thee wed." I suggested that perhaps Z had a wish to be married to me so that we would always be together, and therefore we would never have to experience any more of these painful separations. Z's expression of homosexual transference proved too much, and he instantly retorted, "You're crazy. I don't wanna marry you!" But I felt that in spite of his conscious denial, he knew that I experienced a deep appreciation of his sense of loss and betrayal.

In the following session, Z entered and asked me somewhat sheepishly whether these sessions would be "confisential"—his own attempt to pronounce the word "confidential". I reminded him of our particular confidentiality policy at the Young Abusers Project, whereupon he told me that he had something very important to tell me. As a 7-year-old boy, he once had the opportunity to watch his mother and father fighting. His mother got so mad that she ran into the kitchen, pulled a large carving-knife from the kitchen drawer, and wielded it menacingly over his father's head. Although she did not strike the father with the knife, the father became highly distressed, and he suffered a fatal heart attack right there on the spot. Z had never communicated this story to anybody before. The many social workers and probation officers knew only that Z's father had died from a heart attack, but nobody had heard about the background to the heart attack. Z must have believed that his mother had actually murdered his father, as indeed she did, in a way. This important piece of biographical information helped me to gain a much better understanding of Z's penchant for being threatening to others.

I now developed a greater comprehension of his fantasy of using a knife to carve up an anonymous White man, and to cut his body into a million pieces. I also began to formulate thoughts about the way in which Z used his own penis as a cutting knife that penetrated the bodies of little girls, who may have come to represent his own teenage mother in fantasy, whom Z wished to kill, in part, for depriving him of his father. The story of the death of Z's father also shed more illumination on Z's wish to pursue a fighting career and to have a gang of security officers protecting him from violence.

Z's capacity to speak about a real-life incident between his mother and his father represented a huge developmental advance. He no longer felt the urgency to fill the session with fantasmatic talk of Mike Tyson and Michael Jackson; at last he had begun the long and painful process of speaking about real people from his actual biological family. Thereafter, he even began to talk about his index offences, though scantily, whereas during the first two terms he had refused to admit that he had ever raped little girls at all.

As the long summer break loomed, Z began to look more and more depressed, but less and less vicious. The quality and quantity of his language changed markedly, so that he spoke in larger amounts about actual people and events and did not indulge in quite so much fantasy in the sessions. He became angrier as well, and on one occasion he ripped the dust-jacket off a book on my shelf. I told him that he must not do this, and that, until I felt that he could better manage, he no longer had my permission to touch my books. This imposition of a helpful boundary seemed to contain him further, and he presented in a much more relieved way, knowing that at least one adult in his life would not permit him to become violent in action, only in words.

In the penultimate session before the end of the first year of treatment, Z stuck a saliva-soaked piece of chewing gum on the wall of my consulting-room. Although I felt quite angry initially, and also rather tempted to tell him to remove his chewing gum at once, I ultimately regained my own internal composure and I interpreted Z's chewing-gum gesture as a deep-seated wish to be stuck to my wall over the break, so that he would not have to endure yet another long separation.

Conclusion

This discussion of Z, a young adolescent sex offender, represents only a fragment of a complex, ongoing psychotherapy treatment. Such an essay provides no more than a glimpse into a very emotionally charged clinical interaction. Although we cannot at this stage of the work make any definite conclusions about the ultimate capacity for psychotherapy to transform the mind of a juvenile paedophile, my colleagues and I have received much encouragement from the fact that since we launched our psychotherapy programme at the Young Abusers Project, not one single boy has re-offended during the course of analytic treatment. Thus, though we can offer no assurances as to the ultimate efficacy of psychoanalytic psychotherapy for young sex offenders, we do have enough evidence to suggest that psychotherapy may actually perform a very powerful preventative function.

The treatment of forensic patients remains a relatively uncharted territory, as many psychotherapists still harbour fears—sometimes justifiably—about working with aggressive patients (cf. Welldon, 1993, 1994). But in view of the relative inefficacy and the arguably sadistic nature of castration and other somatic treatments for paedophiles (Freeman, 1979), we must begin to find a more humane way of understanding the origin and the maintenance of behaviours and fantasies. By working with young children and adolescents, we have a rich opportunity to observe the development of paedophilia *in vivo*, before the personality structure has become rigidified. In this way, we perform a potentially valuable service to the community by intervening with young paedophiles before they have become invariant paedophiles, whose crimes can shatter the lives of untold numbers of children and their families.

CHAPTER FOUR

The usefulness of self psychology in understanding and treating a case of homosexual paedophilia

Daniel P. Juda

This chapter briefly reviews the two predominant psychoanalytic theories regarding the aetiology of homosexual paedophilia (child molestation): the Freudian-based approach and the Kohutian-based approach. Both theories recognize the importance of early (pre-oedipal) developmental issues as being implicated in this disorder, yet each suggests important differences in what these early developmental issues are and their importance for the interpretation and analysis of clinical case material. A case history of a homosexual paedophile is presented to illustrate the usefulness of the self-psychology approach in understanding certain cases of this hated and feared disorder. Special emphasis is placed on the notion of the selfobject, specifically, the use—by the offender—of his child victims as mirroring and idealizing objects in order to make up for inadequate and destructive archaic self-objects.

Although much as been written about sexual deviance, beginning with Freud and continuing to the present time, rarely is paedophilia mentioned and even more infrequent are psychoanalytic accounts of homosexual paedophilia. Indeed, the first systematic account of paedophilia did not appear until 1964 when Mohr, Turner, and Jerry published a book based on their review of the literature and their research at the Forensic Clinic of the Toronto Psychiatric Hospital in affiliation with the Department of Psychiatry at the University of Toronto. This excellent book, however, emphasized the social significance of the deviant behaviour rather than the psychological dynamics of individual offenders. Other, more recent, accounts of this serious disorder favour alternative explanations, notably behavioural (Abel, 1976; Abel, Barlow, Blanchard, & Mavissakalian, 1975; Abel, Blanchard, & Barlow, 1981; Langevin, 1983). In order to elucidate the psychoanalytic perspective on paedophilia, I conducted a new review, in the process of which I learned that a bifurcation exists in the theory. On the one hand are the Freudian-based theoreticians, who emphasize biologically based psychological development as being implicated in the aetiology of the perversions (e.g. libidinal and aggressive drive derivatives; oedipal-castration issues; structural—id, ego, superego—conflicts). On the other hand are the self-psychology-oriented theoreticians, who emphasize subjective/experiential self and narcissistic development (e.g. the use of externalized selfobjects to maintain coherent and stable self- and object representations). This chapter reviews briefly these two psychoanalytic hypotheses about paedophilia, focusing whenever possible on the homosexual paedophile. The homosexual paedophile case presented will, hopefully, illustrate the usefulness of the Kohutian orientation in making sense of the clinical data.

The term *paedophilia* was introduced into the technical literature by Krafft-Ebing (1912), who wrote:

> There are cases in which the sexually needy subject is drawn to children not in consequence of degenerated morality or physical impotence, but rather by a *morbid disposition*, a psychosexual perversion, which may at present be named

paedophilia erotica. [Mohr, Turner, & Jerry, 1964, p. 12, emphasis added]

It is the meaning of the term "morbid disposition" which is important and which is interpreted so differently by the two theoretical perspectives mentioned. The term "morbid disposition" is, of course, merely descriptive and, thus, otherwise quite useless, as it lacks explanatory significance. In his review of the early literature on paedophilia, Cassity (1927) writes:

> The studies of this subject made by the older psychologists were limited principally to descriptive observations, the actual psychological mechanisms responsible for the neurosis being usually either neglected in toto or casually dismissed by vague conjectures. [p. 191]

He then cites as examples of these pseudo-psychological explanations Krafft-Ebing's "morbid disposition", Ellis's motivation through the frustration of normal sexual urge, Bleuler's (1924) opinion that the actual impotency in elderly roués is solely responsible for the perversion (a view still held by many in the laity), and Stekel's (1923) belief that the perversion stems from persistent infantile sadistic propensities.

For many years, these "theoretical" (e.g. pseudo-psychological) descriptions and the popular notions of the paedophile coincided. On the theoretical level, the paedophile was pictured as having an acquired mental illness such as senile dementia, chronic alcoholism, or mental debility due to epilepsy, injuries to the head, apoplexy, or syphilis (Howell, 1982). The psychoanalytic position in which the paedophile was considered to be behaving from weaning trauma, unresolved incestuous wishes, or infantile sexuality was all too often interpreted as supporting the popular image of the paedophile as a pervert or dirty old man. Until recently, neither the theoretical nor the popular stereotype of the paedophile received much serious attention. Yet, as Mohr, Turner, and Jerry (1964) have shown, neither image bears much relationship to reality: "It is well established from large scale sample studies, including our own, that paedophilic offenders rarely suffer from psychotic mental illness." In a more recent study comparing convicted rapists with child molesters, Henn, Herjantic, and

Vanderpearl (1976) conclude that the paedophile is the less distinguishable offender.

> Over three-fourths of the rape defendants fell into the categories of personality disorder or psychiatric illness. A different picture emerges for those charged with child molestation; personality disorders are not predominant, and only 6% of those defendants were found to be antisocial. The dominant diagnosis is sexual deviance (pedophilia) without other disorders. [quoted in Howell, 1982, p. 110]

Another myth about paedophiles that scientific investigation has erased is the popular belief that paedophilia and homosexuality, if not synonymous, are nonetheless inextricably intertwined. However,

> pedophilia should not be confused with homosexuality, even when it deals with a same-sex relationship. The National Center [National Center on Child Abuse and Neglect, 1978] cites evidence that most men who sexually abuse male children are heterosexual in their adult orientation. No offenders with a homosexual [adult] orientation were found in a study of 175 males convicted of sexual assault against children. This study suggested that the adult heterosexual male constitutes a greater risk to the underage child than does the adult homosexual male. [Groth & Birnbaum, quoted in Howell, 1982, p. 110]

Freudian-based theories

Mohr, Turner, and Jerry (1964) write that early psychoanalysts such as Hadley (1926) and Cassity (1927)

> see the causal factors [of pedophilia] in the weaning trauma, incestuous wishes, and resultant psychic impotence and psychic distortions [NB: in intrapsychically originated difficulties]. Their view follows Freud's formulation that the choice of an immature sexual object is a result of an unresolved Oedipus complex. The mature female implies mother, and hence a child is substituted. If the immature object chosen is of the same sex, the interpretation is based on [Freudian] narcissism; the pedophile sees himself in the object and identifies with his mother.

These themes were further developed by Roche (1950) and Socarides (1959). Castration anxiety, which in analytic theory can be expected to arise out of unresolved oedipal strivings, is emphasized by Fenichel (1945) and Happell (1925), as quoted by Cassity (1927). . . . Freud's (1920a) dictum that "perverted sexuality is nothing but infantile sexuality, magnified and separated into its component parts" was also followed by Allen (1949, 1962) who uses the term infanto-sexuality and assumes a fixation on an early level of psychosexual development. . . . Freud, aside from his psychodynamic theories, also saw the pedophile as one who is cowardly or has become impotent. [Mohr, Turner, & Jerry, 1964, pp. 12–13]

This latter quote from Freud illustrates how difficult it was for Freud (and, indeed, many others following him) to study the paedophile objectively. As we shall discuss more at length below, this aversion to accepting adult–child sexual interplay and intercourse and examining this liaison clinically and objectively may have led to serious distortions on the part of psychoanalytic theoreticians regarding the aetiology of paedophilia and the homosexual (same-sex) form of the disorder.

Gillespie (1956) quotes Freud's famous phrase: "Neuroses are, so to say, the negative of the perversions."

Thus perversion is represented as the persistence of the infantile. Looked at from the point of view of the *Three Essays* [Freud, 1905d] perversion is seen as a vicissitude of instinct, or to express it in later terminology, as an id phenomenon. In the *Three Essays* Freud seems to regard it as a more or less direct manifestation of component instincts, and therefore scarcely capable of further reduction. It is this aspect of Freud's early formulation which I think may be responsible for the relative sparseness of psycho-analytic writings on this subject, for it conveys the impression that little more can be said; and perhaps even more important, it suggests that the therapeutic outlook is a gloomy one and hence tends to discourage clinical work with the perversions. [Gillespie, 1956, p. 396]

In spite of this seemingly non-heuristic conceptualization of the perversions, Freud elsewhere provides valuable clues for alternative means of construing perversion. In "A Child Is Being Beaten" (1919e), Freud recognizes that sexual perversions might have to be regarded as *defensive formations* rather than more simply as components of infantile sexuality that had evaded defence. Thus, as Gillespie points out, much remained to be added to the notion that "neurosis is the negative of perversion".

> The necessary additions [should] include the part played by the superego, a concept just beginning to emerge in 1923; the central importance of castration anxiety; the role of aggressive impulses and the death instinct and the related anxieties, together with erotization as a defense against anxiety; the role of denial and splitting of the ego and of the object in the defensive process; and the relation of perversion to reality sense and to psychosis. [Gillespie, 1956, p. 398]

Thus, the aetiological conceptualization of paedophilia broadened during Freud's career to include his later metapsychological contributions (e.g. id, ego, superego; aggressive instinctual vicissitudes; defensive manoeuvres, etc.). This theoretical line of development is echoed a generation later by others who attempted to shed light on the sexual perversion of paedophilia. Hirning (1947), for instance, commented that all sexual offences against children have a common fundamental psychopathology that prevents the individual from seeking sexual contact with a mature individual of either sex. He explained that a mature woman represents a mother figure or incestuous object, while a child represents the patient as he would prefer to be himself—that is, a small child. Roche (1950) also supports this hypothesis. Socarides (1959) reports a case in which, he feels, "severe libidinal frustration and the consequent overpowering aggression . . . [play] a crucial role" in the development of perversion (quoted in Kurland, 1960, p. 395).

The early psychoanalytic account of the perversions (fetishism, masochism, sodomy/bestiality, paedophilia, and necrophilia) is summarized by Eidelberg (1954):

> They are caused by the presence of infantile wishes and unconscious defenses, the end result of this defense *is accepted by the total personality*. . . . Similar to neurotics, they are unable to separate love from hate. . . . Perversions are not caused by a simple breakthrough of the id, and a passive acceptance by the ego of the infantile wishes. In the structure of the perversion, it seems that the energy used as counter-cathexis is not altogether

substituted for that of the original wish, but is used to "dilute" it. [pp. 249–250; emphasis added]

This, more-or-less standard, Freudian account, in which it is assumed that the paedophile has developed a sufficiently stable and coherent "total personality" to "accept" the consequences of poorly integrated infantile wishes and so forth, is significantly different from a finding that Eidelberg (1956) himself reports two years later. It is unfortunate that Eidelberg did not appear to fully understand the import of this new contribution:

> The idea that one may play two roles at the same time, either by masturbating or by selecting a partner who represents the self, seems to be the result of an unconscious fear of not being able to survive after *being cut off from the parents.* [pp. 288–289; emphasis added]

Here we have one of the rare early offerings hinting at the relevance of two (i.e. the parental–child dyad) in this sexual deviation, a deficit in the self structure, and, perhaps even more significantly, the suggestion that sexual deviation may not be sexually motivated but defensively motivated—in this case, to ward off the fear of annihilation (i.e. of the self).

Arlow (1954) summarized a panel discussion on sexual perversion in which the points of view of Devereux, Muensterberger, Rado, Axelrod, Bak, Zilboorg, Glauber, Bychowski, Sperling (Otto and Melitta), Kolb, Johnson, Friedman, and Feldman apparently coincided:

> A brief sketch of the outstanding elements stressed at the Panel, in general, would contain the conclusion of an increasing integration of psychoanalytic theory and practice in the field of perversions. The aggressive drive, the significance of which in comparison to the libido was appreciated only within recent years in analysis, was in the forefront of the reformulation of the theory of perversions. The importance of identification of narcissistic object choices as defenses against destructive wishes directed toward the object appeared in almost every contribution. The deleterious effects of distorted object relations which damage the developing superego through the corrupting influence of seduction, suggestion, and permissiveness, show how considerations of problems of ego psychology were honored. [p. 69]

Happily, the panel mentions the potential relevance of object relations in the aetiology of sexual perversions, yet the overwhelming impact of Arlow's summary is still primarily Freudian-oriented in the manner discussed above.

Typical of the research to substantiate these early psychodynamic views of paedophilia is the 1957 study by Hammer of the psychoanalytic hypothesis of castration anxiety as the motivating force for sexual offenders. Sixty Sing Sing prisoners were given projective examinations (including Rorschach, TAT, Blacky, and Bender Gestalt). Blind global ratings by three psychologists of the degree of feelings of castration and phallic inadequacy on a five-point rating scale gave sexual offenders a higher incidence of such feelings than were true for twenty nonsexual offenders examined. These results were taken as evidence to support the hypothesis. (However, the sexual offenders were not all paedophiles.) Indeed, a variety of similarly suggestive (though not conclusive) data has been gathered by the use of projective techniques, and significant differences were found on various tests (Cutter, 1957; Glueck, 1955; Hammer, 1954; Toobert, Bartelme, & Jones, 1959). Toobert, Bartelme, and Jones (1959), for instance, compared paedophiles with general offenders. They found that the MMPI profile was elevated over the general offender on the Mf and Pa scales. An examination of the items differentiating the paedophiles from other offenders showed the paedophile to be sexually dissatisfied, with strong religious interests, feelings of *inadequacy in his interpersonal relations,* sensitive to the *evaluations of others,* and with a good deal of guilt.

However, summarizing this body of research, Mohr, Turner, and Jerry (1964) correctly conclude: "The work in personality assessment is not yet at a stage which would allow succinct generalizations regarding the personality traits of pedophilic offenders" (p. 93).

As for the clinical case material regarding paedophilia, the literature is particularly sparse. Only isolated cases of the psychoanalytic treatment of paedophilia have been reported, and these cases lack an adequate presentation of the clinical material (Cassity, 1927, 5 cases; Hadley, 1926, 1 case; Karpman, 1950, 1 case; Socarides, 1959, 1 case). Karpman' s case, of an adolescent heterosexual paedophile with a pubic-hair phobia, is a good example. Although much is made of this paedophile's phobia, very little early subjectively experienced interpersonal history is presented. This case argues that the paedophilic orientation evolved from a pubic-hair phobia rather than from self-structural deficits, but it does not give the reader sufficient data to make up his or her own mind on this point. Socarides reported the remission of symptoms in his case of a chronic homosexual paedophile while still under treatment; Conn (1949) reported excellent results in the use of brief psychotherapy with which he claims to have effectively treated seven of eight heterosexual paedophiles and three homosexual paedophiles. But in all of these reported cases, the early subjectively experienced object-relations history is too sparse to ascertain the pathogenic weight that should be given to a Freudian versus a Kohutian orientation. It would appear that seeing one's patients "from Freud's shoulders" leads to selective selection of the important data to be accounted for and, more specifically, to the omitting of data regarding self- and object structuralizations.

In summary, Lester (1975), writing more than a decade following Mohr, Turner, and Jerry's classic work, states that "psychoanalysts have not devoted much thought to the pedophile" (p. 154), and Howell (1982), seven years later, again notes how remarkably little is written about paedophilia.

This conspicuous scarcity in the literature has led some (notably Peters, 1976, and more recently Masson, 1984) to suggest that psychoanalytic theory has been skewed as a result of the strong aversion to addressing the problem of paedophilia. Accounts of actual acts have been reported (too often these psychotherapists insist) as fantasy, thus resulting in the overestimation of fantasy explanations in psychoanalytic theory. Howell (1982) writes:

> The idea of adults abusing children sexually is something that many people do not want to think about, much less discuss and investigate. The conspiracy of silence surrounding pedophilia affects all levels of society from the doctor who examines the child (Danjani, 1975) to the parent and child himself. The very lack of professional research material relating to pedophilia is an indication of societal reluctance to confront the issue. [pp. 101–102]

As Mohr, Turner, and Jerry (1964) write: "Although the general public concerns seem to center around pedophilia, the least material available is on this deviation" (p. 7).

Evidence from more recent research of homosexual paedophiles is beginning to establish the significance of early (pre-oedipal) developmental difficulties as being critically implicated in the aetiology of this deviant behaviour. Fitch (1962) found homosexual paedophiles to be "immature". Kurland (1960) noted the following traits in paedophilia: *early infantile deprivation; fear of maternal separation;* inability to directly express aggression; some degree of grandiosity; one or more episodes of depersonalization; and being a loner. Gebhard, Gagnon, Pomeroy, and Christianson (1965) found that homosexual paedophiles *came from broken homes* and had *poor relationships with their parents*. They also had a good deal of *homosexual experience* around the time of puberty and had a bad *relationship with their fathers* and a *poor one with their mothers*. Bell and Hall (1971) analysed 2,368 dreams of a single child-molester patient whom they call Norman and concluded that

> all of his conflicts, confusions, concerns, preoccupations, projections, actions, and traits are expressions of *an infantile character*. Chronologically Norman is an adult; psychologically, *he is a child, an infant, possibly even a fetus*. When this is fully appreciated, then everything that can be learned from his dreams falls into place. It is the central fact of his being. The evidence of Norman's infantile personality will be considered under the following headings: (1) polymorphously perverse disposition; (2) *dependency*; (3) identification with children; (4) confusion of gender; (5) failure of control; (6) preoccupation with the body; (7) feminine identification; (8) *fetal identification*; (9) *externalized superego* [p. 19; emphasis added]

Smaller-scale studies of child molesters have also revealed their infantile character structure. Kielholz (1951) found infantile behaviour and delayed physical and emotional development in one case he studied. Stricker (1967) had 64 male paedophiles rate the Blacky pictures on twenty-one scales of the semantic differential. Their responses indicated an immature and feminine orientation. A study of 120 male paedophiles in San Quentin (Toobert, Bartelme, & Jones, 1959) ascertained that they had strong religious interests and were *inadequate in interpersonal relations*. Finally, Cutler and Ederer (1958) have argued that recidivism in sexual psychopaths may be due, in part, to their *inability* to cope with life outside an institution.

Thus, Gillespie (1967) observed that "the importance of the oral factor in various perversions has been increasingly stressed" (p. 27). Neo-Freudian theorists have had to take this finding into account, yet the integration of these findings into the classical Freudian orientation is insisted upon, even to the point of rendering the theory confusing, awkward, and sometimes even doctrinaire. Gillespie (1967), for instance, writes:

> No analyst experienced with perverts can doubt that the castration complex is in fact extraordinarily prominent in these patients . . . we are dealing not with an either–or, that is, either with defense against castration anxiety or defense against some earlier, pregenital danger situation, but rather with a specific modification of castration anxiety, determined in its form by earlier, pregenital, and especially oral developments. . . . By standing on Freud's shoulders it may be possible for us sometimes to see further than he could, but if we abandon that position and rely on our own stature alone, our horizon is apt to become very limited. [pp. 27–28]

But, by standing on Freud's shoulders, Gillespie sees the landscape through Freud's eyes, although he does "see" farther than did Freud (e.g. the need to include "some earlier, pregenital danger situation" into a comprehensive theory of perversion). Gillespie (1967) continues:

> In conclusion, I wish to suggest that what characterizes perversion and makes it different from neurosis or psychosis is a special technique of exploiting the mechanism of splitting the ego [a pregenital mechanism of defense], by which the pervert avoids psychosis, since a part of his *ego* continues to accept reality and to behave fairly normally in the nonsexual sphere. The split allows his mind to function on two levels at once—the pregenital, oral-sadistic level corresponding to psychosis, and the phallic level, where his conscious mental content bears so much resemblance to the repressed content of the neurotic. This may explain why it has proved so difficult (as Glover, 1933, pointed out) to place the perversions satisfactorily in a developmental series of psycho-pathological states. [pp. 39–40]

It is difficult to ascertain how Gillespie's idiosyncratic employment of the defensive mechanism of splitting (Freud, 1940e [1938]) has accounted for the "oral factor" in paedophilia, nor how a descriptive term such as "oral sadistic" accounts for the data uncovered above regarding the crucial role played by an "infantile, inadequate, dependent" personality in the aetiology of this dreaded form of sexual perversion. Rather, Gillespie appears to be attempting to include the new and crucial data in the theory. However, his formulations appear almost doctrinaire and terribly awkward. Furthermore, Mohr, Turner, and Jerry's research suggests that psychosis is not a factor in paedophilia—latently or manifestly.

Leonard (1930) clearly admits his bewilderment regarding the enormous diversity of clinical symptoms represented in the sexual perversions when he writes that "no specific concept of classification, etiology or psychodynamics has been established so far" (quoted in Ruitenbeek, 1967, p. 42).

Hadley (1926) uses the word "clumsy" to describe early attempts to incorporate pre-oedipal factors into a Freudian theory of paedophilia. He writes that while

> pedophilia in the chronologically adult person might preferably by interpreted as a regressive mechanism, it seems clumsy to refer to regression when the libidinous tendencies have not proceeded to higher biological aims. [quoted in Cassity, 1927, p. 192]

Ruitenbeek (1967) also wrote about this theoretical effort:

> Robert C. Bak attempted to bring the general theory of perversions into the framework of the dual instinct theory, emphasizing especially the role of the aggressive drive. He pointed out that the element of fixation of the libidinal drive at the earlier stages of development alone would not suffice to account for the development of perversions, since such drives could undergo sublimation or repression. Our concepts of fixation, moreover, were developed historically almost solely in relation to the libidinal drives. Complex though the factors may be in that situation, the complexity is manifoldly compounded when one considers simultaneously the associated vicissitudes of the aggressive drive. In the early undifferentiated phase, primary narcissism must be conceived as referring to a cathexis of the self with both libido and aggression. Fixation at this phase is considered as a regressive defense against uncoordinated, uncontrolled aggression stimulated by the deprivations of the

earliest oral phases. Partial regression to this phase, often called secondary narcissism, leads to the narcissistic object choice. This type of object choice is based on an identification with the object of the opposite sex as a defense against aggressive impulses directed toward the object. The failure of the ego either to sublimate or to repress representatives of these drives, Bak feels, lies in the inability of the ego to neutralize aggression, a direct consequence of pregenital fixations. The ego, according to clinical experience, may master some of the aims of aggression better than others. In general, it appears that the earlier the stimulation of aggression, the less is the ego's capacity for neutralization. This early incapacitation influences the development of the ego and weakens its ability to cope with subsequent manifestations of aggression. A consequence of this distorted development is a disturbance in the relatedness of objects and a tendency toward uncontrolled, indiscriminant, preverbal aggressive discharges. [pp. 60–61]

Clearly, the drive-theory/structural-model construct is struggling. As has been the case before, historically, when psychopathology was discovered to be deeply rooted in pre-oedipal complications (e.g. schizophrenia), the theory simply proved too cumbersome, too instinctually oriented, and generally inadequate. At this point the question must be asked whether paedophilia is always the result of infantile libidinal-wish frustrations that manifest themselves in drive-component perversions in an attempt to ward off castration anxiety, or if instead this behaviour is "prophylactic," purposive, and in the service of the self and its needs. To shed light on the problem, the contemporary theory of self psychology may prove useful.

Self-psychology contributions

If the homosexual paedophile is not homosexual, if he does not suffer from the traditional psychiatric disorders (DSM-IVR), and if the traditional psychoanalytic hypotheses regarding sexual deviance are not always adequate, are skewed due to a bias in favour of fantasy causation instead of a reality-based subjectively experienced pathogenesis, then what can we say—psychodynamically—

about this under-investigated deviant? We have seen that very few psychoanalytic writings have appeared about the homosexual pae-dophile. When we examine the literature on perversions in general, we find that most analyses of perversion revolved about the oedi-pal conflict, the structural model (id, ego, superego), and the drive theory with its vicissitudes. These early formulations, however, though no doubt useful in analysing some aspects and perhaps even instances of perversion, have not spawned a sufficient general theory of paedophilia. Data regarding early subjectively experi-enced object relations and their impact on the development of self- and object representations simply are not adequately accounted for in too many (perhaps even most) cases of paedophilia. The neo-Freudian approach appears to be severely limited and has proven sterile in generating an adequate psychoanalytic account of child molestation. It appears, therefore, that new psychoanalytic notions must be introduced.

Recent advances in psychoanalytic theory (e.g. Erikson, 1963; Kohut, 1971, 1977, 1978; Stolorow & Lachmann, 1980), forensic psychology (e.g. Hogan & Jones, 1983; Kaplan, 1980), and attach-ment theory (e.g. Ainsworth, 1972, 1979; Bowlby, 1958, 1969, 1973, 1977, 1980) provide converging evidence to support the theory that how early object relations are subjectively experienced signifi-cantly relates to intrapsychic structuralizations. In particular, a comprehensive theory of the aetiology of homosexual paedo-philia—in this case—must recognize that the formation of self- and object representations is *an interpersonally based subjectively experi-enced intrapsychic developmental process* and not simply a genetically propelled process that unfolds in a predetermined manner when given a "good-enough" environment in which to unfold. Once this point has been digested, it is natural to reconstrue the meaning of the child molester's behaviour as a desperate attempt to utilize the victim to replace inadequate archaic selfobjects in order to help him (or her) to maintain a sufficiently cohesive, stable, and posi-tively coloured self-representation and thus avert a deterioration and possible disintegration of his (or her) self (e.g. psychological fragmentation and/or annihilation). This hypothesis further sug-gests the possibility that the sexual aspect—so prominent in the paedophile's *behaviour*—is not a central motivating force, but rather only a *means* by which to keep himself, intrapsychically, from falling apart. This would account for the insignificantly small number of homosexual paedophiles who are, in fact, homosexual in their adult sexual orientation.

The early Freudian-oriented analysts sometimes hinted at the critical role played by the early *object experiences*. Hadley (1926), for instance, wrote: "From the viewpoint of this sucking impulse, one may see . . . almost a compulsion to repeat an experience of such cherished import" and that "this desire to repeat an experience, to repossess an object or an object substitute as near like the one which so erotically charmed him in childhood is of particular significance to the understanding of the pedophilia" (quoted in Cassity, 1927, p. 192). (For an elaboration on the persistence and central role of the repetition compulsion in human development, see Juda, 1983.) Socarides (1959) brilliantly noted in his case study that the paedophiliac's acting out served to avoid the onset of a psychosis that otherwise would have developed, and, therefore, the paedophilia functioned as "a *prophylactic device*" (quoted in Kurland, 1960, p. 395, emphasis added). Kurland (1960), himself, takes us one step closer to the contemporary view of paedophilia when he reports that the findings from the more recent psychological testings indicate that the paedophile is "Of an orally fixated, extremely dependent individual who has *never developed any clear sense of self*" (p. 396, emphasis added).

These early findings and converging data on the critical role played by early object relations on the development of human personality have been incorporated into an alternative psychoanalytic theory not only regarding the formation of intrapsychic structures in general, but of the perversions as well. Kohut (1977) writes:

> I trust I have succeeded in demonstrating . . . the relevance and explanatory power of the hypothesis that the primary psychological configurations in the child's experiential world are not drives, that drive experiences occur as disintegration products when the self is unsupported. . . . When the child's self-assertive presence is not responded to by the mirroring self-object, his healthy exhibitionism—experientially a broad psychological configuration even when single body parts, or single men-

tal functions, are conspicuously involved as representatives of the total self—will be given up, and isolated sexualized exhibitionistic preoccupations concerning single symbols of greatness (the urinary stream, feces, phallus) will take over. . . . That the perversion, i.e., *the sexualized replica of the original healthy configuration* [emphasis added], still contains fragments of the grandiose self (exhibitionism of parts of one's own body) and of the idealized object (voyeuristic interest in parts of the body of others) is to be understood as a vestige of one aspect of the original self-object constellation: it was, transitionally, subject oriented (*self*-object) in the one instance and transitionally object oriented (self-*object*) in the other. The deepest analysis of either one of these two clinical manifestations does not, however, lead to a bedrock of drives, but to narcissistic injury and depression. [pp. 171–173]

This quotation is typical of Kohut's orientation, which places the drives in the service of the self, versus the Freudian orientation, which places the self in the service of drives. The implications of this reorientation for the treatment of paedophilia is critical in order to avoid a recapitulation of the devastating narcissistic injuries (relating to destabilizing and disintegrating self- and object representations in the face of historically consistent empathic failures) that created the conditions for the paedophilia to develop in the first instance.

Kohut (1978), in a later formulation, describes the victim of perversion as being utilized as an idealized selfobject—that is, as a necessary condition for intrapsychic cohesion and stability in the developmentally arrested offender.

The symptoms of narcissistic personality disorders are the result of the defective condition of the narcissistic structures: they are manifestations of a disease of the self. The disease affects either the grandiose self or the archaic omnipotent selfobject (the idealized parent imago). Specifically, these components of the self are either fragmented or enfeebled. The development of other parts of the personality, for instance, intelligence or drives, may have progressed comparatively undisturbed. But the narcissistic structures remained fixated in their development. In their archaic form they were either repressed or split off from the other parts of the psyche. In the latter case they can strongly dominate the patient's behavior from time to time, for example, in the form of addictionlike praise-seeking or *addictionlike search for idealized selfobjects*. Both these strivings can also be sexualized: we then have the different forms of sexual perversion.

Conflicts over drive aims (classical structural conflicts) are secondary in narcissistic personality disorders. In some cases the patient is involved in innumerable object relations, which can create the impression that drive related conflicts *caused* his psychic illness—conflicts, in other words, which concern the patient's intense love or intense hate. However, these love or hate relationships are either defensive—attempts to ward off, through an exaggerated experience of love or hate relations, the loss of the archaic selfobject, which would lead to fragmentation of the self—or they are not expressions of object-love or object-hate at all, but of the need for selfobjects in lieu of self-structure. [pp. 556–557; emphasis added]

Kohut's theory of the aetiology of perversion, therefore, states that the perversion is purposeful, that it is an attempt to replace inadequate and destructive (i.e. insufficiently empathic) archaic selfobjects with desperately needed idealizable selfobject substitutes (e.g. victims) in order to serve a developmentally vital narcissistic function: "the maintenance of the stability and cohesion of the self" (1978, p. 554). In the case presented below, the "fragmented components of the self" quality of the paedophile will prove most striking in both his self-portrait and in a recurrent nightmare he reported while in prison—that is, while he was removed from his desperately needed selfobjects/victims.

Although the literature specifically related to paedophilia is relatively sparse, and still rarer for the homosexual paedophile, the psychoanalytic movement has nevertheless entered into a fundamental paradigm clash with Kohut's contributions to a general theory of psychopathology and to a specific theory of perversion. Both the Freudian and the Kohutian approaches suggest that the earliest stages of development are heavily implicated. However, the neoclassical approach embeds the aetiological roots in a drive/structure theory, while Kohut claims that perversions are manifestations of an inadequately formed self. With the recent contribution of Stolorow and Lachmann (1980), we have both an elaboration of

Kohut's view and an attempt to incorporate the neoclassical point of view into a more general theory of perversion.

> When perverse sexual fantasies and acts occur in developmentally arrested individuals, in whom self and object representations are insufficiently structuralized, this function of early psychosexual experience may be revived in order to shore up a precarious and imperiled representational world. In such cases, it is not, contrary to what Freud (1905d) maintained, the erotic experience per se that has been fixated and then regressively reanimated; instead, it is the early infantile function of the erotic experience that is retained and regressively relied upon—its function in maintaining the structural cohesion and stability of crumbling, fragmenting, disintegrating self and object representations.
>
> This is not to say that structure maintenance is the only aim of perverse sexual fantasy and activity. Like any complex psychological product, sexual perversions are multiply determined and serve multiple functions (Waelder, 1936; Brenman, 1952; Lachmann, 1975), the motivational importance of which will vary from one patient to another. For neurotically organized patients, perversion may function principally as a regressive defense against oedipal conflicts and reassurance against the threat of castration (Freud, 1927e; Fenichel (1945) or as a hostile, vindictive triumph over traumatogenic early object images (Stoller, 1975). However, for structurally deficient, developmentally arrested patients, the motivationally most urgent function of perverse activity is likely to pertain to an impelling need to restore or maintain the intactness of self and object representations which are threatened with dissolution. [Stolorow & Lachmann, 1980, pp. 149–150]

Here, at last, we have a more comprehensive theory to account for the wide variety of types of perversion cited in the literature (neurotic to psychotic to structurally deficient). It then behoves the analyst to ascertain the level of development of the patient in order to correctly understand the motivation or aim of the perversion, and to provide the patient with empathically based interpretations and interventions. But, most importantly, the self-psychological orientation helps us to construe perversion as functional in many cases, and not as a "fixed erotic experience regressively reanimated". It is interesting to note that Stolorow and Lachmann do not claim that perversion is the result either of developmental arrests or of the classical neurotic conflicts; rather, the body of their work appears to imply that either process (perhaps even both processes) may be implicated depending upon the particular case under investigation. Yet, to date, one would be hard pressed—in the specific instance of homosexual paedophilia—to find a single reported case in which the clearly overriding aetiological roots were imbedded in drive theory and not in selfobject-related self-deficits.

The following case history of Howard (a fictitious name) will, hopefully, illustrate the usefulness of the more recent self-psychology orientation in teasing out neurotic-appearing and seemingly clear "castration"-anxiety issues from underlying self-structural deficits in the aetiology of this homosexual paedophile's criminal lifestyle.

The case of "Howard"

The case of Howard, a 34-year-old male homosexual paedophile, will hopefully provide clear clinical evidence to support the Kohutian approach to understanding the aetiology and psychological function of this hated perversion. Specifically, I would like to provide here clinical data to illustrate the following:

1. the lack of intactness of Howard's self-representation;
2. Howard's utilization of the male child-victim (the other) as a selfobject in lieu of self-structure (i.e., in order to "restore or maintain the intactness of self and object representations which are threatened with dissolution");
3. that Howard's perversion ("the sexualized replica of the original healthy configuration") contains fragments of the grandiose self ("exhibition of parts of one's own body") and of the idealized object ("voyeuristic interest in parts of the body of others"); that these sexualized fragments are not clinical manifestations embedded in drives but, rather, in narcissistic injury (e.g. in consistent empathic failures and their consequences in his inadequately formed representational world);
4. the relatively undisturbed development of another part of Howard's personality (e.g. his intelligence).

Howard was referred to treatment by the courts as a condition of his parole following the completion of the first year of imprisonment of a five-year sentence for having committed paedophilic acts on several 10- to 14-year-old boys. When I first encountered Howard he appeared ugly—both in appearance and in his mannerisms. He was unkempt, seemed to have huge, almost swollen lips, which, together with his oversize nose, made him look like a caricature. He wore loose-fitting, cheap, poorly kept clothing, and when he opened his mouth, a rotten, blackish set of teeth was exposed. I will never forget the first moment our eyes met: Howard looked prepared to be responded to as a heinous specimen (this reminded me of how the Elephant Man must have felt when he encountered a new person); yet, when I smiled warmly and gently shook the hand of this six-foot child-man, he was so moved that he let out a tremendous sigh of relief, smiled broadly from ear to ear (like an infant discovering smiling with its mother), entered the office, sat down, and wept with joy for a full five minutes. A mirroring transference seemed to have formed instantaneously. Indeed, for the first two years of treatment, Howard never once moved anywhere but further and further into a mirroring transference. It was as if his "addictionlike search for [an] idealized self object" had come to an end and the business of undergoing his development could now—finally—begin.

Just how poorly formed Howard's self-representation was remained obscure for several months, as he was able to utilize his well-developed intellectual capabilities to maintain an adult-like verbal relationship. This was further enhanced by Howard's unique self-created treatment procedure: He began to write poems or long letters—sometimes ten pages—which he would bring to each session and give to me. This continued for the first two years.

He never asked me if I read these letters, and he rarely discussed their content directly with me. Instead, he assumed that I knew and understood every detail contained in his epistles. Furthermore, he considered these letters as the treatment itself. For instance, he would say: "You can see how much I understand about myself now from my last letter" or "You are the first person who ever really knew how I was because you understand everything about my poem" (which I did not, often, understand and which, even less often, did we ever discuss together). In this manner, and in many similar circumstances, I soon realized that my function was to allow him to experience himself as competent, grandiose, superior, deeply aware, and so forth; in other words, my mirroring function was desperately needed by Howard to shore up a self-representation that was forever dissolving or threatening to do so. Thus, I became a selfobject for Howard.

One day, in the middle of a session about six months into the treatment, Howard asked me for a piece of paper and, with a proud look on his face, drew a self-portrait. The result, depicted in Figure 1, astonished me. Not only was I unprepared to experience the severity of the deficits in Howard's self-representational world (which, in spite of the obvious utilization of me as a selfobject, had remained obscured by his intellectual capabilities), but I was even less prepared for this intellectually adult-like man to be so proud of his creation. His entire self-image was contained in his nose and one eye. This is the self-portrait of a schizophrenic, yet there were

Figure 1

no other indications that this man suffered from a thought disorder. I had to conclude that I had been given an exact pictorial representation of Howard's self-representational world and that Howard's pride and exhibitionistic pleasure in this creation arose from his subjective experience of being able to "see" himself at all—and for me to be able to see him as well. To Howard, this presentation was not experienced as fragmented, but as having substantial parts. This became even more clear as Howard grew extremely impatient when I asked him about the lines around the neck, above the head, and below the head. He answered (obviously injured by my empathic failure to recognize the "important" areas of the portrait): "angel's wings," a "halo", and "I don't know, could be demons and things down here." He then quickly began to talk about the nose and eye and how these parts of the self-portrait clearly illustrated how he was able to experience his universe in a more comprehensive way now that he had been in treatment with a "good person" for a while.

It is exciting to see from a drawing (Figure 2) by Howard fourteen months after his initial self-portrait (which more or less marked the half-way point of Howard's four-year treatment), how his self-representational world had developed—pictorially. In this self-portrait, Howard shows an increasing stabilization of his self-representational world with this bust-like production, which no longer is embedded in religious symbolic selfobject fragments. (Religion was and remains a core aspect of Howard's self- and object representational world. Throughout his childhood and adulthood, Howard's major constructive selfobject experiences came from his relationship to his priests. Later, towards the middle of his treatment, Howard became an instructor of religion to children in his church, under the supervision of his apprentice priest who was aware of his paedophiliac history). This new self-portrait contains a more complete head, with hair, chin, mouth, nose, eyes, neck, shoulders, and necktie. Interestingly, Howard did not spontaneously offer to make this drawing, but was asked to do so—if he wished—by me. Also, Howard did not show as much excitement or interest in this work as in the earlier one; indeed, he was quite critical of it and not altogether pleased with it. [Note: Figure 1 has no mouth, which certainly seems relevant to the Freudian view that perversions stem from oral fixations: if orality is the core of this

Figure 2

disorder, why is the mouth missing? why are only the nose and one eye present?]

Howard's recurrent nightmare

When Howard was imprisoned—and thereby removed from his selfobject-victims—one would expect the serious loss of "self-structures" to induce a fragmentation of the grandiose self and the idealized object; furthermore, one would anticipate that this disso-lution occurring within Howard's representational world would manifest itself in some sexualized manner, not because some

> erotic experience per se has been fixated and then regressively reanimated; [but because] instead, it is the early infantile func-tion of the erotic experience that is retained and regressively relied upon—its function in maintaining the structural cohe-sion and stability of crumbling, fragmenting, disintegrating self and object representations. [Stolorow & Lachmann, 1980, p. 149]

Howard reported that when he was placed behind bars he soon began to dream a particular nightmare again and again:

> I dreamed that *a flying cock would try to get into my mouth*. What terrified me was that I wanted to suck it, and this made me afraid that I was homosexual. I would wake up shaking and sweating and hoping I would never have that dream again. But it would come back many times in that year I was in jail.

What strikes me about this nightmare is that Howard is not frightened by the image of a disembodied penis (which one might have expected if he were suffering, from castration anxiety). Indeed, he longed for this part-object, as an infant does the nipple. What created the terror was the injury incurred to his fragile self-image (his conscious heterosexual orientation symbolizing his being masculine and, therefore, acceptable and desirable) as he experienced himself as homosexual (i.e., as a social pariah and, therefore, deflated and fragmented). [*Note*: Howard is terrified of identifying himself as homosexual, yet his paedophilic victims were male children. This apparent contradiction is startling from our point of view; however, from a paedophile's point of view, this seeming contradiction seemingly evaporates. Difficult as this is to accept, it does seem to correlate with research findings (see above) that suggest that paedophiles who choose male children as their victims are, nonetheless, *not* homosexual in their adult object choices. Within this paradoxical phenomenon lies an important secret of the same-sex paedophile, a secret perhaps best revealed with a self-psychological key: the victim is not so much a sexual object as a selfobject.]

This extraordinarily clear symbolic representation of the fragmented sexualized regressions Howard needed to employ in order to maintain his representational world (e.g. sucking a disembodied penis) was also revealed in his exposés of his actual sexual encounters with young boys. In the many accounts he gave of these occurrences, Howard never spoke about his victims as whole persons who responded to him as a whole person. Rather, he focused either on what the boy did to him (e.g. fondling and fellatio and urinating into Howard's mouth) or on what he did to the boy (e.g. fondling and fellatio). When I asked how he felt the victim experienced this sexual intercourse, Howard was pleased and proud to explain how happy the victims were both at "ejaculating and pissing in my mouth and being loved—'cause most of them were not loved at home—and in sucking me and touching me, too."

Perhaps the saddest moments in treatment came when Howard would describe—with a warm glow reminiscent of an infant being gurgled to by his mother—how his little child-victims would always smile at him, accept him, and reflect his "love" feelings towards them back to him. I believe that the choice of a child-object is necessitated because of the "innocence" of children that enables them to respond as mirroring and idealizing objects, albeit unwittingly. That is, children are, often, incapable of rejecting an adult who masks his disorder in affectionate behaviours, especially if the children are, themselves, suffering from inadequacies in their familial object relations. Indeed, Howard's victims were always those children who lived on the psychological fringes, did not form peer relationships, did not come from adequate homes (psychologically), and craved paternal objects themselves.

When asked how he knew his victims felt loved by him, Howard grew extremely testy and reacted precisely as he did whenever I had reacted to him with an empathic failure. He simply could not entertain a thought that anyone—the victims, his priest, his mother, or myself—could feel differently from his needs. This hyper-egocentric position is reminiscent of the pre-operational stage of development (ages 2–7 years) in which children have simply not developed the perceptual and cognitive capacity to see things from a point of view different from their own. The feeling from Howard's accounts of his sexual exploits was never that he committed a crime but, instead, that he had committed an act of love. He had no more insight regarding the vital psychological function of these acts (i.e. to addictively reconstruct "the sexualized replica of the original healthy configuration"—that is, a mirroring archaic selfobject—in order to prevent his internal self-representations from fragmenting) than he was aware of the meaning of his nightmare. Indeed, he did not become aware of me as a separate, independently functioning individual until near the end of the treatment. For example, when a progress note needed to be written to his probation officer, Howard would write what *he* expected the note to say. When I then wrote what I felt was appropriate, even if it differed from his original instructions significantly, he would not acknowledge the difference but, instead, would act as if he had written my note himself.

Later, Howard began to notice these discrepancies. At first they left him deeply injured, as if I had betrayed him. Indeed, at one point he dropped out of treatment and did not return for four weeks. When he returned, he acted as if nothing had happened. This incident marked the beginning phases of Howard's loosening of the mirroring transference and his adoption of an idealized transference (written about originally by Kohut, 1971). At this point, Howard began to respond to the discrepancies between his written progress notes and mine by taking an extreme interest in my additions and devoting himself to working on the problems I had outlined. Eventually, Howard demanded that I write a progress letter to him; then *he* would decide whether to allow the probation officer to have a copy of it.

Howard's early sexual history

As is so often the case with the perverted, Howard's early life was one of consistent empathic failures arising from his abandonment by his father at age 1 year and his mother's own utilization of him as her desperately needed mirroring-object. The father, an Italian-American who lived near Howard's mother's apartment, was a fire-fighter. Howard was never told why his father abandoned him, and he did not see his father again until treatment terminated when Howard was 38 years old. (Howard, however, continued to visit with me about once or twice a year to discuss his professional aspirations, his despairs, and his longing for a woman's love and a family of his own—which his now emerging castration anxiety prevents him from realizing.) When Howard tracked his father down following the termination of treatment, he was still deprived of an explanation of his past history, as his father was unable to respond to Howard's questions.

Howard's mother, English-born, barely functioned at a secretarial job, constantly complained to Howard about her life and about him, and alternated between bitterly fighting with him (and making him feel guilty for any feeling he might express that was not in harmony with her own) and infantilizing him. For instance, she bathed Howard until he was 16 years old, she tucked him into bed until he was 36; she used to lie with him in bed and fondle him and rub her genitals and breasts against his body. (Howard insists that she never had sexual intercourse with him or made him perform direct genital acts with her.) When the patient was raped at age 10 by an older upstairs male neighbour (who was 16) and reported this to his mother, his mother never responded but, instead, acted as if she had not heard Howard's complaints. As the rapes continued, Howard found himself terribly confused. All his young life, his schoolmates had made fun of him for his obsequious and infantile social skills, his big lips, his almost grotesque appearance. Now, here was a boy who was attracted to him. Howard explained his profound confusion about his rapist as follows: "I hated that he forced me to suck him off and drink his piss and lick his ass hole. But it felt good when I did it." It appears that the rapist became the only other "mirroring" object in Howard's life; furthermore, it is clear that the boundarilessness at home reinforced the acceptability of behaving in a boundariless manner in order to satisfy one's psychological needs. It seems inevitable that one social/sexual skill that Howard had experienced (i.e. rape and sexual abuse) would become his modus operandi for achieving his own developmental selfobject needs with his helpless, "smiling" boy victims in his adult life. One of his poems, which exemplifies both his more developed intellectual (e.g. cognitive) sphere of functioning and its fragmented quality, follows:

> Please don't shadow me
> showly stead,
> nervous patriot,
> workaholic bridle of my eye.
> Make good music. But have it
> that it chances all alone.
> And don't swipe my forhand's trace
> for winking. please,
> when filling seed
> with your own good greed for a place
> to lie holy.

We have in this poem the exhibitionist "showy steed", the fragility of his coherent sense of self, "but have it / that it chances all alone"; the criminal consciousness intermingled with a sexual play on words with "forehand" (i.e., foreplay), in "swipe my forehand's trace / for winking"; the profound confusion of reality in the "good greed" oxymoron (the addictive need for a selfobject-victim); and, finally, the longing to successfully fuse a remote sense of right and wrong (i.e., the superego) into the rest of his personality "for a place / to lie holy."

Howard utilized his superior verbal and writing skills (of which he, was proud) to tolerate the feeling of humiliation he had to endure when the courts sent him to me. His having attended college enabled him to write such papers as, "Dislocating Sources of Inequality; Cultural Deprivation and Difference Theory; Unequal Resources Hypothesis; Within-School Explanations; The IQ Theory of School Performance: Conclusion", which sounds like an intellectualized psychological self-portrait. By doing his analysis himself (as he experienced it), he could be proud of himself. Thus, I received literally hundreds of pages from Howard, such as the dream analysis that follows, which represented but two pages of a six-and-a-half-page epistle presented to me in the second year of treatment. [*Note*: the treatment was relatively successful in that: (1) Howard was able to completely *give* up his criminal behaviour in order to maintain his representational world; (2) he was able to maintain a job; (3) he sought, received, and paid for $3,000 worth of dental work, which significantly improved his face; (4) he dressed well and appeared better groomed; (5) he carried himself well and began to socialize; (6) he began to seriously wonder about forming his own family and of having sexual relations with women (though he was not yet able to do so due to his emerging castration anxiety); (7) he returned to college to finish the requirements for his bachelor's degree; and (8) he successfully terminated his probationary period.]

The dream of 9 September

"I do not recall the details of this dream, but the sense of it is clear enough to denote general progress in comparison with earlier dreams. In the conclusion of my first reported dream, *I found my car parked just outside of a hedged yard. In the yard was a garage with inside-outside walls. Off to the side I recognized a house, but I did not examine it.* The house was a last moment impression of the dream. I believe we said that the car represented my wandering, and that the scene indicated my arrival at a site offering rest, comfort, and security with the hope of establishing a home situation."

(In fact, we had not said this; this was Howard's own interpretation, but he was fused still with me and did not differentiate between us.)

"In today's dream *I was chasing someone—actually, it was a high-speed search* [note: the addictive search of the selfobject]—*through a large mansion. The person I was pursuing (perhaps a young man) eluded me. It seemed to me that he leaped up and over a brink as he (appeared)—at this point I was no longer in pursuit: I was facing him, I saw his face, but I do not remember his image—to disappear, ending the chase. I then became aware of my surroundings. There were long hallways with many doors on either side. At some points the hallways would open into large rooms. One of these rooms I recognized as a living-room, which was richly furnished and decorated.*

"I woke into a state of semi-consciousness, and told myself to remember that the dream was connected to my earlier dream of the garage.

"My simple analysis of the dream is that it confirms the promise of the garage dream. I spent my life chasing a ghost [is this not a beautiful image expressing his elusive search for a "good-enough" selfobject?] and now that the chase has ended, I find myself perhaps in a most reassuring and encouraging circumstance. Long hallways signify that there is much time left in my life; expansive rooms indicate a wide spectrum of activity and interest. Behind each door are new and exciting possibilities, which give me relative freedom in choosing what potentialities will bring my life optimal meaning and satisfaction.

"As to the departure of my ghost, I at first thought that this figure had done himself in. I'm not sure. He may have just decided to leave. What is really important, however, is that I decided to let him go."

(Here, "him" refers to Carl: a symbol of the me-child who was starved for father-love. Carl is in fact the name of a victim-child of Howard's.)

"It of course occurred to me that the mansion setting had reference to a biblical passage: 'The kingdom of heaven is like a mansion with many rooms. I (Christ) am going there to prepare a place for you.'"

If an attempt were made on my part to analyse, discuss, ask for associations to (and so forth) Howard's written work, Howard responded in a startled manner—as if his work should be as clear to me as it was to him, perhaps even that his work was in fact my work—that we were one mind. He could not accept the possibility that more could be gained from exploring together his work, because that would mean his work was not self-evident—that is, that I am not him and did not understand something he wrote. Thus, it became clear that Howard had discovered a most extraordinary means of developing his self- and object representational world. In the protective context of the mirroring and later the idealized transference, Howard literally began to construct his sense of himself in his written words. These exhibitions of his self were: (1) first and foremost to be admired, as if he were undressing in front of me and showing off his beautiful genitals to be admired and desired (as he did each time in a ritualistic manner with his child victims); and (2) as with his drawings, his words were his, were from him, a part of him, were externalizations of his self, mirrored his self to himself. The writings were a sort of transitional selfobject, transitional from victims/analyst/mother/priest as substitutes for self-structures, to his own ability to be his own self. Thus, Howard would come to each session with an envelope (with only his name printed on the envelope) filled with these writings, throw them on the table as if establishing yet another aspect to his self, and then rarely even mention them again. If I had never read one word in these notes, he would never have known. To him, it was a given that his transfer of the papers to me was tantamount to my knowing—as he did—what they contained.

It was not acceptable to ask for associations, to "pursue", or to explore the feeling of the imageless ghost and its relationship to his child victims—it was crucial that Howard be allowed to experience the therapist as a mirroring (and later an idealizable) object to make up for his destructive archaic selfobjects.

Conclusion

Hopefully, this brief account of Howard has illustrated that, in this one case at least, homosexual (same-sex) paedophilia did not develop out of a drive-based, castration-related, id/ego/superego model, but, rather, from the need of Howard to attach himself to mirroring and idealizable objects in order to prevent his fragile and destructive archaic selfobject (parental imagos) from fragmenting his self- and object structures.

Howard's case—the recurrent fragment of a phallus and concomitant fellatio wish, the severely disturbed mother (including her incestuous acts) and the abandoning father, the rapes by his neighbour, the sexualization of his self-structural requirements, and the utilization of his intelligence to overcome his deficiencies— is reminiscent of Mr A., whom Kohut (1977) describes briefly as follows:

> Mr. A. [see Kohut, 1971, pp. 62–73], whose severely abnormal (latent schizophrenic?) mother provided grossly inadequate mirroring for him as a child and whose idealized father-image was shattered traumatically, recalled early in his analysis that as a child he drew people with large heads supported by bodies consisting of a pencil-line trunk and pencil-like limbs. [Note: compare this with Howard's self-portrait in Figure 1]. Throughout his life he had dreams in which he experienced himself as a brain at the top of a substanceless body. As the analysis progressed he became able to describe the causal (motivational) connection between the dreadful feelings of emptiness from which he suffered and certain intensely sexualized fantasies to which he turned when he felt depressed, in which he imagined himself subduing a powerful mate figure with his "brains," chaining him through the em-

ployment of some clever ruse in order to imbibe, via a pre-conscious fellatio fantasy, the giant's strength. [*Note*: this is reminiscent of Howard's fellatio fantasies and behaviours—both in his nightmare and in his criminal acting-out behaviour.] From early on he had felt unreal because he experienced his body-self as fragmented and powerless (in consequence of the absence of adequate joyful responses from the maternal selfobject) [*note*: as was true in Howard's case with his incestuous and selfobject cannibalizing mother] and because the barely established structure of his guiding ideals had been severely weakened (in consequence of the traumatic destruction of the paternal omnipotent selfobject) [*note*: this was also true in Howard's case with the traumatic abandonment of his father when Howard was a year old]. Only one fragment of his grandiose-exhibitionistic self had retained a modicum of firmness and power, his thinking processes, his "brains," his cleverness. [*Note*: Howard utilized his "brains", his most intact developed self-structure, to shore up his own depression and gross self-inadequacies as best he could.] It is against this background that we must understand the nonsexual significance of the perverse sexual fantasy that accompanied his masturbatory activities. The fantasy expressed the attempt to use the last remnant of his grandiose self (omnipotent thought; the ruse) in order to regain possession of the idealized omnipotent selfobject (to exert absolute control over it—to chain it) and then to internalize it via fellatio. [*Note*: this scenario manifested itself not only in Howard's recurrent masturbatory fantasies, but in his paedophilia as well.] Although the masturbatory act gave the patient fleetingly a feeling of strength and heightened self-esteem, it was, of course, unable to fill the structural defect from which he suffered, and thus had to be repeated again and again—the patient was indeed addicted to it. [*Note*: Howard too was addicted to these criminal/self-restorative acts as he repeated again and again these behaviours with victim after victim.] The successful filling in of the structural void could, however, ultimately be achieved in a nonsexual way via working through in the analysis. This resulted, not in the incorporation of magical power, but in the transmuting internalization of idealized goals which supplied narcissistic sustenance to the self [*note*: this successful transmutation of internalized mirroring and idealized goals also occurred in Howard's case in his four-year-long analysis which, also, resulted in sufficient narcissistic sustenance to the self for the progress—reported above—to have occurred]. [pp. 125–127]

When Kohut writes that the "idealized father-image was shattered traumatically", this is reminiscent of the traumatizing abandonment Howard experienced at age 1 year when his father deserted him. This early trauma was further severely replicated when Howard was raped repeatedly after age 10 years by a six-year-older male neighbour. The subsequent posttraumatic stress disorder (PTSD) that developed in Howard (e.g. his recurrent nightmares, his fragmentation, his generalized numbing and aborted development, etc.), reinforced and exacerbated his earlier object horrors (e.g. maternal incestuous behaviour) and severe narcissistic (e.g. cannibalizing of his self) demands placed on him by his mother, the father's abandonment, and so on. It might be useful to investigate, in other cases of homosexual paedophilia, whether similar traumatizing and re-traumatizing early experiences—outside the family as well as inside the family—are present and further push these paedophiles-in-the-making towards acting out sexually with their child victims. From a clinical point of view, the question needs to be asked: Should one treat the PTSD first, or the early self-structural deficits first? In Howard's case, he answered this question by essentially "forcing" me to act as a selfobject and, within that relatively safe and stable dyadic cauldron, propelling himself towards getting his primitive early developmental needs met. Insofar as focusing on these rapes and maternal incestuous acts was concerned, it was therapeutically helpful if it allowed Howard to empathize with himself. Examining this part of his life too deeply, examining the significance of traumatic sexual acts on others too thoroughly, threatened to shatter his own developing healthy self-concept, as it would force him to examine how his own traumatizing criminal acts had shattered others. This work came much later in the treatment when he was sufficiently narcissistically repaired to tolerate this "new" assault on his self.

I believe that homosexual paedophilia may be a behavioural manifestation of self-structural deficiencies that are the result of subjectively experienced inadequate mirroring and poorly idealizable early parental objects. It is not always adequate to simply analyse the bizarre and varied vicissitudes that result after these early failures of selfobject formations have done their damage—such as the various aggressive and libidinal fantasies/behaviours that formulate and create serious distortions about one's self- and body representations, as well as of one's object representations. To focus exclusively on these important intrapsychic processes is to recapitulate the early devastating empathic failures and exacerbate the narcissistic defects in these patients. Rather, it is necessary to become an adequate mirroring and later omnipotent object, to utilize whatever adequate capacities have survived or are strong enough to develop rapidly, and to allow these patients the opportunity to experience the transmuting internalizations that Kohut writes about so eloquently. This view is supported not only by the case of Howard, but by Kohut himself, who writes:

> Before leaving the topic of perversion, I will, in passing, add for the sake of completeness that there may well exist another type of sexual aberration in which the self is in essence intact. [Note: Kohut is not claiming to have ever encountered such cases—only that they could, theoretically, exist.] In these instances, the abnormal sexual aims would have established themselves because of a drive regression motivated by a flight from oedipal conflicts, especially under the pressure of castration anxiety. Cases of this type, however, in which a firm self participates actively in the search for specific pregenital pleasure—not, in other words, as self that attempts to gain cohesion and substance with the aid of perverse activities—*are rarely encountered in the analyst's clinical practice*; I would assume that such individuals will not feel the need for therapy as strongly as those whose central psychopathology is a fragmenting or enfeebled self [Kohut, 1977, pp. 127–128; emphasis added]

In other words, homosexual paedophilia is a disorder that frequently requires a serious deficit in the offender's self-formation which prevents him or her from being able to empathize with the victim/selfobject—just as an infant has not developed the capacity to experience reality from the mother's point of view. Paedophilia, if seen from the perspective of a "single-axis" theory (i.e. along a Freudian line), leads to an inadequate theory of the disorder, inadequate treatment techniques, and, what is worse, a recapitulation of the devastating early empathic failures by the analyst and by society. Freud, himself, was aware that he had focused his main creative effort towards unravelling the intricacies of genetically based intrapsychic vicissitudes, and that this single-minded focus prevented him from adequately accounting for the effects of subjectively experienced object relations on self-structuralizations, which prevented him from developing a context in psychoanalytic theory for the "self" (Balint, 1968). As Ornstein (1974) wrote:

> As we are now able to see with hindsight and from the perspective of Kohut's contributions, this was the major hindrance to truly *new* conceptualizations and to meaningful progress in the psychoanalytic treatment of patients with narcissistic personality disorders. Freud himself sensed (1914c) that what was missing in his single-axis theory related to the question of how the infant or child dealt in his psyche with the inevitable disturbances to his original narcissism. He wrote: "The disturbances to which a child's original narcissism is exposed, the reactions with which he seeks to protect himself from them and the paths into which he is forced in doing so—these are themes which I propose to leave on the one side, as an important field of work which still awaits exploration" (p. 92). It is precisely this exploration that Kohut has undertaken. He offers us a *new* theory of narcissism, which supplements Freud's single-axis theory, spells out the two separate developmental lines of narcissism, and makes a major contribution toward a psychoanalytic theory of the self. [pp. 128–129]

Even if, eventually, cases are presented that suggest that paedophilia arises from the establishment of abnormal sexual aims due to a "drive regression motivated by flight from oedipal conflicts, especially under the pressure of castration anxiety", the question of the self-deficits must still be addressed. Until and unless these questions can be answered, negatively, we can no longer assume that paedophilia is primarily or even usually an oedipally based, single-axis-oriented disorder.

CHAPTER FIVE

Some comments on ritualized paedophilia and the sexual abuse of children

Wilfred Abse

Incidents involving child molestation have, in my clinical experience, occurred most frequently when a male adult, heterosexually adjusted, though poorly, has engaged in brief sexual contact with a prepubertal girl when intoxicated, by either alcohol, marijuana, cocaine, or some other "recreational" drug. The regressive erotic expression, including de-repression with loosening of impulse control, is quite temporary, sometimes forgotten; sometimes remembered with remorse, sometimes indignantly denied (especially when apprehended). The classic paedophiliac in contradistinction from such fleeting disordered behaviour, compulsively engages repeatedly in sexual relations with a prepubertal child. In DSM-IV (APA, 1994), paedophilia is defined when the following criteria are met:

A. Over a period of at least 6 months, recurrent, intense sexually arousing fantasies, sexual urges, or behaviours involving sexual urges, or behaviours involving sexual activity, with a prepubescent child or children (generally age 13 years or younger).

B. The fantasies, sexual urges or behaviours cause clinically significant distress or impairment in social, occupational, or other important areas of functioning.

C. The person is at least age 16 years and at least 5 years older than the child or children in Criterion A. [p. 190]

Groth, Hobson, and Gary (1982), from work with 500 convicted offenders, concluded that two categories of paedophiles were recognizable among these felons—those fixated and those regressed. These were in about equal numbers in their large sample from court or prison. In the "fixated", there had been obligatory attraction to younger children since adolescence. Sexual contact with age mates had been seldom and then often forced on them. Usually they were unmarried, childlike in appearance and attitude, and more comfortable with children than with adults. They were primarily homosexual and attracted to boys. The regressed type among these felons had usually adjusted heterosexually until abandonment or loss of an adult partner, and the paedophilic behaviour was often alcohol-related.

In Robert Louis Stevenson's (1886) fictive case, the fiendish behaviour of Mr Hyde before his murder of Sir Danvers Carew took the form of trampling down a child, leaving her screaming on the ground (p. 5). In the alcohol-related regressed type of paedophilic behaviour of criminals, the fury of frustration may be embedded in the acting out, and the child is then at considerable physical risk. In more frequent clinical practice, libidinal fixation and regression in the superego–ego organization are differently weighted aetiological variables in different patients, as occurs in psychoneurosis. J. Laplanche and J.-B. Pontalis (1973) in their excellent encyclopaedic work note:

> V. In a famous formulation, Freud connects and contrasts neurosis and perversion: "Neuroses are the negative of perversions." . . . The dictum is too often given in an inverted form: perversion is described as the negative of neurosis; this amounts to treating perversion as the brute, non-repressed manifestation of infantile sexuality. In point of fact, researches of Freud and the psycho-analysts on the perversion reveal that they are highly differentiated conditions. Of course, Freud does often contrast them with the neuroses in so far as, in the case of perversions, the mechanism of repression is absent; but

at the same time he is at pains to show that *other* forms of defence come into operation here. His last works, especially those on fetishism (3b, 4), emphasize the complexity of these defences: disavowal of reality, splitting (*Spaltung*) of the ego, etc.; these are mechanisms, moreover, bearing significant resemblance to those found in psychosis. [p. 309]

Swanson (1968) noted correctly that men who become sexually involved with children are actually a heterogeneous group and it is necessary to take account of a variety of personalities and situations. It is clear, however, as Finkelhor (1979) amply illustrated, that adverse early traumatic experiences in the primary family play a crucial role in creating vulnerability to becoming a perpetrator or a victim of sexual abuse. Sexual preoccupation with children can result from an intensely pleasurable childhood experience in the context of a dysfunctional family and can be adverse to growth and development. The famous literary model for this is Humbert Humbert of Vladimir Nabokov's *Lolita*, who became fixated at an early developmental stage.

An example of this latter sort was a 20-year-old patient on probation following arrest for sexual abuse of a prepubescent 12-year-old girl; after psychiatric evaluation, he entered into psychoanalytic psychotherapy which continued for more than a year. From an affluent and influential family, he was the only child of recently divorced parents. In his late teens he became enamoured of his 11-year-old cousin, who lived nearby. A good scholar with an artistic bent, he had been the recipient of prizes at the school he had attended as a day student, and he had later had much acclamation for his good conduct and achievements. For the most part studious and socially quite inactive, he had masturbated with fantasies of his cousin, who soon became his playmate. She too had suffered from her parents' divorce and currently (at the time of her seduction) had a stepfather whom she apparently felt was quite unsatisfactory; so she and the patient developed a mutual sympathy. Indeed from the patient's story, developed during analytic sessions, he found it hard to pronounce who seduced whom, though at the beginning he blamed himself and felt he had disgraced his family, as well as bringing himself into disgrace. They had been discovered together nude by the girl's mother in her house. She had immediately called the police.

In analytic work, he expressed much anger with his parents, especially his mother, whom he regarded, probably correctly, as a cold, calculating woman. I gathered the impression, through his revelations, of a woman evincing narcissistic phallic character disorder with much injustice-collecting at home, who had frustrated and provoked his professionally successful father largely through her lack of affection towards him, though she had maintained a wonderful polished social façade that had indeed facilitated the father's career. The patient ruefully acknowledged how much he had enjoyed the affection and sexual stimulation afforded in his interaction with his cousin, including mutual masturbation and inter-crural intercourse. A reduction of castration anxiety and enhancement of self-esteem with more adequate identification with his father led to his dating a young woman only one year his junior, and he celebrated his 21st birthday with her.

Some of the details of phantasies elucidated during the three-times-a-week analytic sessions with this patient in London are redolent of some of the psychopathology embedded in Karpman's case published in 1950, and which it happened I was able to discuss with him about two years later in Washington, DC. In his case the paedophile was actually seduced when he was 7 years old by a very hairy woman. She ordered him to disrobe and placed him on top of her. He experienced an indescribable sense of horror on seeing her pubic hair and was frightened that he would be enmeshed in it and devoured, so much so that he was completely immobilized. As an adult he could not bear to see women's pubic hair and finally convinced his wife to shave hers so that he could enjoy intercourse. This patient of Karpman's did not especially want young girls, but he became involved with them sexually *faute de mieux* since they did not have what he feared most (Karpman, 1950, 1954).

In the case of my London patient, the phallic mother of phantasy prevailed, and there was no discovery of actual traumatic sexual events of the sort elaborated by Karpman. Cassity (1927) underscored the early loss of the breast (abrupt weaning), and this traumatic factor was of considerable importance in the pathogenesis of the paedophilic acting-out of this 19-year-old student. The acting-out had contained retaliative dominating and controlling phantasies provoked by early maternal oral deprivation and compounded by the continued domineering and cold, controlling behaviour of the unhappy mother of his youth.

Such a patient as this is a very far cry from the twice-convicted paedophile charged with raping and murdering 7-year-old Megan Kanka reported in the *Washington Post* (p. 1, 31 May 1997). This man's crimes sparked the national movement to notify communities when sex offenders move in and led to the passage of the so-called Megan's Law in many states and in the Congress. In the report in the *Washington Post*, it was stated:

> During jury selection, his lawyers indicated they would present evidence he was sexually abused as a child, but no details emerged. His prior convictions involved pulling down the pants of a 5-year-old girl and an attempted assault on a 7-year-old he had choked unconscious.
>
> In the confession he gave to police, he said he had been "slipping" in the weeks before Megan's murder and was "getting these feelings for little girls." Megan, in particular, excited him, he said. He said his heart raced and his palms became sweaty when he saw her.
>
> He showed no emotion throughout the trial, and he said nothing except on the last day of testimony when the judge asked if he was satisfied with his defense and if he had understood that he had a right to testify and a right to remain silent. He answered "yes" to each question.

In a later opinion the following month (*Washington Post*, 3 June 1997), Richard Cohen succinctly put the case against the death penalty for the perpetrator, Jesse Timmendequas, writing:

> Timmendequas's life, as portrayed by his lawyers, is one for which the adjective Dickensian is inadequate. His father, they said, was some sort of a beast. He forced the boy to have oral and anal sex with him, fondled him and compelled him to watch as he had sex with his other children.
>
> The mitigating circumstances do more than mitigate. They sicken and they shock, but there is more. The father tortured and killed the children's pets and told them the same would happen to them if they told anyone what he had done to them. One of the things Jesse Timmendequas said nothing about was his father's rape of an 8-year-old girl, a neighbor. He witnessed it.

As for Jesse Timmendequas's mother, she too is a collection of mitigating circumstances. She had 10 children by seven different men—and seven of the children were either given to the state or taken from her. She neglected her children, favoring her lovers and she was, it appears, a drunk.

Timmendequas might be mentally impaired on account of fetal alcohol syndrome. As it is, he is a dullard, a dud of a man who shows little intellect, no emotion—so forgettable that one of his high school teachers told the *Newark Star-Ledger* that none of his colleagues could remember having taught Timmendequas.

"That's odd because a name like Timmendequas is hard to forget," said Donald Lindberg, the teacher.

These circumstances do not merely mitigate against the death penalty—they chase it from the room. It's clear Timmendequas never had a chance. He is a monster, created and shaped by his parents—who might still be alive. (No one ever appeared for Timmendequas in the courtroom.) He was unnoticed, a nullity, thrust into society so twisted and sick as to be a menace to one and all. He is a sex pervert, a man addicted to little girls. He was jailed twice for such crimes and then he killed Megan Kanka.

What was he doing out of jail? He knew who he was and what he was like—what little girls did to him, how his palms broke out in sweat when he saw Megan across the street and he had to go into the house to be away from her. He was a calamity waiting to happen, one of those weird kids we have all known from school, whose family life was a mess, we knew, and whose father drank and whose older brother was already in jail and . . . We knew that kid.

So what is to be done with Timmendequas? He is sick with a disease for which we have no cure. We never had a cure and so we had to wait—didn't we?—for him to commit some crime for which he either could be imprisoned for life or executed. If he were a dog—one that had been beaten as a pup and then bit someone as an adult—we would put him to sleep, kill him and recognize, of course, that the dog was a victim of the person who beat him as a pup.

It is the same with Timmendequas, only of course he murdered and raped a little girl. I do not forget that. But what is the point of putting him to death? Will it deter others like him? Hardly. In Timmendequas's warped logic, he had to kill

Megan after he molested her because he was afraid she would tell her parents what had happened. But he lived just across the street—in a house with two other sex offenders. They were the obvious suspects. Deterrence? Timmendequas wasn't capable of the thought.

Death will ensure Timmendequas never again molests another person. But life in prison would serve just as well. His death will not deter another such crime and it will someday be seen as an obscenity—like the shackling of the insane or the exiling of lepers. We kill what we cannot cure. We now know Timmendequas's mitigating circumstances. What, though, are ours?

Unfortunately, such cases of paedophilic murderous perversion are conflated in the public mind with those akin to the Humbert Humbert of *Lolita*. Moreover, there are large ranges of lived experience of conative character, and of observed behaviour disorder such as predatory paedophilia, which elude our usual vicarious introspection and reflection. Nor can such phenomena be adequately explored, however expertly, in survey analysis. Case studies are also required; those in analytic depth are especially valuable. So far, these latter are few in number. In this genre are Greer and Volkan's patient, the so-called Dogman (see chapter two herein) and Socarides's (1988) clinical study of the case of Jenkins. Both cases are in the extreme range of narcissistic pathology, exhibiting sadomasochistic perversion and overt borderline psychotic features. Socarides (1988) writes:

> Of special significance are those individuals who engage in sadomasochistic perversions and who show overt borderline features. They are classified as preoedipal type II narcissistic perverts, at the extreme range of narcissistic pathology (Kernberg, 1980a, 1984a, 1984b, 1986). They are characterized by generalized impulsivity, lack of anxiety tolerance, a disposition to explosive and chronic rage reactions, and tendency to severe paranoid reactions (Kernberg, 1980a, 1984b). Some of them engage in "joyful" types of cruelty fantasies. They are self-mutilative, and the combination of paranoid and explosive personality leads them to severe aggressive attacks upon themselves or others in order to secure orgastic relief. Since their aggression is not integrated into a superego structure, they are capable of engaging in sadomasochistic acts with willing part-

ners to the point of potential or actual damage to themselves or others. During the course of psychoanalytic therapy an unrelieved and continuous incursion of reality into their narcissistic grandiose structures may produce an alarmingly intense disintegration of the self-concept with threats of fragmentation, regressive experiences, paranoidal psychotic like transferences, and an intensification of perverse activities. [p. 149]

Building upon Edward Glover's (1932) ego-nuclei conceptual model and my application of it to schizophrenia (Abse, 1955), Volkan (1995) describes the infantile psychotic self, a reflection of primitive ego nuclei consolidated and split off from the more adult self. This infantile psychotic self periodically dominated in Greer's case to be described below; at other times its influence was in a lower key. In the Dogman case (see chapter two), in a five-year analytic psychotherapy William Greer treated a paedophilic wife-beater whose recurring facial grimaces made him look like a snarling dog. The patient presented himself "as if he were two entirely different men, one of which outside his home dominated as a competent, restrained, and respected plant manager. In the second year of analysis, Greer reported a waning of interest in his masochistic wife accompanied by an increased interest in a pubescent girl across the street whom the couple had befriended after their son went away to school. In his regression:

> Joseph [the patient], overcome by erotic fantasies about this girl, became overtly seductive with her, and she readily reciprocated. When his wife was out of the room the girl would sit on Joseph's lap and tickle him, much to their mutual delight. She would brush against him with her exposed thighs, and pause over his hand. Joseph began reporting memories of being intensely aroused by his sister's sexual activities with her boyfriends when he had accompanied them on dates. He told Greer of his boyhood fantasy of his sister performing fellatio on him. He also remembered the incredibly intense excitement he felt when he had fondled his drunken aunt's breasts and how he rushed into the next room to masturbate to relieve his tension. As he put it, "Lust has no scruples." Meanwhile, he became "afraid of everybody and everything". He thought he would feel safer if he went incognito, so he purchased a pair of dark glasses that he wore everywhere.

Later in the second year of analytic work, Joseph (the Dogman) reported a phantasy in which he had sucked the girl's breast so voraciously that she became desiccated and died. Then

> [t]he therapist told him that he was continuing to remember his childhood in his fantasies about this girl, and that fantasies could be better analysed than actions because actions would actually change the external world. Joseph was clearly driven to recreate a mother–child experience, but because in reality his experience with his mother had been replete with frustrations, his experience with the girl eventually allowed his aggression (the wish to "kill" her) to surface. The therapist interpreted that his first flagrantly paedophilic activities and then his fantasies about the girl were his major resistance to owning his angry, hungry, helpless, and humiliated core (his infantile psychotic self). He further explained to him that, as a child, he had been subjected to many humiliating events and was recalling them by sexualizing them and by re-enactments. Although trying to change his helplessness and humiliation through experiencing sexual pleasure might provide temporary release from tension, it took real courage to allow himself to verbalize these impulses and feelings. Joseph responded well and spoke of how he had been sexually abused as a teenager, being kissed and fondled without actual intercourse. This theme was further expanded in a dream in which he saw his son as a statue with a knife stuck in it. His associations brought feelings about his own sexual abuse and his jealous rage at the sight of his infant son at his wife's breast. In turn, he had sucked his son's penis in order to kill him. By now, both meanings of his paedophilic activities—the wish to have a nurturing mother and the wish to kill the "bad" mother—were understood.
>
> Joseph ceased his paedophilic activity and his involvement with the young girl. This was accompanied by an increased rage towards his therapist; he spontaneously revealed that as a child, even after his mother's death, he used to have fantasies of killing her. He seemed to be owning and expressing the "bad" affects of his infantile psychotic self instead of using paedophilic and related actions as a defence against them.

There followed three years of further analytic psychotherapy.

The work of Socarides (1988) and of Volkan (1995) concerning the pre-oedipal origins of paraphilias calls up many questions so

far incompletely answered. The current psychoanalytic metapsychological framework remains too unintegrated and, in this context, certainly has been inadequately addressed. Yet it is apparent
that the boundaries of what is self and what other in relatedness
at different segments of time, what is external and internal, with
corresponding alterations of consciousness and affect states reflecting the basic degree of separateness of a person in the individuation process, fluctuate widely and excessively at different
times in those afflicted with paedophilic disorder. The earlier contributions of Glover (1932, 1968), of Kohut (1971, 1972, 1977), of
Mahler (1968, 1975), as well as of Federn (1952) remain fertile
ground to be ploughed again in relation to the solid groundwork
provided by Freud (1909d, 1923b) and Janet (1907)—and, I may,
add in relation to the early brilliant insights of both Adler (1907)
and Jung (1940).

Child victims of Satanic cults

Showalter (1997) asserts that many years of lawsuits and intensive
investigations have unearthed no proof that Satanic cults "even
exist" (p. 173). Among others, she cites the 1990 ten-week hearing
in the High Court in Britain concerning alleged nefarious events in
Rochdale. Twenty children were taken out of their homes by social
workers in 1990 following reports of participation by parents in a
Satanist cult. These reports emanated from the tale of a 6-year-old
boy detailing the witnessing of murders of babies, drugging and
caging of children, and people digging up graves. Another case
cited by Showalter was that which took place in the Orkney Islands
in 1991. Nine children then were removed from their homes after a
villager reported peculiar practices by families that included
Quakers and Jews. "Children told investigators about participating
in Satanic rites with people dressed as Ninja Turtles. After an
inquiry that cost six million pounds, charges against the adults
were dismissed and social workers were then criticized for their
suggestive questions. In some cases, the pressure of evangelical
Christians, along with horror films, evidently supplied the imagery
and plot for imaginative narrative" (p. 171). Certainly hysterical

contagion exists. People make contact with one another, interact, and form all kinds of relationships, including those of instinctive identification. They have phantasies—and they act them out. Of course hysterical epidemics occur. Two kinds of stories prevail in epidemics of rumours concerning Satanist cruelties: charges by children of sexual mauling, and recovered memories of adults— among them many who had remembered nothing prior to psychotherapy bent often on a kind of treasure hunt for sexual trauma in early life or adolescence or both.

Thus it happens frequently that even following the investigations and court hearings, as in the 1983 McMartin preschool case in California which cost $15 million dollars and issued in dismissal, the fire of fiction when ignited is not readily extinguished. After the McMartin case, many women later charged that their children had been ritually abused in day-care centres and nursery schools. Overzealous police, social workers, and physicians who performed rectal and genital examinations, investigated further. They utilized anatomically correct dolls, inviting the children to show and tell what had happened, and they asked leading questions. We are in a thorny thicket when trying to get to know when the fantasies were first acted out, whether in actual ritual abuse or later in the alarums and excursions of hysterical parents and police and social workers; or whether the reports are an amalgam of both. The thematic emphasis on incest, infanticide, forced breeding, and conspiracy in Satanic cult stories is a powerful instigator of rumours. These encompass fundamental taboos that, when touched upon, can generate a good deal of disowning projection of dormant unconscious infantile phantasy. Showalter (1997) notes that alleged victims of Satanic cults describe conspiracies by huge, intergenerational, secretive criminal organizations that maintain total control over their members and victims. The leaders are said to avoid detection by living "in disguise" as normal members of the community. She writes:

> Fears of punishment and revenge by the cult for betraying its secrets become so vivid in clinical settings that hospital workers themselves begin to develop hypervigilant panics. In *Shattered Selves*, University of Maryland professor James Glass describes the atmosphere of Sheppard-Pratt Hospital while an SRA [Satanic Ritual Abuse] patient was being treated: "Sud-

denly books, police reports, compendia of newspaper articles
on cults materialized; staff whispered in the hallways. . . .
Many wondered if they should change their phone numbers or
find dummy addresses or even take secret vacations from
work, to throw off any would-be pursuers. People were careful
whom they spoke with, and a few staff members refused to talk
with me about anything to do with cults because they sus-
pected that they and I were being 'watched'." Finally even
Glass succumbs: he starts to believe that his car is being followed, that the cult is breaking into his office, that a suspicious
stranger at his undergraduate lecture is a "cult plant." In
Glass's view, it doesn't matter whether the terrors of SRA are
real; but he overlooks his own evidence of the suggestibility of
perfectly normal people to the paranoid histories of satanic
ritual abuse. [p. 174]

Elaine Showalter is not handicapped by clinical experience. All that
she writes about exaggeration and contagion, about hysterical his-
trionics and fictive narratives, the recovered-memory movement,
and male hysteria is, in my opinion, clinically sound nonetheless.
She does write:

Of course, the sexual, physical, and emotional abuse of children
is a terrible reality. My quarrel in this book is not with the
realities of child abuse, or the vigorous investigation of *children's* complaints, but with the ideologies of recovered memory
and the process of accusation based on adult therapy. Feminism
has a strong enlightenment, rationalist tradition of debate and
skepticism, whose memory I attempt to recover and reassert.
We betray our tradition if we succumb to easy answers. Our
primary obligation must always be to the truth. [p. 158]

Yet it remains, in my opinion, necessary to assert that though
Satanist groups do not practice at night behind every bush and
hedgerow, hysteriform disease is rampant and that Satanist abuse
in particular does exist.[1] As Charcot exclaimed in regard to negative
neurological findings in cases of hysterical paralysis: "Ça n'em-
pêche pas d'exister." The truth, after all, can sometimes be stranger
than fiction, and it is certainly more complex. My clinical experience attests that one or both parents of patients with multiple
personality disorder[2] sometimes belong or have belonged to
Satanist cults and that cult-based ritualistic abuse as defined by

Finkelhor, Williams, and Burns (1988) is a vehicle for sexual and physical torture utilized by sadistic predatory paedophiles. As Hale and Sinason (1994) write of their countertransference experience in dealing with ritually abused patients, "taking in the reality of another's real-life hellish experience, in addition to the phantasies and feelings about it, is very different from work with those with a relatively impinged-on inner life" (p. 280). It is even more psychologically remote from the viewpoint of library research by a scholar writing of the relation of hysterical epidemics to modern culture.

McFadyen, Hanks, and James (1993, found in Bentovim & Tranter, 1994) in a clarifying definition of ritual abuse called it "the involvement of children in physical, psychological or sexual abuse associated with repeated activities (ritual) which purport to relate the abuse to contexts of a religious, magical, supernatural kind" (Sinason, 1994, p. 102).

Over a hundred years ago, Freud, in 1897, wrote to Wilhelm Fliess from Bergasse 19 partly concerning the witch stories he heard from his patient, noting:

> I am beginning to grasp an idea: it is as though in the perversions, of which hysteria is the negative, we have before us a primeval sexual cult, which once was—perhaps still is—a religion in the Semitic East (Moloch, Asbarte). Imagine, I obtained a scene about the circumcision of a girl. The cutting off of a piece of the labium minor . . . sucking up the blood, after which the child was given a piece of skin to eat.
>
> Perverse actions, moreover, are always the same—meaningful and fashioned according to some pattern that some day will be understood.
>
> I dream, therefore of a primeval devil religion with rites that are carried out secretly, and understand the harsh therapy of the witches' judges. [Freud, 1985, p. 227]

Though there remains a pervasive deficiency of studies containing careful observations of witchcraft and sorcery in the literature on folk peasant societies of this century, exceptions include that of Nutini and Roberts (1993) with which Freud's surmise concerning long ago may be compared. An excerpt reads:

> By 2:30 in the afternoon Nutini had gone to Tlaxcala City to fetch the chief medical officer of the state of Tlaxcala, with

whom he had arranged to share information concerning the bloodsucking witchcraft. Unfortunately, the doctor was out of town, but Nutini managed to interest his deputy in coming to Xolotla and examining the corpses.

The deputy medical officer was a young fellow, no more than four or five years out of medical school, who had occupied his post for about a year, but he did not know about bloodsucking witchcraft in rural Tlaxcala. Nutini asked him bluntly and specifically to diagnose the cause of death of the seven infants and the circumstances under which he thought they had occurred, which under no circumstances was he to verbalize to the parents of the infants and to other concerned people. Nutini also asked him to refrain from making any comments regarding the tlahuelpuchi or from in any way making disparaging remarks or from questioning the belief in bloodsucking witchcraft. He was extremely cooperative. Being quite well briefed by his chief regarding the phenomenon at hand, knowing that it would do little good to tell those concerned the physical nature of the deaths or to offer any advice regarding future incidence, and contravening in no way his code of ethics as a physician, he agreed to the following plan. The physician would examine the cadavers or corpses carefully and later discuss with Nutini the causes, circumstances, and his general medical opinion concerning the death of the infant. He would tell those concerned the approximate time of death and would express vague uncertainty about the cause of death. If asked for advice, he would offer none, except to suggest that they should do what they thought best for such circumstances, and that he would think of something later. The young physician was a bright fellow who understood the ethnographic aims perfectly. He did not want in any way to influence or bias the subsequent sociological investigation of the epidemic by anything that might be said or done. He understood also that, if anything practical was to be gained from the medical viewpoint of preventing infant death, it was certainly more logical and advantageous to know in detail the sociological dimensions of the phenomenon and the belief system which underlay it. [pp. 135–136]

Bentovim and Tranter (1994) worked with three children involved in ritual abuse and referred to the Sexual Abuse Assessment and Treatment service of the Hospital for Sick Children,

Great Ormond Street, London. Bentovim (1992) had previously shown in his research that families in which such abuse occurs have rigid boundaries and are either isolated altogether from community networks or else deeply involved with helping agencies. Such families have both a powerful intergenerational transmission of abusive patterns and a set of beliefs, family culture, and ways of relating that sharply contrast with those of the larger society within which they dwell. Bentovim and Kinston (1991) point out that observation of such families shows that they are often on the edge of breakdown patterns. Bentovim and Tranter (1994) write:

> It is possible to see such families as a trauma-organized system (Bentovim, 1992) because of the way that traumatic events experienced by parents and children can have such long-lasting and organising effects on individuals and families. Re-enactment, flashbacks, triggered memories, avoidance and arousal have a pervasive effect on development, much affected by gender (e.g., identification with the aggressor role in boys, and the victim role in girls). Traumatic experiences also influence subsequent choice of partners, based on parallel experiences and interlocking pathology. Many members of a sibship can be affected and an interlocking extended family system can arise, with multiple forms of abuse, transmitted in a variety of patterns (Oliver, 1993).
>
> Characteristic of such families are the blaming of the victim, the deletion and denial of abusive actions by the perpetrator, and the organisation and undermining of potentially protective individuals both within and external to the family. This is achieved by the creation of a powerful boundary in which absolute loyalty is demanded, and the development of a set of stories, beliefs and meanings which justify abusive action. [pp. 101–102]

In the course of therapy of the three children involved in ritual abuse, "Sarah" (age 9) came to describe what she called a devil church to which she was taken notably at Halloween but frequently at other times. Adults at the church would be wearing long black and brown cloaks with hoods, and the windows were covered so it was dark inside. Spells were made in low voices, "different to ordinary talking" (p. 108). She had to drink "some funny stuff" (p. 108) which had a sour taste and gave her a headache. Men and women stood in a circle, and she was tied up by her arms and legs and screamed and wept. Other children were also tied up and screamed and wept. There was a star hanging from the ceiling, and she drew a brown devil with a snake on the top to illustrate further. Rude things then happened, similar things as happened at home; but "My dad did not tie me up when he done it in my bedroom" (p. 109). Sarah told the therapists that she thought of this church often at bedtime and sometimes dreamt about it, but she added: "It was something that really happened" (p. 109). She said the grown-ups told her they would kill her if she told about it.

This child later gave evidence in criminal proceedings against her father and her grandfather, who both received lengthy jail sentences.

In his vivid description of the horrors perpetrated by the two so-called Hillside Stranglers who sexually violated and brutally murdered several teenagers, among other young women, in Los Angeles between October 1977 and February 1978, Darcy O'Brien (1985) reports that shortly after the pair of predatory paedophiles' third killing, the murderers exulted as follows:

During the next few days they talked about what a great success the Jane King murder had been. Angelo recapitulated the pleasures of her shaved pubis. The weekend arrived without any press or television coverage of their latest act. *Impunitas semper ad deteriora invitat*, goes the Latin legal maxim: Impunity always invites to greater crimes. They were beginning to feel invincible. There was no telling what they might be able to get away with. Angelo, still praising Jane King, began suggesting the next logical step: to abduct a very young girl, a schoolgirl, unspoiled, inviolate, barely ripe and helpless; a girl, Angelo emphasized, who did not have anything to shave or only the first fuzzy hints of womanhood. Bianchi said that he had never been with so young a girl but had often fantasized about it, the buttery baby skin, the thin little voice, the hairless smallness. Angelo assured him that there was nothing comparable to very young girls, their helplessness, their fear, their crying out. To make a sacrifice of one—that would be something to make life worth living. If they could find one and "break her in" and then kill her, she would have lived just for them, they would be her beginning and her end. That would be the ultimate snuff.

On Sunday, November 13, four days after Jane King, Buono
and Bianchi drove over to the Eagle Rock Plaza in search of
their vestal virgin. [p. 59]

Of the two, Kenneth Bianchi under hypnosis displayed classic
manifestations of multiple personality and incriminated an alter
ego whom he called Steve. His later insanity plea was denied,
though his testimony became a morass of contradictions congruent
with such a diagnosis (which does not exclude also telling lies) in
the court of Judge Ronald M. George. The dominant member of the
pair, Angelo Buono, involved in this malicious *folie à deux* was an
integrated sadistic psychopathic personality, professedly experiencing sensual joy in his murderous acts, as well as rage and
diffuse hatred of women.

The Hillside Stranglers cases illustrate the appalling dangers
of the association of paedophilic sadists in pairs. Rosen (1979)
pointed out that regulation of self-esteem is one of the major
(deranged) functions of all of the perversions (p. 65). As Rosen
noted from a clinical viewpoint, patients seeking help for perversions present complaints of a disordered narcissistic economy,
with feelings of inferiority and inadequacy and under- or over-
assertion of themselves. On the one hand, they regard their perverse fantasies and acts as a source of pleasure and a boost to
feelings of being powerful with which they do not want to part.
On the other hand, they come to feel a painful diminution of self-
esteem, because of conflict with an embedded ideal self within the
superego. As for those who do not seek help, as with sadistic
felons of borderline psychotic character, the heightened self-regard of power and invincibility is eagerly sought in fantasy and
acting out, without commensurate conflict in one part of the self;
and if any conflict with another ego–superego system exists, it is
quite dissociated. In the pair of murderous felons briefly discussed
here, the dominating partner seemed to be totally lacking in civi-
lized ideals, and his self-esteem maintenance seemed to be largely
dependent on the expression of brutal power.

In groups larger than such pairs, as in Satanist cult practices of
abuse of children, we are bound to notice with Galanter (1989) that
we have not had or taken the opportunity to study firsthand such a
group in action, and we have only the reports of alienated and

decompensated former members. Yet we do know, and concede, that as Galanter writes:

> The psychological forces that mold the intensely affiliated charismatic group cannot be examined adequately through the prism of individual psychology, whether that of the citizen-in-the-street, the clinician, or the researcher. Instead, they must be understood from the perspective of the group as a whole; when properly understood, these forces have a compelling, almost palpable quality. They include group cohesiveness, shared beliefs, and altered consciousness. [p. 16]

It is, of course, well to be understood that psychiatrists are generally very cautious in reporting Satanic cult rituals that may come to their notice in the United States. The litigation fallout from the controversy surrounding memories of abuse has escalated enormously. Thus it is reported in the *Psychiatric News*, 17 October 1997, that a Texas jury awarded $5.8 million to a patient who sued her psychiatrist for malpractice, alleging she had implanted false memories of sexual abuse endured during participation in Satanic cult rituals. Subsequently, in the *Psychiatric Times* of December 1997, the stakes in the debate over recovered-memories therapy were reported as "ratcheted upward" with the indictment of staff members of another psychiatric hospital, including two psychiatrists. The clinicians were accused of perpetrating a "scheme to defraud by allegedly falsely diagnosing patients with multiple personality disorder caused by their alleged participation in a secret satanic cult". Louis Jolyon West, an early scientific observer with Margaret Thaler Singer of cults, cultists, and ex-cultists (West & Singer, 1980), conceded as reported in the *Psychiatric Times* of December 1997 that "there are certainly some recovered memories that ought to raise the index of suspicion more than others". However, he added that "with regard to satanic cult activity, there's a tendency to take a position of all or nothing when the answer is only to be generated by continued digging for the truth". Moreover, as David Spiegel, well-known for his work on the psychotherapy of dissociation as related to trauma (1990), averred, as reported in the same newspaper article:

> I am worried, though, that there is a militant aggressive advocacy group that is encouraging all kinds of restrictions on

therapy, including requirements for disclosures, consent forms and restriction on ordinary, everyday, sensible psychotherapy, and that part of it bothers me.

West (1992) described the "pseudopersonality" of a member imposed within a totalist-type cult and adaptive while in it, such a cult being defined by West and Langone (1986) thus:

> Cult (totalist type): a group or movement exhibiting a great or excessive devotion or deduction to some person, idea, or thing and employing unethically manipulative techniques of persuasion and control (e.g., isolation from former friends and family, debilitation, use of special methods to heighten suggestibility, and subservience, powerful group pressures, information management, suspension of individuality or critical judgment, promotion of total dependency on the group and fear of leaving it, etc.), designed to advance the goals of the group's leaders to the actual or possible detriment of members, their families, or the community. [pp. 119–120]

West postulates a state of dissociation in which members are "split" but not "multiple". As far as paedophile predatory perpetrators who find their opportunities in the sadistic rituals of Satanic cults are concerned, the thrilling ego-states so activated in them while compartmentalized away from their more useful pedestrian waking lives shift readily back to respectable adaptations and are rationalized both at the time and later. A Faustian bargain is struck, analogous, if not identical, with the "doubling" of the Nazi doctors described by Robert Jay Lifton. In the notable and notorious case of Josef Mengele ("Dr Auschwitz"), Lifton (1986) quotes one of the Auschwitz prisoner doctors:

> He was capable of being so kind to the children, to have them become fond of him, to bring them sugar, to think of small details in their daily lives, and to do things we would genuinely admire. . . . And then, next to that . . . the crematoria smoke, and these children, tomorrow or in a half-hour, he is going to send them there. Well, that is where the anomaly lay. [p. 337]

Mengele's misdeeds exceeded in cruelty sending children to their death: far worse was what he made them endure in life, as reported by many survivor witnesses, including those whose contributions concerning his conduct are in Lifton's account. Other accounts, such as that of Simon Wiesenthal (1967), who writes of him under the rubric of "The Man Who Collected Blue Eyes", are, if possible, even more lurid. In the play *The Deputy*, Rolf Hochhuth (1964) created a Mengele-like character known as "the doctor", who is depicted as more evil than Adolf Hitler inasmuch as the split-off "pseudopersonality" (to use West's, 1992, human designation of the other self) entirely lacks human features and persistently dominates in the play. Lifton (1986) worries that Hochhuth thus contributes "to the cult of demonic personality" (p. 338). However much Mengele's psychotic character was formed and embedded in the Nazi biomedical ideology, the fact is that he did develop a demonic-type paranoid personality. It is of importance for psychoanalytic understanding, in my opinion, that his scientific interest, distorted by his preconceptions, became so highly invested in the biology of twinship, especially in his fascination with identical twins. Besides other determinants it may have been a consequence of a subliminal endopsychic perception, heavily defended against, of the "doubling" that Lifton elucidates so convincingly, and which made this fundamentally sadistic creature emblematic of pure Nazi group psychotic mentality.

Note

1. A shocking and comprehensive examination of group sadist paedophilia (whether obligatory or non-obligatory is unknown) may be found in *Treating Survivors of Satanic Abuse* (Sinason, 1994; see also review by Socarides, 1998).

2. In DSM-IV (APA, 1994), multiple personality disorder is named dissociation identity disorder.

CHAPTER SIX

The consequences
of child sexual abuse:
a brief survey

Loretta R. Loeb

The emotional trauma that results from the sexual abuse of children has a profound and lasting effect. It interferes with children's normal emotional and intellectual development and affects their later, adult life and behaviour.

In this chapter I review the writings of several investigators who have worked with persons who have been sexually abused as children and who have observed the long-lasting deleterious consequences of child abuse. Although many of these investigators have provided valuable information on the treatment of these children and adults, I shall not include treatment in this review.

F. Loeb (1977) presented the successful psychoanalytic treatment of an adult patient who had suffered from conversion hysteria. As a child she had slept with her father and had awakened wet with his semen. She had also played with his erect penis while taking baths with him. These experiences were neither traumatic nor psychologically damaging to her until, several years later, she was taught in Sunday school that sex was a sin. Only then did her early sexual experiences with her father come into conflict with her newly internalized external prohibitions and lead to neurosis. She had also been traumatized by an early, painful, long-repressed external experience of having been choked by her schizophrenic mother.

Seymourr Halleck (1963) said that the "Evaluation of many children and adults who have been sexually victimized suggests that they experience disabilities as a result of the sexual assault. The depth and seriousness of psychological trauma is dependent upon such factors as 1) age: 2) sex; and 3) closeness of the victim's relationship to the offender (especially in cases of incest) . . . the child cannot help but experience feelings of anger, guilt, and help-lessness. . . . Symptoms of anxiety and depression may also occur." In addition, he found that "a child's incompletely developed femi-nine or masculine identification may be seriously threatened. The child may be confused, frightened, and be unable to understand what has happened to him."

Halleck stated that many victims are in latency or puberty when they are seduced by an older man. Seductions, he said, take place at the time when the girl is deprived, isolated, or upset. As a result, the girls are on a quest for love, warmth, nurturance, or dependency, and they learn that they can receive such gratification through sexual expression in the context of seduction. Halleck said: "Promiscuity may then appear, in the victim, consequently as a neurotic compulsion." Another consequence, he said, is that "these developing girls who had been sexually abused are unable to achieve orgasm later in life. Promiscuity became the price paid for gratification of more dependency needs."

Susan Sherkow in her (1990) paper uses a psychoanalytic ap-proach to the evaluation of sexual abuse in little girls. She ad-dresses the issues of sexual abuse by looking at the pathogenic effects that appear later in the intrapsychic dynamics of the devel-oping ego of the little girls. Sherkow portrayed the behaviour patterns and mental conflicts that developed in a 2½-year-old girl, Tina, who had been sexually abused by her father during a three-week visit alone with him at his ranch. Tina's mother became suspicious when Tina would stand on the floor, spread her legs in a straddle position, and "pretend she was going to pee on the floor, saying 'Daddy did this'." Tina also began to examine her genital area by spreading her labial lips apart with her hands. She made strange motions with her mouth, rolled her eyes, and used her tongue in the same way that Mrs K. described that Mr K. had licked her breasts. Tina told her brother during a bath, "Daddy put his fishies in my bottom and it hurt," pointing to her anus. On another occasion, she put the arm of a toy doll into her vagina. Another time, she was observed chewing on a leg of a Barbie doll while spreading her own legs. She also played doctor at home, identifying "Daddy" as the "doctor" who played "fishies" and "butterflies" with her. She would say: "Three fishies are going into my vagina," and "Daddy licked my heinie." Tina said, "Fishies give you babies." She also played thrusting games with a thermometer, putting the thermometer in the anus of a doll. Of note about this is that the expression Mr K. used for sex was "I need to take your temperature," according to Tina's mother.

Following the summer vacation with her father, Tina also displayed other disturbances in her behaviour. She was able to sleep only when in bed with her mother. She woke nightly, crying hysterically, saying she heard "men walking", and said men were looking at her while she was sleeping. Tina threw temper tantrums and hit other children. Her appetite was poor, and she had regressed to the use of a bottle, sometimes exclusively. Tina repeated this behaviour with anatomical dolls during her session with Susan Sherkow. In her play she exhibited play reflecting gender confusion. She became agitated at the sight of a doll's male genitalia or in reaction to her own use of the word "penis", saying that "girls do not have penises" and "I do not like the word penis."

Sherkow explained that the developmental phases ordinarily expected in a 2-year-old girl were exaggerated and distorted in Tina. Over-stimulating, excitement, and fear of loss of object, intermingled with increased castration anxiety, could not be contained by any of the defences available to this 2-year-old. Intrapsychic conflict was apparent in Tina's play; for example, she had a compulsive need to "go on a picnic with Daddy" while simultaneously she had intense anxiety about "the lobster" that was in the picnic basket. The wish to be stimulated by her father was met by fear and guilt. The continuing gratification highlighted a feature of the distortion in ego development in these children. For instance, repression is markedly interfered with and impulses previously relinquished are revived, while identification with the aggressor is reinforced. Sherkow explained what would happen if the trauma persisted. Regressive anxieties about the loss of object would be fused with phase-specific loss of anal control, and enhanced early castration anxiety. Ultimately interference occurs with the normal emerging development of feminine-gender identity. Sherkow said that, in an abused child like Tina, one also sees fears of separation and body-part loss. These fears are regressively confused with object loss (invaded by guilt and shame). Ultimately these fears appear to intrude on superego development and decrease impulse control, or these fears may lead to rigid superego development or to superego lacunae. Sherkow's clinical experiences with young girls who had been sexually abused gave her important, hard-to-obtain data about the psychological developmental consequences of sexual abuse in young girls.

In his paper (1994), Brandt Steele presents his findings from thirty years of observing and treating abused children and those who abused them. He felt that psychoanalytic principles were crucially important in understanding the behaviour and psychodynamics of these patients. After taking exhaustive histories, Steele concluded that he "was not just listening to bad, cruel adults, but was seeing grown-up, abused children." The idea of generational repetition of maltreatment was intriguing, for parents were treating their children the way they had been treated. "An abusive father said, 'I swore I would never bring up my kids the way I was raised, but that's exactly what I've done!' The elements, of generational repetition are usually apparent in the abusers' current behaviour and their basic childhood history. . . . Later material emerged indicating that negative perceptions of the abused child and attitudes towards its behaviour have been present since very early, sometimes even before birth." Steele reviewed Klaus and Kennell's (1976) work on the phenomenon of attachment. Steele concluded that "maltreatment can be considered a disorder of attachment." Steele explained that "The bonding to an infant is influenced by the mother's entire previous life and personality, beginning with her attachment to her own mother and her identification with her, and by relationships with all other significant figures." Steele added that "For the helpless infant this is a gamble. He is at the mercy of whatever fate had provided for his attachment." Steele observed that Anna Freud wrote that this infant vulnerability is "Due to their inability to care for themselves, because infants and children have to put up with whatever care is given to them. When child management is not extremely sensitive, this causes a number of disturbances, the earliest of which are usually centred around sleep, eating, elimination, and the wish for company" (A. Freud, 1965, p. 1006). Sexual abusers have a conviction that sexuality is the best way to express love and caring.

Steele stated that "Pedophiles describe how easy it is to find victims by looking for unhappy, lonely, unprotected children who will respond to offers of care and attention. It is sad to find that in many cases of father–daughter incest, the mother herself has been an incest victim, which has contributed to her inability to protect her own child" (p. 1013).

"The maltreated child", Steele stressed, "does not have enough of the good experience to which he can adapt, build into his ego, and be an empathic adult. This lack of empathy is an integral element in the transmission of maltreatment from one generation to another" (p. 1014). Steele observed that "There is a tendency for the victims of all forms of maltreatment to adapt to the abuse as a normal part of life, and integrate it into the ego. The result is a pattern of living with misfortune and mishaps that we call masochism" (p. 1014). Steele refers to an article in which Berliner described this process as, "The child governed by its need for being loved, adapts itself to the hating love object and tends to be the type of child it feels itself supposed to be" (Berliner, 1940, p. 327). The child who fails to get mother's attention will deliberately bump his head or hurt himself and start crying. Steele felt that this behaviour was an example of what Berliner in his 1947 paper called moral masochism, which is characterized by attachment to sadistic love-objects.

Steele highlights one of the most important consequences that occur in sexually abused children. He said, "For victims of maltreatment, the most pathogenic element is that abuse is perpetrated by the very person to whom one looks for care and protection. This poses a dilemma or conflict for which there is no good solution. For very young infants there is no way out except to adapt to the situation and live with it as a normal way of life. Older children can begin to use defenses such as identification with the aggressor, repression, denial, and rationalization, while absorbing less than ideal contents into their developing egos and superegos. . . . It is the lack of protection and sense of helplessness and fear that flood the psyche when the protector is the attacker. This sense of fear and helplessness is also experienced by victims of sexual abuse" (p. 1015). From this awareness, Steele concluded that "A sexual act itself is not necessarily traumatic." Looking and touching are explorative and educational and not traumatic for children from preschool age to adolescence when done with mutually consenting peers (p. 1015).

Steele's data depicted that "Survivors of sexual abuse can talk freely of the hurt and anger against an abusive father, but later reach a deeper level of anger against the mother who failed to protect" (p. 1016). Steele added that, "In addition to having low self-esteem and a negative body image, adult survivors of abuse have an unsure sense of identity or a very mixed-up unintegrated one" (p. 1017).

Another aspect of the effect of abuse, he explains, is that it can be a precursor to delinquency and crime. He explains, "The results of maltreatment in the form of low self-esteem, lack of empathy, empty sense of deprivation, lack of basic trust, resentment against authority, and propensity for aggression form the matrix for development of delinquent and criminal behaviour. With few exceptions juvenile delinquents and major criminals give clear histories of significant neglect and abuse in early life" (p. 1021).

Harold Blum (1996) referred to a range of phenomena currently described under the rubric of child abuse, and he also gave information about the consequences of paedophilia. His paper also addresses the importance of both psychic reality and external reality—that is, the importance of both reality and fantasy in the over-determination of incestuous traumatic abuse and subsequent developmental disturbance.

Blum agreed with Steele's position on child abuse, stating that, "Currently the term seduction may be regarded as an umbrella concept which includes seductive behaviour, sexual harassment, coercive molestation, sexual abuse, and child rape. No child can give informed consent to a sexual relationship" (Blum, 1996, p. 1147).

Blum's observation of a sexually abusing parent's behaviour helps us understand the conflictual situations that abusive parents impose upon their victims. He stated that, "though outwardly presenting a strong, supportive facade, an incestuous parent may

be starved for affection and nurturance and symbiotically dependent. Oedipal jealousy and incestuous demands may simultaneously represent pre-oedipal infantile envy, rage, and omnipotent
control of a narcissistic object."

Shengold (1979), in an excellent paper, says that the earlier the
experience of trauma and deprivation, the more likely it will be
that the child will be overwhelmed and the more extensive will the
damage then be. He asks how experiences of overstimulation and
deprivation influence the motivating fantasies of an individual an
replies: "Soul murder is my dramatic designation for a certain
category of traumatic experiences—those instances of repetitive
and chronic overstimulation alternating with emotional deprivation that are deliberately brought about by another individual. The
term does not define a clinical entity; it applies primarily to pathogenic circumstances rather than to effects."

Shengold had a series of patients who were suffering primarily
not because of unconscious fantasies of cruel and unloving parents
or fantasies of having been seduced as children, but because they
had in fact experienced beatings, torment, and sexual abuse at the
hands of their parents or of parental substitutes. He concludes that
it is the impact of the environment, and that childhood emotional
deprivation, alternating with abuse "has lasting and profound
effect mobilizing certain defenses and structural changes, most of
which tend to interfere with full, free emotional and intellectual
development, and modifying the primal fantasies that motivate
human behaviour." He adds that soul murder has been used in the
recent past against adults in concentration camps and against prisoners of war. From his clinical material, Shengold concludes that
"partial or complete destruction of the developing—or even of the
developed—mental apparatus and sense of identity ('soul') can
occur at any age, but obviously, the earlier the trauma, the more
devastating the effects. Soul murder involves the deliberate traumatization or deprivation by an authority (parent) of his charge
(child). The victim is robbed of his identity and of the ability to
maintain authentic feelings. Soul murder remains effective if the
capacity to think and to know has been sufficiently interfered
with—by way of brainwashing. The need to identify with and to
maintain the illusion of a good parent enforces the difficult resistance of denial brainwashing becomes self-enforced)."

Shengold explains how the abusive parent can be seen as a good parent: it is the same abusive parent who is experienced as bad who must be turned to for relief of the distress that that very parent has caused, and so "the child must break with what he has experienced and must, out of desperate need, register the parent—delusionally—as good. Only the mental image of a good parent can help the child deal with the terrifying intensity of fear and rage which is the effect of the tormenting experiences. The alternative—the maintenance of the overwhelming stimulation and the bad parental imago—means annihilation of identity, of the feeling of the self. So the bad has to be registered as good. This is a mind-splitting or a mind-fragmenting operation. In order to survive, these children must keep in some compartment of their minds the delusion of good parents and the delusive promise that all the terror and pain and hate will be transformed into love. (The compulsion to provoke the parental abuse can be partly understood as the child's need to affirm in action that the next time the contact will bring love instead of hate.)"

Shengold discusses the defence of identification with the aggressor, which enables the former victim, following the compulsion to repeat, and again motivated in part by the delusive wish to make the bad parent good, to play the role of the active sadistic parent. The child who has recovered from the adult's sexual attack will feel enormously confused—in fact, split: "innocent and culpable at the same time—and the confidence in the testimony of his own senses is broken (Ferenczi, 1933)".

"Human beings," Shengold concludes, "are mysteriously resourceful, and some do survive such childhoods, with their sexuality and with their souls not unscarred or unarmed but at least in some part intact. Others are crushed, predominantly or completely—body and soul, sexuality and soul. Despite the vulnerability of children and the prevalence of bad parents, a completely successful soul murder is probably rare. Why this should be so is mysterious; part of the explanation is innate endowment."

Ira Brenner (1996) gave us information on the development of multiple personality as a result of sexual abuse. He explored the role of perverse sexuality as an organizing influence in multiple personality and stated that, "It is hypothesized that various perverse structures may be formed within these seemingly autonomous, amnestic states, in order to contain anxiety and encapsulate the aggression which resulted from early psychic trauma."

Brenner used the word "perversion" as defined in the *Oxford Dictionary*: "1) The action of perverting someone or something; the state of being perverted; turning aside from truth or right; diversion to an improper use; (a) corruption, (b) distortion; a perverted or corrupted form of something. 2) Preference for an abnormal form of sexual activity, sexual deviance. Also, (an) abnormal or deviant sexual activity or behaviour" (*Oxford Dictionary*, 1993, p. 2174).

He went on to say that there is "the reluctance to using the word perversion for it may result in losing sight of definition 1) above, that is, the element of victimization in the development of a sexual deviation. . . . The defensive and organizing influence of perverse sexuality, one of Freud's first discoveries (1905d), may play an important role in multiple personality. . . . An informal review of the presenting complaints of a six-month sample of inpatients with this diagnosis revealed that more than 50 percent feared or actually lost control of ego dystonic sexual impulses. The behaviour ranged from heterosexual and homosexual promiscuity to sadomasochism, pedophilia, bestiality, exhibitionism, *menage à trois*, erotic asphyxia, and kleptomania."

Brenner cites Kluft's (1984) study of thirty-three cases of multiple personality in his paper, who stated that a history of childhood physical and sexual abuse was reported in a high percentage in these cases. However, Brenner states, "It is unclear just how this trauma is related to the formation and function of these dissociated victims of trauma. . . . The clinician may see a similar history of early trauma, severe anxiety, excessive aggression, body image disturbances, and an impaired relationship to reality in multiple personality." Brenner (1994) hypothesized that "it is at the severe end of a continuum of dissociative character pathology in which dissociation is the predominant defensive operation". Brenner refers to his "definition of dissociation as a defence originating in response to the over-stimulation of external trauma, using autohypnotic altered states of consciousness which augment repression or splitting. Depending on factors such as the level of development and integration of the psyche at the time of the trauma, there may be variable disturbances of awareness, alertness, memory, and identity, due to dissociation." This defence, Brenner (1995) then says, "changes in its function, becoming relatively autonomous and warding off anxiety due to the inner danger of intrapsychic conflict. Awareness of the dual nature of dissociation then enables analysis of this defense in a psychoanalytic context. Such an approach is complicated, however, because of the apparent presence of a cadre of personifications (Fairbairn, 1952) which appear to take over consciousness."

The consequences of paedophilia extend beyond what the trauma, itself, may inflict upon a child and produce conflicts and behaviour patterns that interfere with the normal psychosexual development of the child. We must also look at the complex social problems that occur in our culture as a result of the sexual abuse of children. Many times, family relationships are disturbed, and the children find they no longer have a harmonious, domestic life. Today, unfortunately, we hear of children disappearing. Some of these children have been found murdered by the person who had been sexually abusing the child. Also today, child-care workers have become overly concerned about the possibility of child abuse and are falsely accusing adults of being child abusers.

REFERENCES

Abel, G. G. (1976). Assessment of sexual deviation in the male. In: M. Herson & A.-S. Bellack (Eds.), *Behavioral Assessment: A Practical Handbook.* New York: Pergamon.

Abel, G. G., Barlow, D. H., Blanchard, E. G., & Mavissakalian, M. (1975). Measurement of sexual arousal in male homosexuals: Effects of instructions and stimulus modality. *Archives of Sexual Behavior, 4*: 623–630.

Abel, G. G., Blanchard, E. B., & Barlow, D. H. (1981). Measurement of sexual arousal in several paraphilias: The effects of stimulus modality, instructional set and stimulus content on the objective. *Behavioral Research and Therapy, 19* (l): 25–33.

Abse, D. W. (1955). Early phases of ego-structure adumbrated in the regressive ego states of schizophrenic psychosis, and elucidated in intensive psychotherapy. *Psychoanalytic Review, 42*: 228–238.

Adler, A. (1907). *Study of Organ Inferiority and Its Psychical Compensations.* New York: Nervous & Mental Diseases Publishing Company, 1917.

Ainsworth, M. D. (1972). Attachment and dependency: A comparison. In: J. L. Gewitz (Ed.), *Attachment and Dependency,* Washington, DC: Winston.

Ainsworth, M. D. (1979). Attachment as related to mother–infant interaction. In: I. S. Rosenblatt, R. A. Hinde, C. Beer, & M. C. Busnel (Eds.), *Advances in the Study of Behavior, Vol. 9*. New York: Academic Press.

Allen, C. (1949). *The Sexual Perversions and Abnormalities* (2nd edition). London: Oxford University Press.

Allen, C. (1962). *A Textbook of Psychosexual Disorders*. London: Oxford University Press.

Almansi, R. J. (1960). The face–breast equation. *Journal of the American Psychoanalytic Association, 8*: 43–70.

APA (1994). *Diagnostic and Statistical Manual of Mental Disorders. DSM-IV*. Washington, DC: American Psychiatric Association.

Arlow, J. A. (1954). Perversion: Theoretical and therapeutic aspects. *Journal of the American Psychoanalytical Association, 11*. Reprinted in: H. M. Ruitenbeek, *The Psychotherapy of Perversions* (pp. 56–63). New York: Citadel Press, 1967.

Bak, R. (1971). Object relations in schizophrenia and perversion. *International Journal of Psycho-Analysis, 52*: 235–242.

Balint, M. (1968). *The Basic Fault: Therapeutic Aspects of Regression*. London: Tavistock.

Bell, A. P., & Hall, C. S. (1971). *The Personality of a Child Molester: An Analysis of Dreams*. Chicago, IL: Aldine Atherton.

Bentovim, A. (1992). *Trauma Organized Systems—Physical and Sexual Abuse in Families*. London: Karnac.

Bentovim, A., & Kinston, W. (1991). Focal family therapy—joining systems therapy with psychodynamic understanding. In: A. Gurman & D. Kniskern (Eds.), *Handbook for Family Therapy, Vol. 2*. New York: Basic Books.

Bentovim, A., & Tranter, M. (1994). A systemic approach. In: V. Sinason (Ed.), *Treating Survivors of Satanist Abuse* (pp. 100–112). New York: Routledge.

Berliner, B. (1940). Libido and reality in masochism. *Psychoanalytic Quarterly, 9*: 322–333.

Berliner, B. (1947). On some psychodynamics of masochism. *Psychoanalytic Quarterly, 16*: 459–471,

Bleuler, E. (1924). *Textbook on Psychiatry*, trans. A. A. Brill. New York: Macmillan.

Blos, P. (1979). *The Adolescent Passage*. New York: International Universities Press.

Blum, H. (1996). Seduction trauma: Representation, deferred action, and pathogenic development. *Journal of the American Psychoanalytical Association, 44*: 1147–1164.

Bowlby, J. (1958). The nature of a child's tie to his mother. *International Journal of Psycho-Analysis, 39*: 350–373).

Bowlby, J. (1969). *Attachment and Loss, Vol. 1: Attachment.* New York: Basic Books.

Bowlby, J. (1973). *Attachment and Loss, Vol. 2: Separation, Anxiety and Anger.* New York: Basic Books.

Bowlby, J. (1977). The making and breaking of affectional bonds. *British Journal of Psychiatry, 130*: 201–210.

Bowlby, J. (1980). *Attachment and Loss, Vol. 3: Loss, Sadness and Depression.* New York: Basic Books.

Boyer, L. B. (1961). Provisional evaluation of psycho-analysis with few parameters employed in the treatment of schizophrenia. *International Journal of Psycho-Analysis, 42*: 389–403.

Boyer, L. B. (1967). Office treatment of schizophrenic patients: The use of psychoanalytic therapy with few parameters. In: L. B. Boyer & P. L. Giovacchini (Eds.), *Psychoanalytic Treatment of Characterological and Schizophrenic Disorders* (pp. 143–188). New York: Science House.

Brenman, M. (1952). On teasing and being teased, and the problem of moral masochism. *Psychoanalytic Study of the Child, 7.*

Brenner, I. (1994). The dissociative character—A reconsideration of "multiple personality". *Journal of the American Psychoanalytical Association, 42*: 819–846.

Brenner, I. (1995). Letter to the Editor. *Journal of the American Psychoanalytical Association, 43*: 300–303

Brenner, I. (1996). On trauma, perversion, and "multiple personality". *Journal of the American Psychoanalytical Association, 44*: 785–814

Campbell, D. (1994). Breaching the shame shield: Thoughts on the assessment of adolescent child sexual abusers. *Journal of Child Psychotherapy, 20*: 309–326.

Campbell, D. (1997). *On Pseudo-Normality: A Contribution to the Psychopathology of Adolescence.* In: B. Kahr. (Ed.), *The Legacy of Winnicott.* London: Karnac.

Cassity, J. H. (1927). Psychological considerations of pedophilia. *Psychoanalytic Review, 14*: 189–209.

Cohen, R. (1997). *Washington Post*, 3 June, Section A.

Conn, J. H. (1949). Brief psychotherapy of the sex offender: A report of a liaison service between a court and a private psychiatrist. *Clinical Psychopathology, 10*: 347–372.

Cutler, S., & Ederer, F. (1958). Maximum utilization of the life table in analyzing survival. *Journal of Chronic Disorder*: 699–712.

Cutter, F. (1957). Sexual psychopathy and psychological differences. *Psychological Newsletter, 9*: 41–46.

Danjani, A. S. (1975). Symptomatic gonococcal infestation of children: A seven year experience in metropolitan Detroit. *Michigan Medicine, 74*: 755–758.

Deutsch, H. (1942). Some forms of emotional disturbance and their relationship to schizophrenia. *Psychoanalytic Quarterly, 11*: 301–321.

Dorpat, T. L. (1976). Structural conflicts and object relations conflict. *Journal of the American Psychoanalytic Association, 24*: 855–875.

Eidelberg, L. (1954). *An Outline of a Comparative Pathology of the Neuroses.* New York: International Universities Press.

Eidelberg, L. (1956). Analysis of a case of a male homosexual. In: S. Lorand & M. Balint (Eds.), *Perversions: Psychodynamics and Therapy.* New York: Random House.

Eissler, K. R. (1958). Notes on the problem of technique in the psychoanalytic treatment of adolescents: With some remarks on perversion. *Psychoanalytic Study of the Child, 13*: 223–254.

Erikson, E. H. (1950). Growth and crisis of the healthy personality. In: *Identity and the Life Cycle* (pp. 50–100). New York: International Universities Press.

Erikson, E. H. (1963). *Childhood and Society* (2nd edition). New York: W. W. Norton.

Fairbairn, W. R. D. (1952). *An Object Relations Theory of Personality.* New York: Basic Books.

Federn, P. (1952). *Ego Psychology and the Psychoses.* New York: Basic Books.

Fenichel, O. (1945). *The Psychoanalytic Theory of Neurosis.* New York: W. W. Norton.

Ferenczi, S. (1933). Confusion of tongues between the adult and the child. In: *Final Contributions to the Problems and Methods of Psychoanalysis* (pp. 156–167). New York: Basic Books, 1955.

Finkelhor, D. (1979). *Sexually Victimized Children.* New York: Free Press.

Finkelhor, D., Williams, L., & Burns, N. (1988). *Nursery Crimes: Sexual Abuse in Day Care.* Newbury Park, CA: Sage.

Fitch, I. (1962). Men convicted of sex offenses against children. *British Journal of Criminology*, 3: 18–37.

Freeman, M. D. A. (1979). The law and sexual deviation. In: I. Rosen (Ed.), *Sexual Deviation* (2nd edition, pp. 376–440). Oxford: Oxford University Press.

Freud, A. (1949). Some clinical remarks concerning the treatment of cases of male homosexuality. *International Journal of Psycho-Analysis*, *30* (3): 195.

Freud, A. (1965). *Normality and Pathology in Childhood. Writings, Vol. 6.* New York: International Universities Press.

Freud, S. (1905d). *Three Essays on the Theory of Sexuality. S.E., 7.*

Freud, S. (1909d). Notes upon a case of obsessional neurosis. *S.E., 10.*

Freud, S. (1911b). Formulations on the two principles of mental functioning. *S.E., 12.*

Freud, S. (1914c). On narcissism: An introduction. *S.E., 14.*

Freud, S. (1919e). A child is being beaten. *S.E., 17* (pp. 175–204).

Freud, S. (1920a). The psychogenesis of a case of homosexuality in a woman. *S.E., 18.*

Freud, S. (1923b). *The Ego and the Id. S.E., 19* (pp. 12–86).

Freud, S. (1927e). Fetishism. *S.E., 21.*

Freud, S. (1940e [1938]). Splitting of the ego in the process of defense. *S.E., 23.*

Freud, S. (1985). *The Complete Letters of Sigmund Freud to Wilhelm Fliess, 1887–1904* (4th edition), trans. & ed. J. M. Masson. Cambridge, MA: Belknap Press.

Galanter, M. (1989). *Cults: Faith, Healing and Coercion.* New York: Oxford University Press.

Gebhard, P., Gagnon, J., Pomeroy, W., & Christianson, C. (1965). *Sex Offenders.* New York: Harper & Row.

Gillespie, W. (1956). The general theory of sexual perversion. *International Journal of Psycho-Analysis*, 37: 396–403.

Gillespie, W. (1967). Notes on the analysis of sexual perversions. In: H. M. Ruitenbeek (Ed.), *The Psychotherapy of Perversions.* New York: Citadel.

Giovacchini, P. L. (1972). Interpretation and definition of the analytic setting. In: P. L. Giovacchini (Ed.), *Tactics and Technique in Psychoanalytic Therapy* (pp. 291–304). New York: Science House.

Glover, E. (1932). A psychoanalytic approach to the classification of mental disorders. *Journal of Mental Science, 78*: 819–842.

Glover. E. (1933). The relation of perversion formation to the development of reality sense. *International Journal of Psycho-Analysis, 14*: 486–504.

Glover, E. (1968). *The Birth of the Ego: A Nuclear Hypothesis*. London: Allen & Unwin.

Glueck, B. D., Jr. (1955). *Final Report: Research Project for the Study and Treatment of Persons Convicted of Crimes Involving Sexual Aberrations*. New York: Department of Mental Hygiene.

Greenacre, P. (1968). Perversions: General considerations regarding their genetic and dynamic background. In: *Emotional Growth: Psychoanalytic Studies of the Gifted and a Great Variety of Other Individuals, Vol. 1* (pp. 300–314). New York: International Universities Press, 1971.

Greenacre, P. (1971). Notes on the influence and contribution of ego psychology to the practice of psychoanalysis. In: J. B. McDevitt & C. F. Settlage (Eds.), *Separation–Individuation: Essays in Honor of Margaret S. Mahler* (pp. 171–200). New York: International Universities Press.

Groth, A. N., & Birnbaum, H. J. (1978). Attraction to underage persons. *Archives of Sexual Behavior, 7* (31): 175–181.

Groth, A. N., Hobson, W., & Gary, T. (1982). The child molester: Clinical observations. In: J. Conte & D. Shore (Ed.), *Social Work and Child Sexual Abuse*. New York: Haworth.

Hadley, C. (1926). Comments on pedophilia. *Medical Records, 124*: 157–166.

Hagglund, T.-B. (1978). *Dying: A Psychoanalytic Study with Special Reference to Individual Creativity and Defensive Organization*. New York: International Universities Press.

Hale, R., & Sinason, V. (1994). Internal and external reality: Establishing parameters. In: V. Sinason (Ed.), *Treating Survivors of Satanist Abuse* (pp. 274–284). New York: Routledge.

Halleck, S. L. (1963). Emotional effects of victimization. In: R. Slovenko (Ed.), *Sexual Behavior and the Law*. Springfield, IL: Charles C Thomas.

Hammer, E. F. (1954). A comparison of H-T-P of rapists and pedophiles. *Journal of Projective Techniques, 18*: 346–354.

Hammer, E. F. (1957). A psychoanalytic hypothesis concerning sexual offenders. *Journal of Clinical and Experimental Psychopathology, 18*: 177–184.

Happell, C. (1925). From the analysis of a case of pederasty. *International Journal of Psychoanalysis, 7* (1926): 229–236.

Henn, F. A., Herjantic, M., & Vanderpearl, R. H. (1976). Forensic psychiatry: Profiles of two types of sex offenders. *American Journal of Psychiatry, 13* (3): 640–695.

Hirning, L. C. (1947). In: R. Linder & R. Selinger (Eds.), *The Sexual Offender in Custody: Handbook of Correction Psychology*. New York: Philosophical Library.

Hochhuth, R. (1964). *The Deputy*. New York: Grove Press.

Hodges, J., Lanyado, M., & Andreou, C. (1994). Sexuality and violence: Preliminary clinical hypotheses from psychotherapeutic assessments in a research programme on young sexual offenders. *Journal of Child Psychotherapy, 20*: 283–308.

Hoffer, W. (1954). Defense process and defense organization. *International Journal of Psycho-Analysis, 35*: 194–198.

Hogan, R., & Jones, W. H. (1983). A role-theoretical model of criminal conduct. In: W. S. Laufer & J. M. Day (Eds.), *Personality Theory, Moral Development, and Criminal Behavior*. Lexington, MA: Lexington Books.

Howell, S. (1982). Twisted love: Pedophilia. In: J. Scherer & G. Shepherd (Eds.), *Victimization of the Weak: Contemporary Social Relations*. Springfield, IL: Charles C Thomas.

Hurry, A. (1990). Bisexual conflict and paedophilic fantasies in the analysis of a late adolescent. *Journal of Child Psychotherapy, 16*: 5–28.

Janet, P. (1907). *The Major Symptoms of Hysteria*. New York: Macmillan.

Juda, D. P. (1983). Exorcising Freud's "daemonic" compulsion to repeat: The repetition compulsion as an adaptational/developmental process. *Journal of the American Academy of Psychoanalysis, 2* (3): 353–375.

Jung, C. G. (1940). *The Integration of the Personality*. London: Routledge & Kegan Paul.

Kahr, B. (1996). Donald Winnicott and the foundations of child psychotherapy. *Journal of Child Psychotherapy, 22*: 327–342.

Kahr, B. (Ed.) (2001). *Forensic Psychotherapy and Psychopathology: Winnicottian Perspectives*. London: Karnac.

Kaplan, H. B. (1980). *Deviant Behavior in Defense of Self*. New York: Academic Press.

Karpman, B. (1950). A case of pedophilia (legally rape) cured by psychoanalysis. *Psychoanalytic Review, 37*: 235–276.

Karpman, B. (1954). *The Sexual Offender and His Offenses*. New York: Julian Press.

Kern, S. (1973). Freud and the discovery of childhood sexuality. *History of Childhood Quarterly, 1*: 117–141.

Kernberg, O. F. (1975). *Borderline Conditions and Pathological Narcissism*. New York: Jason Aronson.

Kernberg, O. F. (1980a). "Contemporary Psychoanalytic Theories of Narcissism." Paper presented at the American Psychoanalytic Association, December.

Kernberg, O. F. (1980b). *Internal World and External Reality: Object Relations Theory Applied*. New York: Jason Aronson.

Kernberg, O. F. (1984a). Malignant narcissism and its relationship to perversion—The Sandor Rado Lecture, 4 June (P. R. Muskin, reporter). *Bulletin of the Association for Psychoanalytic Medicine, 24*: 38–43.

Kernberg, O. F. (1984b). *Severe Personality Disorder: Psychotherapeutic Strategies*. New Haven, CT: Yale University Press.

Kernberg, O. F. (1986). A conceptual model of male perversion. In: G. Fogel, F. M. Lane, & R. S. Liebert (Eds.), *The Psychology of Men* (pp. 152–180). New York: Basic Books.

Khan, M. M. R. (1965). *Intimacy, Complicity, and Mutuality in Perversions* (pp. 18–30). New York: International Universities Press.

Kielholz, A. (1951). Perversion und sexuelle Erziehung. *Psycho. Berater Gesundes Prokt. Lebensagesalt, 3*: 452–458.

Klaus, M., & Kennell, J. (1976). *Maternal–Infant Bonding*. St. Louis, MO: Mosley.

Kluft, R. (1984). Treatment of "multiple personality": A study of 33 cases. *Psychiatry Clinical of North America, 7*: 9–29.

Kohut, H. (1971). *The Analysis of the Self: A Systematic Approach to the Psychoanalytic Treatment of Narcissistic Personality Disorders*. New York: International Universities Press.

Kohut, H. (1972). Thoughts on narcissism and narcissistic rage. *Psychoanalytic Study of the Child, 27*: 360–400.

Kohut, H. (1977). *The Restoration of the Self*. New York: International Universities Press.

Kohut, H. (1978). *The Search for the Self, Vols. 1 & 2.* New York: International Universities Press.

Krafft-Ebing, R. von (1912). *Psychopathia Sexualis* (12th edition). New York: Rebman.

Kramer, S. (1983). Object-coercive doubting: A pathological defense response to maternal incest. *Journal of the American Psychoanalytic Association, Suppl. 31* (5): 325–351.

Kurland, M. (1960). Pedophilia erotica. *Journal of Nervous and Mental Disorders, 131* (5): 394–403.

Lachmann, F. (1975). Homosexuality: Some diagnostic perspectives and dynamic considerations. *American Journal of Psychotherapy, 29*: 254–260.

Langevin, R. (1983). *Sexual Strands: Understanding and Treating Sexual Anomalies in Men.* Hillsdale, NJ: Lawrence Erlbaum.

Lanyado, M., Hodges, J., Bentovim, A., Andreou, C., & Williams, B. (1995). Understanding boys who sexually abuse other children: A clinical illustration. *Psychoanalytic Psychotherapy, 2*: 231–242.

Laplanche, J., & Pontalis. J.-B. (1973). *The Language of Psycho-Analysis,* tr. D. Nicholson-Smith. London: Karnac, 1988.

Leonard, S. (1930). Fetishism in statu nascendi. *International Journal of Psycho-Analysis, 1.*

Leonard, S. (1967). The therapy of perversions. In: H. M. Ruitenbeek (Ed.), *The Psychotherapy of Perversions.* New York: Citidel, 1967.

Lester, D. (1975). *Unusual Sexual Behavior: The Standard Deviations* (chapter 19). Springfield, IL: Charles C Thomas.

Lichtenstein, H. (1961). Identity and sexuality. *Journal of the American Psychoanalytic Association, 9*: 179–260.

Lifton, R. J. (1986). *The Nazi Doctors.* New York: Basic Books.

Loeb, F. (1977). Conversion hysteria stemming from child abuse. *Journal of Clinical Psychoanalysis, 6* (1).

Loewald, H. W. (1960). On the therapeutic action of psychoanalysis. *International Journal of Psycho-Analysis, 41*: 16–33.

Mahler, M. S. (1965). On the significance of the normal separation–individuation phases with references to research in symbiotic child psychosis. In: M. Schur (Ed.), *Drives, Affects, and Behavior, Vol. 2* (pp. 161–169). New York: International Universities Press.

Mahler, M. S. (1966). Developments of symbiosis, symbiotic psychosis and the nature of separation anxiety. *International Journal of Psycho-Analysis, 46*: 559–561.

Mahler, M. S. (1968) (in collaboration with M. Furer). *On Human Symbiosis and the Vicissitudes of Individuation*. New York: International Universities Press.

Mahler, M. S. (1971). A study of the separation–individuation process: Application to borderline phenomena in psychoanalytic selection. *Psychoanalytic Study of the Child, 26*: 403–424.

Mahler, M. S. (1972). One the first three subphases of the separation–individuation process. In: *Selected Papers of Margaret S. Mahler, Vol. 2* (pp. 119–131). New York: Jason Aronson, 1979.

Mahler, M. S. (1975). *The Psychological Birth of the Human Infant*. New York: Basic Books.

Masson, J. M. (1984). *The Assault on Truth: Freud's Suppression of the Seduction Theory*. New York: Farrar, Straus, & Giroux.

McFadyen, A., Hanks, H., & James, C. (1993). Ritual abuse: A definition. *Child Abuse Review, 2*: 35–41.

Mezey, G., Vizard, E., Hawkes, C., & Austin, R. (1991). A community treatment programme for convicted child sex offenders: A preliminary report. *Journal of Forensic Psychiatry, 2*: 11–25.

Modell, H. (1965). On having the right to a life: An aspect of the superego's development. *International Journal of Psycho-Analysis, 46*: 323–331.

Mohr, J. W., Turner, R. E., & Jerry, M. B. (1964). *Pedophilia and Exhibitionism*. Toronto: University of Toronto Press.

Nabakov, V. (1955). *Lolita*. Paris: Olympia Press.

National Center on Child Abuse and Neglect (1978). *Hearings, U.S. Congress, Committee on Crime: Sexual Exploitation of Children*, H2647, April.

National Children's Home (1992). *Children Who Abuse Other Children*. London: National Children's Home.

Nutini, H. G., & Roberts, J. M. (1993). *Bloodsucking Witchcraft: An Epistemological Study of Anthropomorphic Supernaturalism in Rural Tlaxcala*. Tucson, AZ: University of Arizona Press.

O'Brien, D. (1985). *Two of a Kind: The Hillside Stranglers*. New York: New American Library.

Oliver, J. E. (1993). Intergenerational transmission of child abuse: Rates, research and clinical implications. *American Journal of Psychiatry, 150* (9): 1315–1329.

Ornstein, P. H. (1974). On narcissism & beyond: Highlights of Heinz

Kohut's contributions to the psychoanalytic treatment of narcissistic personality disorders. *Annual of Psychoanalysis, 2*: 127–149.

Peters, J. J. (1976). Children who are victims of sexual assault and the psychology of offenders. *American Journal of Psychotherapy, 30*: 398–421.

Roche, P. Q. (1950). Sexual deviation. *Federal Probation, 14*: 3–11.

Rosen, I. (Ed.) (1979). Perversion as a regulator of self-esteem. In: I. Rosen (Ed.), *Sexual Deviation* (2nd edition, pp. 65–78). New York: Oxford University Press.

Rosenfeld, D. (1992). *The Psychotic: Aspects of the Personality*. London: Karnac.

Rosenfeld, H. A. (1965). *Psychotic States: A Psychoanalytic Approach*. London: Hogarth Press.

Rosenfeld, H. A. (1985). Psychosomatic symptoms and latent psychotic states. In: R. Langs (Eds.), *The Year Book of Psychoanalysis and Psychotherapy, Vol. 1* (pp. 381–398). Emerson, NJ: New Concept Press.

Ruitenbeek, H. H. (Ed.) (1967). The psychotherapy of perversions. New York: Citadel.

Sachs, H. (1923). On the genesis of sexual perversions. In: C. W. Socarides (Ed.), *Homosexuality* (pp. 531–546). New York: Jason Aronson, 1978.

Sandler, J. (1960). On the concept of the superego. *Psychoanalytic Study of the Child, 15*: 128–162.

Schwartz, L. (Panel Reporter) (1973). Techniques and prognosis in the treatment of narcissistic personality disorders. *Journal of the American Psychoanalytic Association, 21*: 617–632.

Shengold, L. (1974). The metaphor of the mirror. *Journal of the American Psychoanalytic Association, 22*: 97–115.

Shengold, L. (1979). Child abuse and deprivation: Soul murder. *Journal of the American Psychoanalytic Association, 27*: 533–557.

Shengold, L. (1988). *Halo in the Sky: Observations on Anality as a Defence*. New York: Guilford Press.

Sherkow, S. (1990). Evaluation and diagnosis of sexual abuse of little girls. *Journal of the American Psychoanalytic Association, 38*: 347–369

Showalter, E. (1997). *Hystories: Hysterical Epidemics and Modern Culture*. New York: Columbia University Press.

Sinason, V. (1992). *Mental Handicap and the Human Condition: New Approaches from the Tavistock*. London: Free Association Books.

Sinason, V. (Ed.) (1994). *Treating Survivors of Satanic Abuse: An Invisible Trauma*. New York & London: Routledge.

Socarides, C. W. (1959). Meaning and content of a pedophiliac perversion. *Journal of the American Psychoanalytic Association, 7*: 84–94.

Socarides, C. W. (1985). Depression in perversion: With special reference to the function of erotic experience in sexual perversion. In: V. D. Volkan (Ed.), *Depressive States and Their Treatment* (pp. 317–334). New York: Jason Aronson.

Socarides, C. W. (1988). *The Preoedipal Origin and Psychoanalytic Therapy of Sexual Perversions*. Madison, CT: International Universities Press.

Socarides, C. W. (1998). Review of V. Sinason, *Treating Survivors of Satanic Abuse: An Invisible Trauma* (1994). *Psychoanalytic Books, 9*: 262–266.

Sperling, M. (1959). A study of deviate sexual behavior in children by the method of simultaneous analysis of mother and child. In: L. Jessner & E. Pavenstedt (Eds.), *Dynamic Psychopathology in Childhood* (pp. 221–242). New York: Grune & Stratton.

Spiegel, D. (1990). Hypnosis, dissociation and trauma. In: J. L. Singer (Ed.), *Repression and Dissociation: Implications for Personality Theory, Psychopathology and Health* (pp. 121–142). Chicago, IL: University of Chicago Press.

Steele, B. (1994). Psychoanalysis and the maltreatment of children. *Journal of the American Psychoanalytic Association, 42*: 1001–1025.

Stekel, W. (1923). *Störungen des Trieb und Affektlebens, IV*. Berlin, Vienna: Urban & Schwarzenberg.

Stevenson, R. L. (1886). *The Strange Case of Dr. Jekyll and Mr. Hyde*. London: Longmans & Company.

Stoller, R. (1975). *Perversion: The Erotic Form of Hatred*. New York: Pantheon.

Stolorow, R. D., & Lachmann, F. M. (1980). *Psychoanalysis and Developmental Arrests: Theory and Treatment*. New York: International Universities Press.

Stricker, G. (1967). Stimulus properties of the Blacky to a sample of pedophiles. *Journal of General Psychology, 77*: 35–39.

Swanson, D. W. (1968). Adult sexual abuse of children: The man and circumstances. *Diseases of the Nervous System, 29*: 677–683.

Toobert, S., Bartelme, K., & Jones, E. (1959). Some factors related to pedophilia. *International Journal of Social Psychiatry, 4*: 272–279.

van Dam, C. (2001). *Identifying Child Molesters: Preventing Child Sexual Abuse by Recognizing the Patterns of the Offenders.* Binghamton, NY: Hawarth Maltreatment and Trauma Press.

Vizard, E., Hawkes, C., Wynick, S., Woods, J., & Jenkins, J. (1994). *Roots of Juvenile Sexual Offending (II): Assessment Issues.* Unpublished manuscript.

Vizard, E., Monck, E., & Misch, P. (1995). Child and adolescent sex abuse perpetrators: A review of the research literature. *Journal of Child Psychology and Psychiatry and Allied Disciplines, 36:* 731–756.

Vizard, E., Wynick, S., Hawkes, C., Woods, J., & Jenkins, J. (1996). Juvenile sex offenders: Assessment issues. *British Journal of Psychiatry, 168:* 259–262.

Volkan, V. D. (1976). *Primitive Internalized Object Relations: A Clinical Study of Schizophrenic, Borderline and Narcissistic Patients.* New York: International Universities Press.

Volkan, V. D. (1981). *Linking Objects and Linking Phenomena.* New York: International Universities Press.

Volkan, V. D. (1986). Suitable targets of externalization and schizophrenia. In: D. B. Feinsilver (Ed.), *Towards a Comprehensive Model for Schizophrenic Disorders* (pp. 125–153). New York: Analytic Press.

Volkan, V. D. (1992). Nesne iliskileri Kurami ve Psikosomatik Hastaliklar [Object relations theory and psychosomatic illnesses]. In: A. Cevik (Ed.), *Scientific Papers on the First Psychosomatic Symposium* (pp. 1–42). Antalya, Turkey: Roche.

Volkan, V. D. (1995). *The Infantile Psychotic Self and Its Fate.* Northvale, NJ: Jason Aronson.

Waelder, R. (1936). The principle of multiple function: Observations on over-determination. In: S. A. Guttman (Ed.), *Psychoanalysis: Observation, Theory, Application.* New York: International Universities Press, 1976.

Welldon, E. V. (1993). Forensic psychotherapy and group analysis. *Group Analysis, 26:* 487–502.

Welldon, E. V. (1994). Forensic psychotherapy. In: P. Clarkson & M. Pokorny (Eds.), *The Handbook of Psychotherapy* (pp. 470–493). London: Routledge.

West, L. J. (1992). "Pseudopersonality." Paper presented at American Family Foundation Conference, Arlington, VA.

West, L. J., & Langone, M. D. (1986). Cultism: A conference for scholars and policy makers. *Cultic Studies Journal, 3:* 117–134.

West, L. J., & Singer, M. T. (1980). Cults, quacks and non-professional psychotherapists. In: H. Kaplan, A. Friedman, & B. Saddock (Eds.), *Comprehensive Textbook of Psychiatry, Vol. 3.* Baltimore, MD: Williams & Wilkins.

Wiesenthal, S. (1967). *The Murderers Among Us: The Simon Wiesenthal Memoirs,* ed. with introductory profile by J. Wechsberg. New York: McGraw-Hill.

Winnicott, D. W. (1960). String. *Journal of Child Psychology and Psychiatry and Allied Disciplines, 1*: 49–52.

Winnicott, D. W. (1965). *The Maturational Processes and the Facilitating Environment.* Madison, CT: International Universities Press, 1980.

Woodbury, M. (1966). Altered body experiences. *Journal of the American Psychoanalytic Association, 14*: 273–303.

Zweig, S. (1933). *Mental Healers.* London: Cassell.